Rod Laver

AN AUTOBIOGRAPHY

Rod Laver

with Larry Writer

ALLEN&UNWIN

First published in Australia in 2013 by Pan Macmillan Australia Pty Limited

First published in Great Britain in 2014 by Allen & Unwin

Allen & Unwin
c/o Atlantic Books
Ormond House
26–27 Boswell Street
London WC1N 3JZ
Phone: 020 7269 1610
Fax: 020 7430 0916
Email: UK@allenandunwin.com
Web: www.allenandunwin.co.uk

A CIP catalogue record for this book is available from the British Library.

ISBN 978 1 76011 124 3

Set in 12.75/17.5pt Fairfield by Midland Typesetters, Australia
Index by Sue Jarvis
Printed and bound by CPI Group (UK) Ltd, Croydon, CR0 4YY

10 9 8 7 6 5 4 3 2 1

*For Mary
and my family*

Contents

Foreword
by Roger Federer

IF YOU REALLY LOVE THE SPORT YOU PLAY THEN YOU MUST study its history to understand how it has evolved into the sport we know today.

Few sports have a longer or richer history than tennis and no player occupies a bigger part of that history than Rod Laver. From my earliest tennis memories, Rod 'the Rocket' Laver stood above all others as the greatest champion our sport has known.

Winning all four majors in the same calendar year to complete the Grand Slam, on two separate occasions no less, is one of the greatest feats a player can accomplish. In 1962, Rod became only the second man to do this. Seven years later, Rod conquered the game's Everest again to become the first player – man or woman – to have won the Grand Slam for a second time. No male player has completed the Grand Slam since.

When you consider the greats who have graced the world circuit since Rod's second Slam in 1969 – Connors, Borg, McEnroe, Becker, Edberg, Lendl, Sampras, Agassi, Nadal and Djokovic – you realise just how hard it is to do. Three of us, Andre, Rafa and myself, have won all four majors but not in the same year.

This monumental achievement is what sets Rod Laver apart. This is his unique contribution to tennis history.

It wasn't until the Australian Open in January of 2006 that I actually met Rod. It was just a few days before that well-recorded occasion when, in front of 15,000 screaming centre court fans and a worldwide television audience, I broke down and cried just after Rod presented me with the Sir Norman Brookes Challenge Cup.

I was pretty relaxed but certainly tired after winning the match. When they called my name to collect the trophy from Rod Laver, in that great Melbourne Park stadium that bears his name, the magnitude of the moment finally hit me. I realised how fortunate I was to be presented the Norman Brookes trophy by Rod himself. This was a moment I will never forget.

There is a footnote to these events. At our first meeting on the Tuesday before the final, Rod and I had a chance to get to know each other. We discussed my shyness early in my career. Similarly, Rod mentioned that he, too, was shy as a young player. It was at this moment that I realised Rod and I had a lot of similarities, and I really felt comfortable in his presence.

Seeing this, my then coach and good friend of Rod's, Tony Roche, arranged for Rod and me to get together after my quarter-final and semi-final matches. Tony had told me so many classic stories about Rod and the good old times from his playing days, so it was really great to be able to hear some of those experiences directly from Rod. It was very inspiring meeting someone like Rod, who is such an important part of the fabric and legacy of our sport. There is no doubt my chats with Rod over those few days gave me added impetus and inspiration in my quest for back to back Australian Open crowns.

Since those heady moments in Melbourne, Rod has witnessed my two most recent Wimbledon final victories – the marathon five setter against Andy Roddick in 2009 and then against Andy Murray in 2012. I wouldn't presume to call Rod my lucky charm, but his presence at any tournament is not only motivational – it also helps to bring out the best in my game. I have always appreciated it when the greats come back to the arenas in which we play, but Rod's presence is always incredibly special.

Rod retired from the circuit just a few years before I was born so I never witnessed his exquisite skills live. I have watched film of him playing in finals and was mesmerised by his all-round game and incomparable court coverage. Rod seemed to have no weaknesses and while always a true sportsman on court, he was also a man of steely determination, and was incredibly strong under pressure. Rod always brought his best game to the big stage, whether it was a Grand Slam or a Davis Cup final.

Rod changed from being an amateur player to a professional one, aged 24, after claiming the Grand Slam in 1962. As a result he was ineligible to play in the amateur-only grand slam championships – the Australian, the French, Wimbledon and the US – until a few months before his 30th birthday in 1968, when these tournaments became open to professionals as well as amateurs. In the interim Rod missed playing for 21 grand slam titles. We can only guess how many of these he might have won.

Rod made a huge contribution to the game of tennis over his 22-year career, which started in 1956. His enormous talent was largely responsible for changing the way tennis was played. For example, Rod was the first player to master and consistently use hard hit top spin on both his forehand and backhand sides. For a left hander this was exceptional because, before the Rocket started wielding that massive left arm, no southpaw had been able to perfect the top-spin shot off the backhand side. So this was quite a feat, given the small head on those old wooden racquets. By this time Rod was on the path to becoming the No. 1 player in the world. Every other player realised they would have to eventually emulate his top-spin skills or be left behind. The result was that by the time the 1970s were in full swing, it was virtually impossible to win a big tournament unless you hit top spin like it was second nature. Rod Laver literally forced others to change the way they played the game and rethink their own playing style, technique and tactics.

Rod was also a primary catalyst for the introduction of open tennis in 1968, which completely revolutionised the structure of world tennis and, in turn, changed the game forever. By the second half of the 1960s, Rod was universally recognised as the best player in the world, with his closest rivals for that mantle being mainly drawn from the professional ranks, including the great Pancho Gonzalez and Australian stars like Lew Hoad (Rod's own hero) and Ken Rosewall. As a result, the separation of the professional players from the amateur-only grand slam tournaments was becoming increasingly intolerable to anyone who had the best interest of tennis at heart.

The four grand slam events were beginning to lose their lustre as a result of not having all the best players compete. Many of the amateur officials were hugely resistant to change for fear of losing their influence and, often, total control of their country's players. So it is to the eternal credit of a few forward-thinking tennis administrators – notably Herman David, the chairman of the All England Club – that the momentous decision was taken to introduce open tennis in 1968. This breathed renewed life into the game and enabled the continuing evolution of tennis into the great world sport it is today. Tennis had entered the modern era and Rod had played his part.

Rod is quite simply one of the nicest individuals I have ever met. He is warm, generous and good-humoured. He conducts himself with an endearing humility that promotes his status as not only a tennis great but a genuine legend of world sport.

Family comes first with Rod, and my wife Mirka and I have the deepest admiration for Rod's absolute devotion in caring for his beloved wife, Mary, during her final years. His personal attributes of total commitment and inner strength were in play once again. Previously, Mary had been instrumental in Rod's recovery from a debilitating stroke in 1998 and Rod reciprocated in full, until her passing in November 2012.

In the following pages, Rod tells the extraordinary story of a talented but shy freckle-faced kid from outback Queensland who, with the right support from the right people at the right time, was able to fulfil his father's dream of having a son win Wimbledon and then go on to become the world's greatest tennis player.

Rod loves tennis and everything about it and this shines through on every page. After you've finished reading his story, you will understand so much more about the game we love.

Roger Federer
September 2013

Acknowledgements

So many friends and colleagues made wonderful contributions to this book, and to the life and career in tennis that it chronicles. Thank you to you all, and to anyone else I've inadvertently omitted.

Larry Writer came to my home in Carlsbad, California, over some weeks in October 2012 armed with a tape recorder and hundreds of questions that made it easy, and a pleasure, to talk about the events of my life. Then Larry helped me to put my memories and thoughts into the words that you are about to read.

My gratitude to my manager Stephen Walter, a fine man and a dedicated one, who has always had my best interests at heart.

There is no more knowledgeable tennis man than Geoff Pollard, vice-president of the International Tennis

Federation, president of the Oceania Tennis Federation, chairman of the ITF Rules of Tennis Committee and Technical Commission, and president of Tennis Australia from 1989–2010, and I thank Geoff for reading the text for accuracy and making invaluable suggestions and amendments.

The tennis skills and winning mentality bestowed upon me by my coaches, the late Charlie Hollis and Harry Hopman, are detailed in the pages that follow. Suffice to say that without those special men I could never have been the player I was.

For their camaraderie and fair but ferocious competition I thank my peers from Australia's golden age of tennis: Ashley Cooper, Roy Emerson, Neale Fraser, the late Lew Hoad, John Newcombe, Tony Roche, Ken Rosewall, Frank Sedgman and Fred Stolle. I also pay tribute to their wives: Helen Cooper, Joy Emerson, Thea Neale, Jenny Hoad, Angie Newcombe, Sue Roche, Wilma Rosewall, Jean Sedgman and Pat Stolle. A cheer, too, to non-Aussies Charlie and Shireen Pasarell, Butch and Marilyn Buchholz, Ray and Susan Moore, and Cliff Drysdale. I thank my friends the late Frank Gorman, Jim Shepherd, and the late Mr and Mrs Cereal Shepherd, who took me under their wing when I was young.

John and Roberta McDonald are friends who have given generously of their wisdom, friendship and tennis knowledge. It was John who introduced me to his mate the late Charlton Heston and his wife Lydia, for whom nothing was too much trouble. Chuck Heston showed me and the other tennis players of the day that movie stars can be as in awe of sports champions as we are of them.

I thank the author and businessman Robert Edsel for his friendship and his inspiration. I am similarly in the debt of my old friends Tony Godsick, who now has the honour of managing Roger Federer, and his wife Mary Jo Fernandez.

What an honour it is that the great Roger Federer has taken time out from his peerless career to pen the foreword to this book. I appreciate and am humbled by Roger's kind and generous words. For her friendship and kindness, too, I thank Roger's wife Mirka.

I am so grateful to my sponsors Rolex, Adidas and the ANZ Bank. They have had my back through thick and thin. The ANZ was my first bank as a lad, the rosewood Rolex I treated myself to three decades ago has not missed a beat and Adidas has been producing the Rod Laver shoe for more than 40 years. We have history.

Bud Collins happens to be one of the finest tennis writers and personalities who ever lived. I'm proud to count Bud and his wife Anita as friends. In 1971 Bud and I collaborated on *The Education of a Tennis Player*, a book of which I am very proud and which was a wonderful resource for this memoir, each page jogging my memory as I looked back into the past.

Without the belief, guts and know-how of the late sports promoter and businessman Lamar Hunt and his son-in-law Al Hill Jr, professional tennis as we know it could never have happened. We all owe a debt to Lamar and Al, and to Lamar's wife Norma.

In the gypsy pro years, a promoter with integrity who staged his events professionally and didn't skip town before his players were paid was worth his weight in gold. Pat Hughes was one such promoter, as well as an excellent player and Dunlop sports administrator in London.

IMG, headed by the late Mark McCormack and with Jay Lafave as my representative, for many years managed my career to perfection.

I admired the late Adrian Quest as a tennis player and a tennis journalist. I thank him for his lifelong support and wisdom. I am grateful, too, to all the other fine tennis writers who covered my career accurately and with insight.

Thank you to Chris Clouser, friend, businessman and chairman of the International Tennis Hall of Fame at Newport, Rhode Island. He and his wife Patti have been staunch allies.

The Wimbledon championships were, and remain, special to me, and under the chairmanship of Philip Brook, the All England Tennis Club is in the very best of hands. As are the Australian championships, with Steve Wood as chief executive officer of Tennis Australia.

I thank Wick Simmons and his wife Sloane. Wick, chairman of Nasdaq Stock Market Inc. and former president of Shearson Lehmann and Prudential Securities, gave great, much-needed business advice, and was a good friend and tennis partner.

Tom Gross gave wonderful service as an instructor with Laver–Emerson Tennis Holidays and is still one of the best MCs in the business.

For helping to make this book a reality, I thank John Tall for so generously and painstakingly sourcing and supplying many of the photographs that grace this book, Jennie Fairs for her meticulous research, and Tom Gilliatt, director and non-fiction publisher, and Jo Lyons, editor, of Pan Macmillan, my publisher. Thanks also to publicists Tracey Cheetham and Eve Jackson. For putting Stephen Walter and me in touch with Pan Macmillan in the first place, I owe a debt to the fine Australian writer Les Carlyon.

Last, and most of all, I thank my much-loved, much-missed wife, the late Mary Laver, for her love and her courage, for sharing my life journey, for broadening my horizons, and for helping me to understand that there is more to life than tennis and that family is everything. Love, too, to my son Rick, his wife Sue and their daughter and my grand-daughter Riley. Loving thoughts also to my late parents, Roy and Melba, and brother Bob, to my sister Lois and her husband Vic, and my brother Trevor and Trevor's wife Betty, whose marvellous and encyclopaedic self-published recounting of my career, *The Red-Headed Rocket from Rockhampton*, was as affectionate as it was accurate and, like *The Education of a Tennis Player*, a priceless resource for this book. Another of Betty's blessings is her wonderful work scouring the Laver photograph albums to find many of the candid family shots in our photo sections. And by welcoming me into their lives, Mary's children Ann Marie Bennett and Ron and Stephen Benson, Ann Marie's husband Kipp and Ron's wife Julie have given me a gift I treasure.

Acronyms

ATP	Association of Tennis Professionals
ILTF	International Lawn Tennis Federation
ILTPA	International Lawn Tennis Players Association, later changed to International Tennis Players Association
IMG	International Management Group
IPA	International Players Association
IPTPA	International Professional Tennis Players Association (LA)
ITPA	International Tennis Players Association
LET	Laver–Emerson Tennis
LTA	Lawn Tennis Association (Yugoslavia)
LTAA	Lawn Tennis Association of Australia
NTL	National Tennis League
WCT	World Championship Tennis

Chapter 1

Bush boy

TENNIS WAS A BIG PART OF MY LIFE FROM AS FAR BACK AS I can remember. What else was a kid to do? Growing up in those years when my family and I were moving around rural Queensland, I can't remember a house, backyard or paddock that wasn't littered with tennis racquets and tennis balls . . . along with, of course, footballs, cricket bats and six stitchers. And it wasn't just me. If you lived in Australia in the '40s and '50s, those golden, more innocent times before the public tennis courts that were ubiquitous on Australia's rural and suburban blocks were banished by houses, flats, offices, parking lots, factories and shopping malls, tennis was what you played. It was every bit as much a national pastime as cricket, footy and swimming. A tennis racquet was as prevalent in a boy's life then as PlayStations, iPods and mobile phones are today. That being so, and with tennis-mad parents, brothers, in-laws and mates like mine, I had little choice but to play the game.

I was born on 9 August 1938, just one month before the American Donald Budge won the first ever tennis Grand Slam, in Rockhampton's Tannachy Hospital, the third child of Melba (named after Dame Nellie, naturally) and Roy Laver. My brother Trevor was six years older and Bob had four years on me. Sister Lois arrived nine years after I came along. Dad was a cattleman, a loving, caring father but, like most bushies, a tough, hard bloke who treated his own farm injuries (mainly because there was no hospital handy). Home for us was Langdale, a 9300-hectare cattle property an hour's drive from the town of Marlborough, which is 96 kilometres north of Rocky. My father, who was raised in Gippsland, Victoria, was one of 13 kids, eight of them boys, so the Laver brothers were able to field the best part of a cricket or football team and four tennis doubles teams in local comps. My mother also hailed from a sporting family, the Roffeys. Mum's mother, Alice Roffey, rode horses until she passed away at age 90.

Queenslanders have always been tough, self-reliant people, but, apart from the heat, tropical rain and those beautiful old wide-verandah Queenslander homes, rural Queensland in the 1940s would be all but unrecognisable to anyone who has known it only in modern times. Most roads were unsealed, and I remember kangaroos bounding alongside the family car as we travelled the long distances from town to town, farm to farm. When I was a boy, with World War II being waged, the federal government introduced measures to aid the war effort. There were blackouts and brownouts in the cities and larger towns to deter Japanese air raids, food was rationed and fun was too, with sporting events confined to weekends. Mum and Dad had to carry personal ID cards. There were fewer blokes about because many were serving overseas. Short back and sides was the hairstyle of choice for Queensland men, the vast majority of whom smoked rollies and wore wide-brimmed felt hats and suit coats in a heatwave.

There was no TV back then, so radio was the main source of entertainment and war news. The newsreel that was screened before the cartoons and the double movie bill at the local picture theatre was another way of keeping up to date with how we were faring against the Germans and Japanese. Churches on Sundays were full to brimming. After church, people gathered in the church hall to devour sandwiches and tea and talk about the weather and its effect on crops, after which it was home for a Sunday roast with family and friends, no matter how hot the day. Eating out on a Sunday was impossible for the simple reason that pubs and cafes were not allowed to open on the Sabbath. Other days, when restaurants were open, proprietors insisted that male patrons wear a collar and tie. Lew Hoad told me how difficult it was to dine out when he was a young player travelling the rural Queensland tournament circuit. He said he was routinely abused and denied entry by restaurant staff if he entered dressed casually. Dressing to the nines can be a challenge when you're living out of a suitcase.

When I was a toddler, Dad's favourite sport was tennis and he was determined that it become ours. To this end my brothers carted great quantities of ant bed – you knock over an ant hill and crush the pebbles into smooth, hard grit, which plays a little like fast clay – and loam, laid it in the yard, surrounded it with a wire perimeter fence, erected a net, scratched out some markings . . . and we had our own tennis court. We rolled and watered it every day to stop it from cracking, or being washed or blown into the next paddock by rain or wind. That upkeep was a small price to pay given the fun we had on that ant-bed court. There was no quarter given or asked when I got a little older and played against my brothers, or against my parents for that matter, and making it even more interesting was that the court's bounce was anything but true so you had no clue where the ball was going to go. Centre court at Wimbledon it was not.

What with tennis on our makeshift court, backyard cricket in wide, grassy paddocks and doing my lessons – reluctantly, I have to admit – by correspondence, life was idyllic on the property for the Laver boys, little blokes with sun hats, T-shirts, shorts and no shoes. With my flaming hair, sticking-out ears and 49,000 freckles, I'm told I was the spitting image of Ginger Meggs in the Sunday newspaper comics. We hunted kangaroos and rode horses, playing at being cowboys. That Langdale paddock became the endless plains of the wild west, even though horses and I got off to an unfortunate start. When I was two, Dad lifted me up into the saddle of one of our horses and led it across the paddock but somewhere along the way I fell off without my father realising and when he reached the stable and saw the empty saddle he hightailed it back to retrieve me.

Life was everything a boy could wish for, so we were not pleased when Dad, who wasn't the only one finding it tough to make ends meet on the land, took us off the property and relocated us all to a house in the backblocks of Marlborough, where he'd found work as a butcher. Trevor, Bob and I attended the tiny local school where I excelled at tennis against my school mates – though unlike my tennis pals, schoolwork got the better of me.

When I was 10, we moved again, to Rockhampton, because Dad, now in his 50s, could make more money butchering in a bigger town. Besides, he and Mum believed my brothers and I would receive a better education at Rockhampton Grammar School than at Marlborough. And, even more importantly, there was a well-organised tennis competition at the Rockhampton Association courts, where my parents played mixed doubles, and my brothers and I singles and doubles. It was about then that I realised I had a better-than-ordinary talent to follow and strike a tennis ball, and being naturally left-handed probably helped me too because lefties were in the minority so I was awkward for others to play against.

We lived on Lakes Creek Road for a while and then moved to a Queenslander in Main Street Park Avenue. I'm told I had a thing for climbing up onto the roof of our house and sitting there, only coming down when I got hungry. I was at Rocky Grammar for three years and then finished my primary education at Park Avenue School near our home before following Trevor and Bob to Rockhampton High School, which they left after completing the first two years. Trev then worked in our cousin Len Laver's sports store and Bob, much to everyone's envy, got a job at Paul's Ice Cream Works.

Right through school, I was a handy cricketer, a batsman and a left-arm spinner who bowled leg breaks. One afternoon when I was 11, I came home after playing cricket for my school and when Trevor asked me how I'd fared I said, 'Oh, okay, I guess, I took nine wickets for seven runs.' I wasn't being modest, it was just no big deal for me. I don't think I even realised these were amazing figures. As far as I was concerned I'd just had a good day and a whole lot of fun.

I was a keen fisherman, sitting for hours on the banks of the Fitzroy River and often returning home in the gathering dusk with a sugar bag filled with fish for dinner. I hear that fishing is one of the most dangerous of pastimes and it certainly proved hazardous for me when, after netting barramundi in the Fitzroy, I suffered a mishap that easily could have ruined my tennis career. I was absent-mindedly digging my fish-cleaning knife into the sand when it hit a rock and somehow the blade sliced into my left hand, my racquet hand, and severed the tendon in my little finger. Another centimetre or two and it could have cut off my fingers or slashed the arteries in my wrist. The cut bled heavily. I staunched the flow by wrapping my hand in my T-shirt and ran home. We lived too far from the hospital to have the cut stitched and the wound, though a nasty one, healed itself in time. To this day I have no feeling in that finger. Playing tennis, I had to alter my racquet grip to compensate for the injury, and my fingers, which forever after would stick stiffly out, were always catching on the left-hand side pocket of my shorts. In the end, Mum sewed up my pocket.

In many respects life today is better for children, but I reckon in some ways we had it very good. Surely playing games in the open air and swimming and fishing for barramundi in Moore Creek and the waterhole at Park Avenue Powerhouse is better than going cross-eyed in front of a computer game screen or living life vicariously watching TV.

We had our movies, but even a night at the flicks was an adventure for us in those long-ago country Queensland days. In Rockhampton there was an outdoor theatre . . . just a big canvas screen set up in a vacant lot with rows of folding chairs in front of it (though you could sit on the grass if you wanted) and a projector that shone its magical rays through hordes of bugs and summer moths up onto the canvas rectangle. Somehow, in my memory, it was always John Wayne rounding up the baddies on that screen, and rain, hail or moonlight we wouldn't leave until the big fella had brought the last black-hatted desperado to justice. Even today, 60 years on and with the Duke long a resident of Boot Hill, I'm one of his biggest fans and will happily watch a western any day of the week. When I was touring on the pro circuit with Alex Olmedo, it bothered him that the Indians always got it in the neck in the westerns we watched at the movies or on the hotel room TV. So Alex, who was an Inca Indian from Peru whose nickname was 'The Chief', would wait until the Indians were winning, usually in the very early part of the movie, and then he'd up and leave before they inevitably bit the dust in the final reel. 'I know we Indians will lose in the end, so I'm getting out of here while we're still ahead,' he'd say.

When Dad was looking for a place for us to live, one of his requirements was that the yard must have sufficient room for us to lay another homemade tennis court. At the Main Street Park Avenue house we were able to clear the scrub and Dad, Bob, Trev and I carted the soil and silt in his truck from the Fitzroy River and laid the court in the clearing. The good thing about silt, apart from being a good playing surface, is that when it dries and it's windy the sand is blown off but when you water it again, more sand rises and holds it all together.

This time, we fitted out our home court for night play by stringing four 1500-watt light bulbs on an overhead wire down the centre of the court. Any of us kids who broke a bulb with a lob or smash was in for it. Those lights were dim, so consequently our eyes grew sharp trying to see the ball in the gloom and the ability I acquired to see the ball clearly and early stood me in good stead right through my career. The Lavers' court was a magnet for local tennis players and was in constant use, as we played against each other and all-comers from kilometres around. One fellow who extended us was the young future champion Mal Anderson. Both my brothers were excellent players. Trevor was possibly the better, but Bob was no slouch and would grow up to be a tennis coach. One thing about Trev, though: when he played his emotions bubbled to the surface. If he was struggling in a match, everyone knew about it. He grumbled and griped and his shoulders sagged. I enjoyed playing against him when he was angry, because his mind wasn't on the match. It occurred to me that it would benefit me to play without emotion – well, without emotion that others could see, anyway. Card players profited from having a poker face so opponents wouldn't know how good or bad their hand was, and I figured a deadpan expression would work in tennis, too.

I was always happy when one of my brothers came home from school before the other, because then he'd be forced to have a hit-up with me. As soon as my other brother arrived, I'd be booted off the court so they could play each other. 'Scram, kid,' they'd say. One solution was to find Mum and she'd team with me to play Trevor and Bob in doubles. If she couldn't, I'd occupy myself hitting against a wall, studying what a ball did on impact after I'd connected with a particular shot: would it shoot forward, spin back towards me or to the side, bounce high or drop dead? I also hit along a grass cricket pitch. One day Dad came home with the wood to build a back wall. My job was to screw the wooden panels onto a wooden frame. I did it wrong and assembled the panels vertically instead of horizontally, which meant that the panels warped. Happily, there was an up-side. When I hit a tennis ball against the wonky wall, the ball came back at me any which way and I had to be in position to return it. All of this helped my reflexes, anticipation and my footwork enormously.

I loved tennis. It seemed the natural game for me to play. I played in the rain and the wind, and under the blistering

Queensland sun, which would soon cause my floppy sun hat to become saturated with sweat. To counter that, on very hot days I occasionally placed wet cabbage leaves inside my hat to keep my head wet and cool. Over the years, some media profiles of me have made out that I never left home without my hat filled with cabbage leaves. Nice story, but not true.

What I loved was the satisfaction of hitting the ball sweetly, the running to ram home a point or save one, the one-on-one combative nature of the game, facing up to an opponent and testing yourself against him. I think only boxing is as confrontational. There is a kinship between the two sports. You have two people facing each other in a contained space, probing for weakness and attacking it. Tennis players and boxers need footwork, timing and stamina.

Chapter 2

Charlie and Hop

Mum and Dad, who were not wealthy, did so much for me. As well as the backyard court, I was never without a racquet and tennis balls, and when they wore out there would always be new ones. When I turned 11, they drove me without complaint to junior tournaments all over Queensland. We'd be up and out of bed at 2 or 3am, with Mum preparing sandwiches and thermoses of tea before Dad drove us from Rockhampton to Bundaberg, Brisbane or wherever else we had to go, hundreds of kilometres – and this was in the days when tough dirt tracks, not asphalt roads, linked the towns. Those road treks could take seven or eight hours, sometimes longer. Not that Dad always watched my every match. He liked to drop me off and say, 'See you at 5,' and in the time in between you'd find him in a congenial pub enjoying a rum and milk and reading his newspaper.

One of the best things they did for me was to introduce the remarkable tennis coach Charlie Hollis into my life. A regular player on our home court in Rockhampton, Charlie was a mate of my father's and a nomadic bachelor who travelled around Australia, stopping here and there to coach children for a couple of years before moving on again. A tall and muscular, fastidiously attired man with carefully combed wavy brown hair, he was a fair player when young and had been an artillery instructor in World War II. He transferred his army *modus operandus* – explain, demonstrate, instruct, correct – to tennis coaching in the '40s and '50s. He bellowed at kids like the sergeant he had been, telling them when they were floundering that they were wasting their time and their parents' money. He liked to bark at his pupils: 'Why defend on the backhand when you can attack! Take the ball on the rise and use the speed your opponent supplies!', 'Up, change, punch!', 'You're playing a smash. Do what the word *says*!', 'Attack! Attack! Attack!'

To Charlie, you were a mug or a champion, with nothing in between. He wouldn't give you the time of day if he thought you had a couldn't-care-less attitude. To him, the three traits every good tennis player had to have were heart, brains and a never-say-die fighting spirit. Whatever he did, it worked, and Charlie became a nationally renowned coach who contributed to the careers of Fred Stolle, Mal Anderson, Daphne Seeney, Roy Emerson, Wally Masur and Mark Edmondson, and yours truly. So influential was he that I have no problem saying that if Charlie's and my paths hadn't crossed I may never have become an elite tennis player. He could have made a swag of money charging for lessons, but looking after his finances was not Charlie's strong suit and money seemed to slip through his fingers. He didn't care, or didn't seem to. He was a free spirit.

Dad, ambitious for his three sons and believing that all of us could be tennis world beaters – 'One of you boys will play at Wimbledon one day,' he'd say – persuaded Charlie, over a rum and milk, to coach my brothers. The first time Charlie laid eyes on me, I was 10 and he was putting Bob and Trevor through their paces. I'd crept out of bed to watch them and was peeping at them through the chicken-wire perimeter fence of our court when he spied me. Before I could run away, he said to Dad, 'Aw, let the little bugger have a hit. I can see he's keen as mustard.' And there, under the 1500-watt bulbs, barefoot and in my pyjamas, Charlie and I had a knock, and I got that ball back over the net more times than I didn't.

At first Charlie thought I was the least likely of the Laver brothers to succeed. I was, after all, a skinny runt, and a left-handed runt at that. Then, after a bit, he saw something in me and changed his mind. 'Rod will be the best of the boys,' he told Dad. 'I'll coach him for nothing, even if he is a midget in need of a good feed. He's got the eye of a hawk. I believe we can make a champion out of him. And something else, Roy – Trevor and Bob, they're like you. Quick-tempered. They blow up too fast. Rodney is more easygoing, a bit shy and self-effacing, like his mother. He's too lackadaisical now, but I reckon if we can give him a killer instinct, it'll be the perfect blend.'

Charlie Hollis taught me many things that he believed a budding tennis player had to know. One of the most important was not to grow complacent and compose eulogies to myself when I was ahead in a set, but to ruthlessly inflict the heaviest possible defeat on my opponent. Grind him into the grass, clay, concrete or whatever other surface we were playing on. In the beginning, I would do what I thought was the fair and decent thing and go easy on an opponent when I had him beat, and this often let him back into the match. Charlie stopped that trait quick-smart. 'Go out there, Rodney, and win as quickly as possible. If you can beat him, 6–0, 6–0, do it. Destroy him. Never relax if you're ahead. Never give him a sniff of getting back into the game.'

He also drummed into me that true champions never, ever give up – 'Chase down every ball, Rodney, even if you haven't a chance of getting to it.' When I was being beaten was when I *really* had to be ruthless and mentally strong enough to claw my way back. If I lost a match without having busted my gut, he was scathing. 'Why did you lose that match, Rodney? I'll tell you! Because you quit halfway through it.'

Charlie taught me to remain positive rather than getting bogged down when I was behind in a match. Whenever he thought I hadn't, he'd give me both barrels: 'So what, you're 1–4 down, don't beat yourself up. If you break back everything will be fine. Put yourself in a position from where you can go ahead.' Because Charlie instilled that optimistic attitude in me, throughout my whole career my concentration was better when I was behind because

I learned to relish the challenge of working hard to regain the lead. Once in an Australian Open final against Neale Fraser I was down by two sets. It was match point against me but I did what Charlie had taught me to do: I hung in there, rode out the best that Neale could hurl at me, battled my way to recover and take the lead, and eventually won the match. I probably didn't deserve to win it but I prevailed because I kept plugging away, telling myself, 'He's not going to beat me! And if he does beat me, I'll make sure he does it the hard way.' It can be a daunting prospect for any player to know that his opponent will never, ever quit. And when I did lose a match, and in my career I lost many, I never dwelled on that loss but consigned it to ancient history and thought only of how I'd win my next.

Charlie made sure I played on clay, concrete and grass courts (the only grass surface in our region was Mr and Mrs Shields' court at their home in the gold-mining town of Mount Morgan, and Charlie wangled it so I got to play there occasionally) so I would learn how to alter my game to accommodate the idiosyncratic tricks and turns of each surface.

He was a stickler for correct form. By putting me through endless drills, he taught me to play every shot – the serve, forehand, backhand, volley, lob, slice and smash – as perfectly as I could. At the Rockhampton Association courts where he coached, he'd make all us kids stand in a straight line and hit imaginary balls. He'd be there facing us like a choreographer, performing all the strokes and then making us mimic exactly what he did, again and again, till we nailed the shot. He'd say, 'Learn the stroke before you hit it. Groove it in. Watch the imaginary ball, now pretend to hit it. Then when you're on the court in a real match it will come naturally to you.' Good form was the talisman of a Charlie Hollis pupil. Whether the kid had the mental smarts and toughness was another matter. Such things are harder to coach.

Charlie also improved my serving by making me serve at a fence just two metres away. That way I didn't have to waste precious time chasing balls. He also made me understand that if I was going to succeed I had to be fitter than my opponent – 'Just think, Rodney, if *you're* tired, the other bloke will be *exhausted*' – and consequently he drove me to the point of collapse. It's a good thing that I was happy to be driven hard. I thrived on sweat, tears and, occasionally, blood. You can have the greatest strokes in the world but you won't be able to hit them properly if you're buggered.

'Just get the ball back over the net and let the other bloke make the mistakes,' Charlie would say. More games were won by simply getting that ball back over the net than by fancy, risky shots that might win a match but also cost you one. By getting your serve in and hitting your volley deep, by relentlessly returning your opponent's best shots, keeping the ball in play, you wear him down physically and mentally.

He encouraged me to put top spin on my forehand and backhand. 'You'll never win a big tournament unless you've perfected those shots.' Top spin enabled me to hit my ground strokes hard but not too deep to a general area. Top spin carried the ball higher over the net. In rallies from the baseline I always put top spin on my forehand, dropping the racquet head below the level of the ball and coming over it with a snap of my wrist. He placed tin cans just inside the baseline and challenged me to hit them with my top-spin drive. No session with Charlie ever ended before I hit 200 shots with top spin, with my coach yapping at me, 'Rodney, get under the ball and hit over it! Under and over! Under and over!' To improve my accuracy, he also marked various areas of the court and demanded that I hit them with my growing repertoire of shots.

Charlie drummed into me to come up with the unexpected in a match. Fool an opponent into thinking you were going to do A, then do B. To pull off this tactic I had to learn to disguise my shots. The wily Czech Jaroslav Drobny hit a marvellous example of a brilliantly disguised shot to beat Ken Rosewall in the Wimbledon final of 1954. Drobny, although an artist with a racquet, was never the fittest player, and he was leading two sets to one and 8–7 in the fourth but running out of steam, and the much fitter Rosewall was roaring back into the match. Ken got it into his head that Drobny would try to finish the match with a fierce serve and so stood at the baseline ready to return the inevitable cannonball, but instead Drobny dinked the softest serve to Ken's backhand. Totally unprepared for such a shot, Ken raced forward but was off-balance and hit the ball into the net. Game, set and match to Drobny.

●

Charlie worked out that I could compensate for my small size by being super-fit and very strong. He told me I needed to do extra conditioning and strength work and he didn't have to tell me twice. I ran long distances in the blazing Queensland heat, did endless push-ups and double knee jumps, and strengthened my left forearm and wrist by relentlessly squeezing squash balls.

After every coaching session, even when my body was aching, Charlie and I would play a couple of sets, and he wouldn't go easy on me either. Charlie was demanding, and never satisfied. When I won my second Grand Slam in 1969, he cabled me from Queensland: 'Congratulations on Grand Slam No.2. Now do it again.'

Mornings, Trevor, Bob and I would rise at 5 and ride our bikes to the hotel where Charlie lived in Rockhampton and I would let myself into his room and take the tennis balls from under his bed without waking him. Then my brothers and I would have a hit together on the Association courts, which were just down the road at the back of a petrol station, before Charlie showed up at 7 for our lesson, after which, hot and sweaty, we had to go to school. When the bell rang at 3.30 signalling the end of our last school lesson, we'd return to the Rocky courts for more coaching. Then we'd cycle home for dinner.

Often Charlie would join us at our dinner table, talking about past tennis champions, such as the great American Donald Budge who, in 1938, was the only men's singles player ever to win a Grand Slam – that is, the championships of Australia, France, England and the United States in a single calendar year. Charlie had seen Budge win the Australian championships in '38 and been deeply impressed by the American's lethal backhand. The Australians Jack Crawford and Norman Brookes, Englishman Fred Perry, American Bill Tilden, the Frenchmen Henri Cochet and Jean Borotra . . . the legends' names tripped off Charlie's tongue. (Years later I played against Borotra in Paris and the experience brought Charlie's history lesson to vivid Gallic life.) He also told me what he knew about the customs of London, Paris and New York, so I'd be prepared when – not if, but *when* – I played in big tournaments there. 'You have to know how to act the part,' he'd say. 'You use your fork like a little savage. You must know how to eat when you go abroad. We want to be proud of you when you're a champion. You're representing the people of Rockhampton, Queensland and Australia.' As well as good table manners, Charlie demanded that I stand straight and dress well, and thought nothing of disciplining me in front of Mum and Dad if he thought I deserved it. He said I should try to be like Gentleman Jack Crawford, the Australian champion of the 1930s, a fine player who fell agonisingly short of a Grand Slam, and was admired for his sportsmanship and generosity to opponents, his classy manners and, by wearing a long-sleeved white cotton shirt and long cotton slacks when he played, his sartorial elegance. 'That's how you've got to carry yourself,' admonished Charlie, 'like Gentleman Jack.'

In the four years that he coached me, from age 10 to 14, Charlie Hollis made me believe that if I continued to apply myself I could be a champion tennis player. At school I even wrote a highly imaginative essay about the day I was selected to play for Australia in the Davis Cup. Thanks to him, I could beat most boys in Queensland my age or a bit older, and was now regarded as the best of the Laver brothers. Bob begged to differ, and he fed me a dose of hard reality by beating me in the final of the North Queensland Junior Under-16 Championships.

My first official win in organised open competition – that is, playing against boys and men of all ages – was when I won the Port Curtis Open Tennis Championships at age 13. Many times opponents underestimated me because I was comparatively small, about 162 centimetres then (173 centimetres, or 5 foot 8 and a half inches, was as tall as I ever grew), and before they realised they'd misjudged me I had won the match. I was 12 when I was beaten by a much bigger boy, Mal Dixon, in the final of the Wide Bay Championships and he reckoned he couldn't see me over the net. Mal's a nice bloke and after I'd made my name in tennis he liked to boast, tongue firmly in cheek, 'I once beat Rod Laver . . . once.' The following year I beat Gilbert Beale of Bundaberg, a tall fellow well into his 20s, in the final of a B grade tournament in Gladstone. Gilbert took it well in his post-match speech: 'I don't mind losing to a slip of a kid, but having to kneel down to shake his hand was a bit rough.'

I was 13, too, when I won the Queensland under-14 singles championships. Before I left for the Milton courts in Brisbane, Charlie gave me a typically terse parting pep talk: 'Rodney, don't come back to Rockhampton without the state title.' In the singles final I beat Barry Spence 6–2, 6–2, and John Sully and I won the doubles title.

My victories earned me selection in the Queensland schoolboys team to take on New South Wales schoolboys in Sydney in the Pizzey Cup interstate schoolboys tournament. On my first trip to the Harbour City, as much as competing in the tournament, I was excited to be billeted at Glebe, Sydney, home of my idol Lew Hoad, whom I'd cheered on when, as a strapping 16-year-old prodigy with matinee idol looks, he came to Rocky to play. I marvelled at Lew's skill, power and laidback manner, which belied his ruthlessness on the court. I had adopted his practice of putting tape over the horizontal strings in his racquet to reinforce them, keep them from breaking and add power to his shot. I pictured myself hanging out with Lew, chatting about tennis into the night and having a hit-up together. Sadly, when I knocked on the Hoads' front door, Mrs Hoad informed me that at that very moment, Lew was playing at Wimbledon. I would get to know Lew well in years to come. They say that often we are disappointed when we finally meet our idols. That was not the case for me with Lewis Alan Hoad.

In 1952, after I'd won the Queensland under-15 championships, Charlie and Dad took me to Brisbane to attend a *Courier-Mail* tennis coaching clinic conducted by Charlie's old mate from his Melbourne days, the famous Harry Hopman. Hopman had been a member of the Australian Davis Cup team in the late 1920s and early '30s, and he and his wife Nell had won the Australian mixed doubles title four times. After his playing days ended, he became the No.1 tennis coach in the world. When I met him he was five years into his 19-year tenure as Australia's Davis Cup captain (under Hop's stewardship Australia would win the Cup 16 times). Although Charlie told me on the long drive south from Rockhampton to Brisbane, 'Now, hear every word Hoppy says and do exactly what he asks . . . but don't listen to anyone except me!' he enthused about Hop's ability to get the best from young players and transform them into champions. He listed a few who had benefited from Hopman's intense, some might say merciless, coaching: Frank Sedgman, Ken McGregor, Lew Hoad, Ken Rosewall, Rex Hartwig, Roy Emerson, Fred Stolle, Ashley Cooper. Not a bad bunch. Charlie had my attention, and so would Harry Hopman when I came under his wing.

A *Time* magazine journalist once called Hopman the most valuable man in Australian tennis, and described him as 'a hard-nosed disciplinarian who demands monastic devotion and impeccable manners from his players'. Too true. He insisted on decorum, wanting Australia to be represented by, as he put it, 'fine young men'. He laid down the law to the kids at his clinic: 'You want to throw racquets on the ground and swear and not do what you're told, then opportunities won't go your way.' He made it clear that it was his way or the highway. The *Time* article went on: 'Hopman bosses an uncompromising talent-hunting organisation that spots promising youngsters and grooms them carefully for the big time. There is no nonsense about higher education: instead, players quit school at 14 or 15, take "employment" from some sporting goods firm, and spend every working minute on the courts.' That journalist got it right. By the time I was 20 I was a battle-hardened player with six years' experience and primed for the cauldrons of Wimbledon and Forest Hills. I suppose the flaw in Hop's philosophy is that when a youngster devotes himself to tennis to the exclusion of all else and doesn't make the grade, he is left high and dry.

Although Charlie had briefed Hop about me, assuring him I was one out of the box and had what it took to be a fine player, the great coach was unimpressed at first sight. Hop was big on personal appearance, and when he first laid eyes on me he didn't think I looked the part, being, as I was, a short and skinny, freckle-faced, crooked-nosed, bow-legged blood nut, and painfully shy to boot. As had happened with Charlie Hollis, Hop revised his opinion when he saw me on the court. Being a protégé of Charlie's and a state champion, I could obviously handle myself well in a match and I had an array of shots that was impressive for a young bloke. Yet the perfectionist Hopman still had a gripe about me. He thought I wasn't strong enough, or speedy enough, and that is why, in the ironic Australian way, he christened me 'The Rockhampton Rocket'. He once explained, 'He was the Rocket – *because he wasn't*. You know how those nicknames are. Rocket was one of the slowest kids in the class, but his speed picked up as he grew stronger. Rod was willing to work harder than the rest and it was soon apparent that he had more talent than any of our fine players.' Like Hop said, I did get quicker, but the name stuck.

After I'd spent some time under his tutelage, Hop told Charlie he agreed with his assessment of me. 'He *is* good.' Praise indeed from this hardest of taskmasters, who, like Charlie, adopted a stern and strict façade to cover a soft and caring heart, and was, with his barking voice, impeccable dress and posture, and precisely parted hair Brylcreemed to within an inch of its life, not a little terrifying.

This coaching clinic in 1952 was also where I got my first taste of Harry's two-on-one training drill, which I reckon was responsible in large part for Australia's tennis success in the Hopman years. One of us would play at the net, and two others would stand back on the baseline, some metres apart. Hop would stand in the centre of the baseline and hit the balls to the bloke at the net, who then volleyed them hard and with accuracy to either of the baseline players. Sometimes there were two at the net and one on the baseline. Whatever the configuration, all three players had to be alert and ready to react and really run to get to the ball. Hop kept those balls rocketing and you'd better be ready. If you missed a volley, before you knew it he would thump another ball straight at you in the same spot. And another, and another . . . Five minutes and you were exhausted. There was no time to breathe. The idea wasn't to hit the balls where the other guys couldn't reach them but to put them where they had a chance of getting to them if they ran really fast. Play that game and you're going to learn to do drop shots, hit angles, play top-spin lobs or ground strokes. Two-on-one conditioned me to adapt to pretty much anything that could possibly happen on a tennis court. It was unrelenting, and improved our accuracy, anticipation and stamina. None of us could last more than 10 minutes if we were doing two-on-ones properly, but I thrived on that gruelling drill, as did all those who let Hop take them to great places in our game.

The dashing Roy Emerson, just a year older than me but by then firmly established as one of Australia's very best youngsters, was among the 24 kids chosen for the *Courier-Mail* clinic, and every chance I got I made sure I shook hands with Emmo, who became a fierce rival, great mate and is a neighbour today in Southern California where I live. Emmo was the fittest of us all. He thrived on Hop's two-on-one drills and when he'd suggest we go for a jog he meant a 10-kilometre run, in soaring temperatures if possible. Roy could manage 100 double knee jumps when the best I could do was 50. He set the fitness standard and just by trying to keep up with him I became fitter. Remembering me from that time, Roy said: 'I saw this tiny little 14-year-old kid. He came up to my waist, and he was wearing a big bush hat. I could barely believe the sight of him. Then he hit a few strokes, all those whippy sorts of things, and you could see all he needed was some size.'

I was told that over the 10 days of Hop's coaching clinic, he noted my keenness to train hard and – sorry, Charlie – willingness to listen to him and put his teachings into practice. Hop thought I had a good all-round game with few weaknesses. He was happy enough with my stroke play and my fitness (he reiterated what Charlie had said, that if I was fitter than my opponent then I'd be well placed to win the fifth set of any match), my footwork, my intensity. However, he felt I needed to further hone my on-court killer instinct. I was still too nice to my opponents and not dispatching them quickly or ruthlessly enough. And he wanted to see me faster and more muscular. If I could do all that, he said, I'd be welcome at his coaching clinics in the future, and I had a remote chance of making it in the world of senior tennis.

Shortly after I returned to Rockhampton, I was laid low by yellow jaundice. I think I caught it from a school-mate. I turned bright yellow and for six weeks I was away from school, too ill and weak to go near a tennis court, and because my liver was damaged my diet was black tea, bread, rice and steak with no fat. To recuperate and because my condition was contagious, I was sent to stay with Dad's sister Fanny at her property near Wowan in central Queensland. The only compensation for being quarantined in Wowan was taking my .22 rifle and going out into the scrub to shoot targets or the kangaroos that were in plague proportions out there. When my liver repaired and my skin took on its previous hue, I returned to Rocky.

I couldn't wait to get back onto the court. Not being able to play tennis had driven me crazy. Among the many things that my parents and Charlie Hollis had inspired in me was a deep love of the game, and now Harry Hopman had his eye on me. If I could have, I would have played and trained all day and night. School work came a very distant second.

It was an easy decision to make at 14 when, after my headmaster at school told me I would have to repeat second year because of all the lessons I'd missed while ill, I closed my textbooks forever and set out to get a job – hopefully one that would synchronise with my tennis. I was certain that tennis would be my life and I didn't see the point in not doing what young Australian players had been doing for decades: trying to land a job with a company that would sponsor my tennis in return for a day's work, giving me the chance to hit thousands of balls, build my strength, sharpen my accuracy and play in as many tournaments as I could. Mum and Dad were in full agreement. So was Charlie Hollis, who prevailed upon former champion and journalist Adrian Quist, who was the managing director of the Dunlop Sporting Goods Company in Sydney, to have a word in the ear of Dunlop's Brisbane manager, Wally Best, and persuade him to employ me. Charlie had touted me to the Slazenger company but they didn't share his faith in his scrawny pupil. Adrian assured Wally that I was a champion of the future, and told him that Dunlop, being a company keen to associate themselves with tennis, would be wise to establish a connection with me that could prove lucrative. Wally took a chance. Dunlop paid me four pounds, seventeen shillings and sixpence a week to be a clerk, messenger boy, loader of tyres onto trucks and, the good bit, exclusively use their racquets and balls and travel Queensland as a Dunlop ambassador playing exhibition matches and spruiking the company's products. Part of the deal, too, was that Dunlop gave me time off work to practise under the watchful eye of coach Ian Ayre (to whom I had to hand over a pound note each time) at the Milton courts. I did this for two hours at lunchtime twice a week, although one hour was occupied catching the tram to and from the tennis complex.

It was on those Dunlop excursions to rural and outback Queensland, often with my fellow employees Lew Hoad, Ashley Cooper, Les Flanders, Graham Lovett and Frank Gorman, that I experienced virtually every kind of tennis court known to man . . . We played exhibition and tournament matches, usually comprising two singles matches and a doubles match, on grass, packed sand, ant bed, clay, mud, gravel and pebbles. The spectator numbers ranged from 500 to 1000. The deal was that if we played in an exhibition or tournament, the organisers would return the favour by buying all their balls that year from Dunlop, and we did the rounds of the sports stores in each town making sure that Dunlop racquets were prominently displayed. Frank Gorman was always a good companion, a funny young man and an excellent player, and of course it was a thrill to be on the road with Lew. I enjoyed his company, and we were friends. He'd grab me and say, 'You and I are driving together today,' and that made me feel 20 foot tall. About the only thing we didn't have in common was that Lew enjoyed a beer or two at the end of the day and at that stage of my life I didn't.

Harry Hopman was pleased when he heard I'd joined the workforce. He firmly believed that school was a waste of time for young tennis players – far better at age 14 or 15 that they be honing their skills against the best in the world. That thinking fitted in well with many young players' parents, like mine, who weren't flush with money and knew their son's prospects of going to university and taking on a professional career were limited. At times in my life, especially before I met my wife, Mary, I have regretted my lack of education. Sometimes I've felt ill-equipped to carry on a conversation with well-read people. I'm naturally shy, but they really sent me scurrying back into my shell. Mary, who was an avid reader and arts lover, encouraged me to expand my intellectual horizons and today I can hold forth with the best of them – and sometimes even make sense!

Because Brisbane was far too big a daily commute from Rockhampton, Mum and Dad arranged for me to board at the home of the elderly Mrs Timms, in the Brisbane suburb of Red Hill. I paid her three pounds a week for bed and board (which left me just one pound, seventeen shillings and sixpence for 'luxuries'). Mrs Timms was kind and looked after me, but I was just a kid, and so lonely and homesick living away from home. The experience toughened me up, gave me a feeling of being my own person, but it was hard for me. It was always a red letter day when my family rang or sent me post. I had a good mate in Frank Gorman, who was as extroverted as I was shy. Frank trained with me and dragged me out and about in Brisbane. When we played against each other, he'd say, 'Let's pretend this point is for the Wimbledon final . . . or a date with Marilyn Monroe!' I believed Frank could have gone on to be a top player, but tragically that was not to be.

I also made the most of my time alone to go to Snowy Hill's Gymnasium around the corner from the Dunlop office, where Frank and I worked out with the boxers, sparring and banging the heavy bag and speed ball to improve my stamina, and hefting medicine balls and lifting weights to build muscle. After trying to discourage me – 'Get rid of that scrawny-looking mug with the awful coordination before he kills himself!' – Snowy saw I was serious and gave me an exercise and weight regime to build up my chest and shoulders. I didn't have to be in a gym to squeeze the tennis and squash balls that were transforming my left forearm into an enormous appendage that Popeye would have envied. Or to plunge my hand again and again into a bucket of sand to strengthen my fingers and wrist.

About this time, I moved out of Mrs Timms' house to live with the family of another young tennis mate, Jimmy Shepherd, and asked for and received a new job at Dunlop, stringing tennis racquets, because I reckoned it would further strengthen my fingers and wrists. I have wonderful memories of staying with the Shepherds. We had night games on their tennis court with Frank Gorman, Mal Anderson, Ashley Cooper, Ken Fletcher and our other tennis pals Dot Linde, Laurie Hasted, Jimmy Moore, Terry Bullock, Barry Green and Neil Swenke. The neighbours would hang over the fence, not believing the tennis they were seeing for free. We all tried to out-do each other at double knee jumps. Jim's sister Shirley and cousin Alison taught me to do the twist. One time someone cracked an egg over someone's head and Mrs Shepherd got mad, or pretended to. Mr Shepherd drove us all to a park 16 kilometres from home and made us run laps and if we shirked it he'd make us run all the way home.

From 1954 to '56 I was a regular participant at junior tournaments in Queensland, and I won more than my share. One fellow who always gave me a tough match was Frank Gorman, who knew my game inside out and had no problems with my left-handed play, because we had spent so much time together on the court. I won every Queensland age championship from the under-13s on, except the under-17s, when Frank beat me. In 1955, I was named Top Junior Boy in Queensland, and made the final of the South Australian State Championships where, in the semi final, I beat a good young player named Bob Mark, who was Australian Junior Champion that year, only to be downed in the final by South Australia's best junior, Barry Phillips-Moore.

When I was invited to partner Max Collins in the senior doubles I jumped at the chance, even though I was much younger than those I'd be up against. Imagine how I felt when we were drawn to play against the mighty Hoad and Ken Rosewall, one of the best doubles pairings in the world, in a quarter final. We didn't win, but nor were we disgraced. I showed I held no hard feelings towards Lew when, that December, his racquets were stolen and I came to the rescue. There was even a small item in *The Sydney Morning Herald* that read: 'Davis Cup player Lew Hoad arrived [in Adelaide] today without three rackets he intended to use in the State Championships. He left them unattended for a few minutes at Essendon Airport and when he returned they were missing. He tried racquets belonging to B. Bowman and J. Hann, but finally settled for one loaned by Queensland left-hander R. Laver.' Talk about a brush with fame. The following year Lew would inadvertently return the favour when he pulled out of the doubles in the New South Wales championships at White City and I was chosen to take his place as Ken Rosewall's partner.

In 1956 I played in the Linton Cup for Queensland – an under-19 competition that allows each state's best juniors to compete and have their future Davis Cup potential evaluated by selectors from the governing body, the Lawn Tennis Association of Australia (LTAA). My Queensland partners were Frank Gorman, Max Collins and Ken Fletcher. I competed in the Queensland Hard Court Titles in both the junior and senior divisions. I won the junior championship, and was beaten in the senior final by Neale Fraser, who was four years older than me. Before the match I was surprised to realise that I wasn't at all nervous at the prospect of playing the accomplished Fraser. I had been schooled by the best and was confident I would acquit myself well against Neale, and so I did. He won a rain-interrupted final 6–4, 12–10, and was generous with his praise afterwards. We would play against each other many, many more times and on far grander stages in years to come. I also took part in Harry Hopman's Queensland coaching clinics again that year, and came away convinced that my game was heading in the right direction.

At that time, the top Australian players were Frank Sedgman, Lew Hoad, Ken Rosewall, Mal Anderson, Roy Emerson, Neale Fraser and Ashley Cooper. What a golden age of Australian tennis. Happily I had the chance to observe, and sometimes even play against, these champions as I played my way around the country and I soaked up lessons that made me a better player. I tried to analyse every facet of their game and work out what made them so good. Doing so gave me a realistic view about how far behind them I was and what I needed to do to reach their level one day. I'd hit shots and tell myself, 'That was just like Sedgman . . . That was a bit like Hoad,' and then the next four would go into the net.

I learned two valuable lessons that served me well my whole career when, aged 16, I was at the 1955 Queensland championships. Ashley Cooper was playing Les Flanders in a round two match. Les was a very tall man whose arms and legs flailed everywhere but he was a most capable player. Les had Ashley down two sets to one and was serving at match point in the fourth set. Ash returned an easy ball that popped up innocuously and I reckon I could hear it begging to be put away. Les, who I'm sure was already envisaging himself in the quarter finals, lined it up and made to smash it not just out of the court but 25 kilometres into the bush. Problem was, with his rush of blood Les mis-hit, connecting not with his strings but the frame of his racquet and the ball looped into the net. He was shattered to have frittered away a winner and his shoulders slumped. Ash snatched the game from him and won that set and then the match.

In the quarter final, Ash faced Lew Hoad and beat him, and he downed Mal Anderson in the semi. The final pitted him against Ken Rosewall and Ash won 6–8, 6–4, 6–4, 6–4. Now, Ash Cooper had won one of the biggest tournaments in Australia, but had Les Flanders not muffed that single shot through over-confidence, it could have been him up there on the dais holding the trophy and Ash would have been a round two loser. The two lessons? Tennis matches hinge on single points, and complacency can beat you as surely as any opponent.

Chapter 3

Innocent abroad

In May 1956, aged 17, I went on a five-month world tennis trip with Harry Hopman. I had no idea he was inviting me to travel with him and Australia's top junior male player, Bob Mark, to compete at the French, Wimbledon and United States championships, as well as other tournaments including the British Beckenham and Queens events in the lead-up to Wimbledon, until Christmas 1955. It was then that a reporter telephoned me in Gladstone, where I was on a fishing holiday with my family, and told me I should get a passport and pack my bags. After I had contacted Harry to confirm that the reporter hadn't been playing a trick on me and he assured me that the trip was on, he just hadn't got around to telling me yet, I knew that the experiences I was about to have would be my junior tennis finishing school and pave the way for my senior career.

The tour was funded by a Tasmanian meat and property millionaire and tennis enthusiast named Arthur Drysdale. At first, Drysdale's plan was for only Hop and Bob to go, until Hop told him it was all too much trouble to take just one boy, so Arthur offered to pay for a second junior so the youngsters would have company. The second junior chosen, even though I was ranked only fourth or fifth then, was me. No matter how much Charlie Hollis had prepared me, for a raw-boned bush kid like me, playing at the biggest tennis tournaments and seeing the world was momentous and the opportunity of my young lifetime. I grew up fast. It thrilled me to think that, just as Charlie said, wherever I played around the world I'd be representing my town, state and country. In the time before we jetted out, Hop signed me up for daily French lessons so I could handle basic conversational French.

I kept a diary of my journey, and my awe at seeing the world for the first time was immense, though you may not get that impression from the somewhat stilted diary entries that follow:

> . . . had lunch on the plane at 1pm then arrived in Djakarta about 5pm. We had a drink and went and saw our first rickshaw . . . arrived in Singapore at 8.30pm and stayed the night at Raffles Hotel and had tea at Raffles. After tea we went for a walk around the town and there was a terrible smell from the drains running down the main streets. Back to the hotel and before I went to bed I washed my underclothes and shirt . . .

Our plane left Singapore at 8.30am for Colombo . . .
After that we headed back to plane and headed off
to Bomb Bay [sic] and arrived at 7.45pm. We were
restricted to the airport [then] left for Karachi . . . Flew
all night [and could] see the Suez Canal below . . .
[In Rome, we] drove through the ruins [the Forum] on
our way to the Quirinale Hotel. After lunch we met a
chap Hop knew in the Olympic Games and he showed
us the tennis courts, the Olympic Stadium and the
swimming pool. Then we went down to some courts
and had a hit. After the hit we put our things in the
pub and went to the American Bar for tea, looked
around the shops and went to bed. We were woken up
by Hop as he had to go and interview Prince Rainier's
father [the why's and wherefore's of this interview
have been lost in the mists of time, but the fact that
it happened gives an indication of Hop's clout] so
we had to travel to Paris all by ourselves. We got
dressed, had breakfast, paid the bill and went around
to the TWA office and got our tickets. We put our
luggage in and went for a walk. We watched some kids
play soccer in a park then while we were looking for
a place to eat, believe it or not, we ran into our flight
steward from Cairo to Rome. We said we hadn't been
to the Colosseum or the ruins so he took us there,
and to Caesar's palace in the centre of Rome where
he used to address the people. We left the steward
and got a taxi back to the TWA office where we
were picked up by the coach and went to the airport.

We got on the plane and stopped at Milan, Zurich and Paris . . .

The following day, Hop, Bob and I visited the red clay courts of the Roland Garros Stadium in Paris, home of the French championships. I couldn't believe how slowly this clay played. I raised a laugh from Hop when I bet him I could serve a ball to Bob at the other end then sit and eat an ice cream before he could hit it back to me. The clay left red stains on your shorts and shirt and shoes, and turned your hair scarlet — not that anyone could tell in my case. I had enormous problems adjusting to this new surface and was eliminated from the French championships in my first match, losing in straight sets to the Dane Kurt Nielsen, who was eight years older than me. Hop was unfazed and encouraging, and told me what Charlie Hollis had, that if I was to be a top tennis player I had to learn to master all surfaces. Debuting at this and the other great champion-ships was not about winning; it was about *learning*.

You'd go onto a clay court expecting to win on such a slow surface and you'd come off beaten, thinking, 'How did that happen?' In time, by watching the best clay players in Europe and playing on clay courts every chance I got, I worked clay out. What you need on clay are patience and legs, because you do a lot of running. Players who win on a clay surface are those who can control the ball, playing steadily and accurately from the back-court, keeping the ball in play and moving it around with changes of speed and spin, and resisting the temptation to over-hit. The defensive player is in his element on clay because of the slower, higher bounce of the ball, which gives him more time and therefore a better chance to return an opponent's forcing shot. Likewise, it blunts your rival's powerful serve, so the best policy is to forget about trying to blast the other bloke, simply make sure your first serve goes in. Before I played a match on clay I studied my opponent to find out what kind of a forehand and backhand he had, and in the match I would move him around, get him out of his groove. I could roll my forehand, keep hitting it deep, force my opponent to move back and stay back anticipating more, then play a drop shot to catch him out of position. Some players are all but unbeatable on clay, such as Spain's Rafael Nadal today, and others struggle, such as the greats of my day, Lew Hoad and Pancho Gonzales, who won 75 percent of their matches on grass and only 40 percent on clay.

Wimbledon, with its fast, smooth grass surface, was more my style than Roland Garros. I had dreamed of Wimbledon virtually since I first lifted a racquet, and I couldn't help remembering how, when I was a little boy, Charlie Hollis had told me I would play there. I knew Charlie, and of course Mum and Dad and my brothers, would be following my progress closely in the newspapers and via radio reports back in Queensland. Hop was a legend at Wimbledon, and he introduced me to the world's tennis elite as well as dukes, ladies and earls. I was grateful to Charlie for having told me which fork to use. At Wimbledon my eyes were out on stalks as I took in majestic centre court and the pristine outer courts, the ivy-covered walls, the big black limousines delivering the high and mighty to this, the finest championship in the world. Was that Donald Budge I just saw getting out of his limo? It was. I was deeply impressed by the fair and knowledgeable crowds who knew what good play was and politely clapped it. From the first I enjoyed playing there because the importance of the place demands that you concentrate. You don't want to be made a fool of on centre court in front of all those fans, and with the world paying attention. There's always a lot at stake, and nowhere to hide.

In my first match I was pitted against the 28-year-old Italian giant, Orlando Sirola, who had been an anti-Nazi freedom fighter in World War II. Talk about David and Goliath. At 201 centimetres Orlando towered over me. When he served, the ball came at me steep and hard, as if he was serving from a perch high in a tree. I weathered the storm and used my speed (yes, I'd picked up my pace by then) to out-manoeuvre the bigger, slower man and take him to deuce 5–5 in the first set, although he ended up winning it 7–5. He also won the second and third sets, 6–4, 6–2 to send me packing from the tournament. I was not disgraced in this baptism of fire on the biggest tennis stage in the world. Bob Mark and I played in the doubles and were knocked out in the first round by Pierre Darmon and Jean-Claude Molinari of France in a hard-fought five-set match.

Realistically, there was never going to be a fairytale win for me at Wimbledon, but I took heart from my performances and vowed to be back the following year. My main mission on Hop's tour was to contest Wimbledon's Junior World Championships. I made the final of the singles, but was towelled up 6–1, 6–1 by the American Davis Cup player Ron Holmberg, and Bob Mark and I made it to the last 16 in the doubles.

After some more matches on the Continent where I was glad to get the chance to make a better fist of playing on clay, we flew to the United States. I sensed that playing in England and on the Continent had taken my game to a higher level. First up, Hop entered me in the US Junior Titles in wonderfully named Kalamazoo, Michigan. On my way to the final, I beat California's top junior, Norm Perry, in three sets, and then the celebrated junior Davis Cup star Donald Dell, before winning the final in three sets and 70 minutes against Chris Crawford in a match during which I attacked the net relentlessly. It took a while to sink in that I was junior champion of the United States, the first Australian ever to hold that title. In the doubles, I teamed with Jim Shaffer of Florida, and we beat Ed Atkinson and Bob Delgado in the final.

I turned 18 the day Bob and I beat French Davis Cup pair Paul Remy and David Haillet in the doubles at the Eastern Grass Court Titles in New Jersey. We didn't win the final there, but I fared better in the Canadian Junior Titles when I won the singles crown.

Hop, Bob and I were at Forest Hills, New York, in September for the US senior titles. In my first singles match I was knocked out in straight sets by Ham Richardson, which gave me plenty of time to watch Lew Hoad progress to the final of the singles. Already in 1956, Lew had won the Australian, French and Wimbledon singles titles, and a victory in the final, over his great friend and doubles partner Ken 'Muscles' Rosewall, would give him the coveted Grand Slam; he would be only the second man since Donald Budge to achieve it. From personal experience, I know that the vast majority of Australian tennis players are good friends and love to party together and do each other favours above and beyond the call of duty, but that doesn't mean we wouldn't rip each other's throat out on the court. This was certainly the case with Lew and Ken. Ken knew how much the Grand Slam meant to Lew, but there was no way he was going to give anything less than his very best, because that would have been disrespecting his mate. Muscles won in four sets, and Lew congratulated him heartily and meant it.

I learned a lot on that trip with Hop, and the best lesson was observing Hoad and Rosewall's mateship, pride, great fighting qualities and grace in defeat and victory in that final. Lew wasn't at his best. I don't know whether he had an off day or if it was nerves. I doubt it was the latter. I don't think Lew had a nerve in his body. No, Ken was simply too good for him on that occasion. At that elite level, any player can beat another. Knowing Lew, who had as much or more natural talent as any player I've seen, he would have regarded the Grand Slam as a feather in his cap and nice to have won, but he wouldn't have lost too much sleep over being thwarted. He took his wins and his losses with a grain of salt. All that mattered to him was that every time he went onto a court he played to the best of his ability.

I played in a number of tournaments throughout the US before Hop, Bob and I arrived back in Australia in October.

Mum and Dad, dressed in their Sunday best and wearing huge grins, were at the airport to greet me. In the photo of the reunion that ran in the *Central Queensland Herald*, you can clearly see the distinct resemblance between my father and me.

I felt my game was improved immeasurably by that tour, and Hop thought it was a positive experience, too. He announced to the media at the airport that he had been pleased with Bob's and my progress and that he considered us Davis Cup players of the future. I repaid his faith by becoming Australian Junior Champion at Kooyong, Victoria, in January 1957. Secretly I was hoping that my name would be read out when the Davis Cup team was announced days after the Australian championships. I'm told Hop pushed for my selection, but the powers that be in the LTAA considered me too young and chose Bob Mark, who was nine months older than me, to accompany Lew Hoad, Ashley Cooper, Neale Fraser, Mal Anderson and Roy Emerson. (Ken Rosewall had turned professional and so was ineligible to play.) My non-selection enraged the head of Queensland tennis, Big Bill Edwards, a portly, autocratic fellow who sometimes occupied two seats in the grandstand to accommodate his 136-kilogram bulk, who railed, 'Laver won the American and Canadian junior singles last year. This season he won the Queensland, Victorian, South Australian and Australian junior titles, and was unbeaten in the Linton Cup. What more has a boy got to do to impress the selectors?' I wasn't concerned by my omission. I knew my time would come and so, Hop told me, did he.

In those days, it was compulsory for 18-year-old blokes to do 176 days of National Service army training, which meant that I had to put tennis on the backburner for a bit. It also cost me a second overseas trip with Hop. I could have deferred my stint as a trainee soldier, but thought it would be better to get it over with then rather than have to serve it later and have it disrupt my senior tennis career. It rankled not to be competing at Wimbledon and New York's Forest Hills again, but I still had the chance to play in local Queensland tournaments. I have no memory of it today, but my sister-in-law Betty Laver, Trev's wife, whose 2001 book *Rod Laver: The Red-Headed Rocket from Rockhampton*, chronicled my career with care and accuracy, wrote that I won the mixed doubles at the Central Queensland Hard Court Championships – *with Mum as my partner!* – as well as taking out the open singles. Brother Trevor made it a real family affair when he won the doubles with his mate George Lucke. I also played in the New South Wales championships and it was a thrill to go up against Wimbledon and US title winner, the American Vic Seixas. He was 34 and I was 19 when we faced off and his experience and court smarts were too much for me, although I snatched a set off him.

I would have played tennis barefoot on hot coals; it was all I wanted to do, yet there were some aspects of amateur tennis in Australia then that did not sit right even with me. So despite still being a pipsqueak in the sport I didn't have to think too long before joining, in November 1957, a group of our best players – current Davis Cup representatives Ash Cooper, Mal Anderson, Roy Emerson, Neale Fraser and

Mervyn Rose (Lew Hoad was now in the pro ranks), as well as Bob Howe, Warren Woodcock, Barry Phillips-Moore, Bob Mark, Neil Gibson and Don Candy – who were seeking better amenities at Australian tournaments. We wanted the LTAA to provide suitable on-court and changing room amenities at tournaments; the toilets and showers were particularly primitive. We saw a need for more reasonable expenses to be paid to cover our basic living costs while we were on the road competing. And we felt umpires had to be provided for every tournament match; many times the lack of an available umpire had resulted in players officiating at their own matches. Other times, inexperienced people were plucked out of the crowd to umpire or be linesmen; we made very sure we didn't hit the ball near the lines. There was a lot right, and a lot wrong, with the set-up then. I was told that once, when a couple of the designated LTAA tour selectors were assigned to run their eye over likely players, they went to a Davis Cup tie (series of matches) and became angry when they saw a couple of kids on the court and ordered them off. A bemused Ken Rosewall and Lew Hoad took their racquets and left. Unbelievably, if this story is true, the selectors were so distanced from the players, they didn't even recognise the two best youngsters in the country. Our delegation did not manage to bring matters to a head. The LTAA greeted our request for a meeting to discuss the issues with stony silence. Most tennis lovers knew we were not troublemakers and thought we had a point.

On 29 November 1957, one of my great ambitions came to fruition when, after I beat Bob Mark, Warren Woodcock and US Davis Cup player Herb Flam in quick succession in lead-up matches, I was selected in the Australian Davis Cup practice squad. They had made me sweat. First, the selectors chose five of the six Davis Cup players and I wasn't among them, but it was made clear to me that if I could string a few wins together to show I was in better form than Bob Mark and Bob Howe, I would join Anderson, Cooper, Emerson, Fraser and Rose in the squad. I'll never forget my match against Herb Flam or, specifically, what happened immediately after it. Usually I was the most reserved of players; I'd learned to be that way, Charlie and Hop having both lectured me on the importance of self-control. My habit, at the end of a match, win or lose, was to approach the net and congratulate my opponent, shake his hand and leave the court with him. This time, I had a brain explosion, and when I hit the winning point against Herb, I ran at the net and hurdled it. Or tried to. My foot got caught and I crashed down on my head. The crowd's cheers turned to belly laughs. Herb looked embarrassed for me. I wished the earth would swallow me whole.

•

The Davis Cup was the brainchild of four members of Harvard University's tennis team who wanted to set up a regular match between American and British players. When agreement on rules and venues was reached between the competitors, one of the American quartet, Dwight Davis, commissioned and paid for a handsome trophy (some say, since decorative additions have been made to the Cup, it now resembles a gleaming golden wedding cake!) designed by William Durgin and crafted by Rowland Rhodes. Officially, the competition was called the International Lawn Tennis Challenge. In time it became known simply as the Davis Cup.

To briefly digress, Donald Budge once told me that the four initially prominent Davis Cup countries, the United States, Great Britain, France and Australia, were known as the 'Grand Slam' of tennis nations and their national tournaments came to retain the title, as did the feat that Don and I achieved of winning all four of those tournaments in a calendar year.

The first Davis Cup tie took place in 1900 when a team representing the United States played a British Isles team at the Longwood Cricket Club in Boston. In 1905, Australasia (a combined team comprising Australian and New Zealand players), France, Belgium and Austria were invited to compete, and by the 1920s, 20 nations were doing battle all over the world each year for the Davis Cup. Early domination by the United States, Great Britain and Australasia was shattered when France's renowned Four Musketeers – Jacques Brugnon, Henri Cochet, René Lacoste and Jean Borotra – ruled the roost from 1927 to '32.

In the '30s, '40s, '50s and '60s, the US and Australia (no longer Australasia) again dominated. The Davis Cup looms large in our tennis history. Harry Hopman won a record 16 Davis Cups as captain and Roy Emerson won a record-breaking eight Challenge Rounds out of the nine he played in, and won 34 out of 38 contested rubbers (individual matches). In the 1970s, it was the turn of Czechoslovakia, Italy, Sweden and South Africa to snare the coveted Cup, and in recent years Spain, Argentina, Serbia, Croatia, France and Germany have become Davis Cup powers.

Until 1971, the nation that had won the Cup the previous year stood back while all the other nations competed in a year-long tournament for the right to take on the Cup-holder in the final, which was called the Challenge Round. Since 1972 all nations, including the champion, compete in the knockout with the last two standing contesting the Davis Cup final.

A changing of the guard of the Australian Davis Cup team was in progress when I made my Cup debut. Past stalwarts Rex Hartwig, Frank Sedgman, Ken McGregor, Lew Hoad, Ken Rosewall, Ashley Cooper and Mervyn Rose had turned, or were about to turn, professional, thereby disqualifying themselves from representing Australia in the strictly amateur Davis Cup ties as well as from amateur tournaments such as Wimbledon and the Australian, French and US titles. New faces had to be found to fill the breach and Neale Fraser, Mal Anderson, Roy Emerson, Fred Stolle and I were tapped on the shoulder to stand up.

When I became a member of the Australian Davis Cup squad in 1957, albeit a very junior member, I found myself stepping into the shoes of giants. Quite frankly, I was in awe of these great players, and great men, and I tried to model myself on them. Lew Hoad was my hero, of course, and Frank Sedgman was another whom I respected immensely.

He was a Davis Cup stalwart and would win 22 Grand Slam events in singles, doubles and mixed doubles. He had superb timing, one of the best volleys of all time (developed hitting against a barn as a boy), and an equally devastating backhand and forehand. Yet just as important to me is that he was, and is, a kind and gracious man. I first met Frank when I was a mere boy playing a junior tournament in Melbourne and he was friendly to me and even hit a few balls my way. I've never forgotten Frank's kindness, and if a starry-eyed kid ever approaches me, you can bet I'll give him or her a smile, a g'day and a good luck, just as Sedg did me.

They were all very different blokes from a variety of backgrounds, but I like to believe that the top Australian players of our golden age in the '50s and '60s – Sedgman, Hoad, Rosewall, Fraser, Emerson, Stolle, John Newcombe, Tony Roche and others – shared special traits. Firstly, to a man they were excellent players with an array of fine strokes, incredibly fit, and cool in a crisis on the court. They played hard, to the death if need be, but fairly, and did not throw tantrums or racquets. They did not let fame make them bigheaded, and were invariably modest in victory and generous in defeat. They knew how to enjoy themselves (boy, did they know how to enjoy themselves!), but they respected each other and their opponents and the game of tennis, and took their role as ambassadors for Australia very seriously by steering clear of trouble. I sure didn't want to be the one to let down that dynasty.

Ask any of the overseas players who faced the Australians, a victory over an Aussie was something to cherish, because it would be hard fought. Consider our record. From 1950 to 1970 Australians won the Wimbledon men's singles 13 times, the Australian championships 18 times, the United States 14 times and the French 10 times. And the Davis Cup 15 times. I've thought long and hard about why we were so dominant in that era. Mostly I believe Australia was simply blessed with an extraordinary group of fine players who all happened along at about the same time. But there are other reasons. I think with the sheer number of Australian kids from all demographic groups who played tennis in the late '30s, '40s and '50s with as much passion as they swam and played cricket and footy, on local courts which, unlike today, seemed to be on every block, it was only natural that Australia produced champions. Our warm, dry, sport-friendly climate, which allowed us to play outdoors all day long and into the twilight, was another factor. So, too, our fresh food, which built strapping kids. Back then, as well, when many overseas countries were still recovering from World War II, on food rations and austerity programs, with their playing fields having become army barracks, their suburbs and cities piles of rubble, Australia was fortunately largely spared deprivation and bomb damage.

There's no doubt, either, that we had more than our share of champion tennis players because of our youth development system in which fellows like Harry Hopman identified likely young players, trained them hard and made tennis their life. Unlike in some other countries where tennis was regarded as a hobby for the privileged, something to be squeezed in between the more important pursuits of university study and climbing the employment ladder, in Australia being a full-time tennis player was a perfectly acceptable career and, though there was precious little money to be had, the travel and glory made it something to aspire to.

On my selection in the Davis Cup squad and inclusion in the group of players who played on the so-called southern circuit, Brisbane, Sydney, Melbourne, Adelaide, to prepare for the Cup, our captain Harry Hopman took me under his wing. He and Stan Nicholls, who ran a Melbourne gym, devised an ongoing strength and conditioning program for me. Early on, when I was still very slight, I lifted heavy weights and dumbbells and did wrist curls and chin-ups to build up my chest and shoulders and general strength. Later, Hop switched me to an agility-focused routine that sped up my reflexes and loosened my muscles. And, of course, with Hop as the drill sergeant, there were endless double knee jumps, star jumps and push-ups, and long runs to boost my cardio and, in the heat, test my resolve to push through the exhaustion barrier and develop mental toughness. Occasionally he'd give me time off to return home to be with my family and fish and water-ski behind my brother Trevor's boat (which I was rather chuffed that he had christened *Rocket*).

Australia played the United States in the Davis Cup Challenge Round at Melbourne's Kooyong on 26, 27 and 28 December 1957. I knew I was there simply to observe and absorb the Cup intensity. I didn't expect to get a match. My major contribution was being orange boy, serving balls, and running errands for Hop and the men who'd be playing in the tie. Mal Anderson and Ashley Cooper won their singles matches against Barry MacKay and Vic Seixas, and our doubles pair Anderson and Merv Rose beat MacKay and Seixas, and we ended up winning three rubbers to two. In 1958, I was again selected in the squad and once more played no matches, but this time the United States got payback. With Alex Olmedo on fire, they beat us three rubbers to two at Brisbane's Milton courts and reclaimed the Cup.

Chapter 4

Into the cauldron

SOME PLAYERS DIDN'T RESPOND TO HOP'S AUTHORITARIAN ways as easily as Lew Hoad and I did. We did everything Hop demanded of us, knowing it was making us better players and men. Frank Sedgman, Ken Rosewall, Bob Mark and Ken Fletcher, on the other hand, rebelled at various times. Bob was often in Hop's bad books for returning to our team hotel after curfew having enjoyed a few beers. One time when we were playing in London and all staying at the Kensington Palace Hotel, Ken Fletcher and Martin Mulligan got back after the captain's appointed hour. They were about to sit down to dinner when Hop said, 'You two blokes, before you eat you're going to run down to the Serpentine and back.' It was a distance of about 10 kilometres. Fletch and Marty asked Hop if he was out of his mind. Hop assured them that he wasn't and told them to get going.

They did, but only ran a short distance before they found a fountain and splashed themselves with water and lay low for an hour before they returned to the hotel, pretending they were covered in sweat after their long run. Unfortunately for them, Hop had followed them and knew exactly what they had got up to. From then on he had little respect for them. He believed that if you had no discipline away from the court you'd have none on it.

In 1958, for the first time, I was holding my own with Australia's best. In March I had a five-set win over fellow leftie Neale Fraser in the quarter finals of the Australian Hard Court titles at Milton. The match went on and on, for four hours and five minutes, in blistering heat, and one set, the third – in those days before tie-breakers – ended up 17–15 my way.

I made the third round of the singles at Wimbledon where I was taken to school by 36-year-old Jaroslav Drobny, a Czechoslovakian refugee who, as I mentioned, had beaten Ken Rosewall with some marvellous subterfuge to win Wimbledon in 1954. We played on the fabled centre court and, I'll admit it, I was a bundle of nerves. Usually I didn't get edgy before a match, but that day I was shaking. In the lead-up my mind was not on the match, but obsessing about protocol at that daunting tennis shrine. A fellow named E.G. Bulley, who was the locker official in the men's changing rooms, came to my rescue and explained that the rigmarole was as follows: my opponent and I come onto centre court together, walking under the gate emblazoned with the words from Rudyard Kipling's poem 'If', then we turn to the Royal Box up behind the baseline and bow, just a respectful dip accompanied by a smile. When the time came, I managed to pull that off, though I was trembling and my throat was dry.

That ordeal negotiated successfully, I took in my opponent and felt much better. Drobny was old and overweight and I figured that if I played my best I would surely beat him by making him run and exhausting him. So much for theories. Drob more than compensated with his slick, surgical technique and control that he had honed over decades at the top level. He lobbed me, chipped me and drop-shotted me, and had *me* scampering all over the place. In no time at all he had me down 6–1, 6–1, and although I lifted for the third set he still beat me 6–4. Drob taught me that appearances may deceive, and never to underestimate a champion.

Never let anyone tell you tennis isn't a contact sport. Soon after Wimbledon, Bob Mark knocked himself out when he and I teamed against Americans Ham Richardson and Alex Olmedo in the United States National Doubles Tournament. We were doing it tough, when Bob scrambled from the baseline to the net to reach a drop shot. He was really flying and when he tried to pull up at the net, he stumbled, his feet shot straight out and he crashed backwards, striking his head on the hard surface. An x-ray in hospital after he regained consciousness revealed an intact skull. Bob recovered in time for the US championships and we made the quarter finals.

Back home in November, Mal Anderson and I, pairing for the first time, won the Queensland doubles title and beat

Ashley Cooper and Neale Fraser in a marathon five-setter in the final of the South Australian, then we beat Ash and Neale again in the Victorian, just before the Davis Cup Challenge Round against the US. I thought, having achieved what we had that year, that Mal and I would be chosen to play doubles in the Cup, but Hop must have thought I was still a bit green and he opted for Neale Fraser to team with Mal.

At the Australian titles in January 1959, Bob Mark and I beat Don Candy and Bob Howe to win the doubles final, but by the time the Queen's Club Tournament rolled around in June, just before Wimbledon, Hop, possibly thinking of the gruelling Davis Cup campaign that lay ahead of us in December when we would try to wrest the Cup back from the high-flying Americans, partnered me with Roy Emerson. That was okay by me. I was a huge fan of Emmo. One year older than me, he was the fittest player I ever saw, and he had all the skills and a fighting spirit. He was a man of strong principles, one of which was never to complain or make excuses when he lost. His strong wrists were the result of milking hundreds of cows back home on his family's dairy farm in tiny Blackbutt in the Queensland bush. With his slim build, open features, shiny black hair and white teeth embedded with gleaming gold fillings, he was a pin-up boy. We were mates off and on the court and I liked to joke that we'd played each other so often we were as familiar as summertime repeats on TV. Over our long careers, Roy was so often my nemesis, as I was his. A victory over him was always sweet and he would cut out his heart to beat me. I always had trouble playing him. He was Mr Consistent. His return of serve was always good, though serving was not his strongest point. He volleyed well. Emmo had a piercing and distinctive laugh on the court and whether he was my opponent or my doubles partner it was music to my ears.

In my singles campaign at Wimbledon that year, I began using a swinging serve. Before, I had relied on a kicking service. The swinging serve soon became one of my trademark strokes. I beat Englishman Alan Mills, who went on to be Wimbledon tournament referee from 1982 to 2005, in four sets to set up a date with Frenchman Jean Molinari in the quarter finals. The match report read: 'Laver won, 6–3, 6–3, 6–0 in a match lasting less than an hour. He began confidently, and broke through immediately, hitting his ground strokes crisply. His left-hand service, which swung away to Molinari's backhand, baffled the Frenchman . . . Laver's backhand forced Molinari into errors at the net. Laver took the third set 6–0 in just 13 minutes. He finished the match with a smash that made the crowd gasp.' In the semi I played the American Barry MacKay, who had beaten Neale Fraser in the quarters. This was possibly the hardest match I had played to date. Barry took the first set 13–11, I won the second 11–9 and the third 10–8. He fought back hard to win the fourth 9–7, before I won the deciding fifth set 6–3. It took us two hours just to play those first two long sets. We received a standing ovation from the crowd.

I had to pinch myself. I was in the Wimbledon final, only the third unseeded player ever to make it through, and my opponent was Alex 'The Chief' Olmedo, the genial Peruvian who was the United States Davis Cup ace. This time when I faced the Royal Box, which was crammed with dukes and duchesses, I had my bow down pat and didn't give protocol a second thought. Alex beat me 6–4, 6–3, 6–4. His powerful serve, speed and accuracy at the net were too much for me. His stronger volleys forced me wide and when I was out-manoeuvred he smashed winners to the open court. I was pleased at saving two match points on my service in the final game. Charlie and Hop had told me, 'Never give up!' and I certainly wasn't about to on that grand stage.

The Wimbledon doubles final took place the day after the singles final and, aching in every bone and muscle, I dragged myself out onto the court to join Bob Mark against Mal Anderson and Neale Fraser in an all-Australian match. We lost. Of course, afterwards there were beers all round. I did notch my first Wimbledon finals win when I teamed with Darlene Hard in the mixed doubles to down Neale and Maria Bueno. No wonder I was feeling weary at the end of that Wimbledon tournament. I had competed in three finals and in reaching them I played 628 games, a Wimbledon record.

Straight after Wimbledon, the Australian Davis Cup team flew to Mexico to prepare for our inter-zone Cup match against the Mexicans at Chapultepec Club in Mexico City. Hop got us there early enough to acclimatise to the 2240-metre altitude which, apart from sapping your oxygen, made the ball fly longer and bounce higher. My dreams came true when I made my Davis Cup debut in the second singles match, then elation became despair when I was beaten in straight sets by Mario Llamas. Mario, in his high-altitude element, played a virtually error-free match. What a let-down. My loss was even more galling because Neale Fraser had won the first singles against Antonio Palafox. We could have been ahead two matches to zero, but were locked up at one-all and it was my fault. Hop remained cool. 'I'm concerned that we gave up our lead, but what's the use of worrying? I think we'll have the edge on the Mexicans in the doubles.' As usual, he was on the money. We won the doubles and the return singles (to my relief I downed Palafox) to claim a four matches to one victory.

After we downed the Mexicans we went on to beat Canada, Italy and India and earned our chance to reclaim the Cup from the United States in the Challenge Round at Forest Hills in August. I redeemed myself after my less-than-stellar performance in Mexico City by wrapping up the tie against Italy when I beat their best player, Nicola Pietrangeli. After the match, Nicola was kind: 'I tell you, that kid is another Lew Hoad. I've been telling everybody for three years how good that kid is going to be. But now I tell you he is even better than I thought he was. Give him two years and he will beat everyone.'

Reporting on our match, former US Davis Cup player Ham Richardson wrote: 'The victory of Rod Laver is further proof of the soundness of Australia's junior development system. When a country is able to lose eight of its Davis Cup stars in a period of eight years, all of them still in their prime when they became professionals, and still produce youngsters of Rod's calibre to fill the breach, a lot of credit is due to the organisers of the game and their many loyal workers. America may chuckle with glee as each Australian champion leaves the Davis Cup picture, but always there seems to be a host of young and gifted aspirants who quickly develop into world beaters.' Added Adrian Quist in his newspaper column: 'Laver has moved into the champion bracket because he now realises he can play well enough to beat anybody. He is a completely natural player with smooth, easy-flowing shots and good reflexes. These attributes are necessary to reach the top, but in the past his reserve, extreme shyness and inability to express himself have been reflected in his game, and he has been beaten by players not in his class.'

In all the Davis Cup campaigns I played under Harry Hopman, Hop ran his usual tight ship. He drove us, made us fitter than any other team, and ensured that we con-ducted ourselves on and off the court as proud and dignified representatives of Australia. Just as well, then, that he never found out about one party in 1958. The Australian Davis Cup team had been invited to a rowdy rooftop shindig in an apartment block in the Back Bay area of Boston and, though it was nothing like some of the problems you read about sportsmen getting involved in today, we made enough of a ruckus for the police to be called. Just as Ashley Cooper was showing off his standing long jump skills a burly sergeant burst onto the roof and said that he was arresting us because our racket was keeping residents awake all over Boston. 'I'm backing the paddy wagon up to the front door downstairs and I'm taking everybody in to Station 16!'

I was terrified and pictured Hop's furious reaction, and Mum and Dad and Charlie back home picking up their morning newspaper and reading how I'd disgraced Australia by being thrown into jail. I seriously considered leaping off the roof and escaping before someone told me that we were five storeys up. When one of us begged the sergeant to forgive us because we were the Australian Davis Cup team, he growled, 'What in hell is the Australian Davis Cup team?' Happily, after giving us all the fright of our lives, he told us he'd let us off. We were as quiet as church mice for the rest of the night. Unusually for Hop, who had eyes in the back of his head and everywhere else, he never did find out. Thank goodness for that, because his wrath would have been spectacular.

The difference between the modest, understated approach to sport adopted by Australians back then and the brash and boastful ways of the Americans was evident in the lead-up to the 1959 Davis Cup Challenge Round when we took on the United States in New York. American captain Perry Jones crowed to reporters, 'We'll knock 'em over five matches to nothing. We've got the material to beat the Aussies and we're going to do it,' and their best player Alex Olmedo trumpeted, 'I told the captain I'll win every match I play in – and I will!' (At this point, I can't not mention that Neale Fraser beat Alex in the first match!)

I suppose there're two ways of looking at it. Apart from our egalitarian national trait of not wanting to appear big-headed and above our station, we relished being the underdog and not talking ourselves up because we then avoided the pressure of everyone expecting you to win. We had no doubts about our ability, we just didn't bang our drum about it. The Yanks, on the other hand, are a self-confident race and if they believed they were the best they had no qualms about telling the world. While we weren't fazed by the Americans' boasts – in fact we used the Americans' crowing as motivation to ram their words down their throats – other nations, if they had doubts about themselves and credited the Yanks' hype, could be beaten before they went onto the court.

I recall the 1959 Challenge Round against the United States with mixed feelings. We zipped the Americans' mouths to beat them three matches to two and brought the Davis Cup back home, but I was far from happy with my performance. In the second singles match I was beaten by Barry MacKay 7–5, 6–4, 6–1, which saw the US draw even with us after Neale Fraser beat Alex Olmedo in the first singles. Australia went ahead 2–1 when Neale and Emmo beat Alex and Earl 'Butch' Buchholz in the doubles, and then, wouldn't you know it, all I had to do was win my reverse singles match against Olmedo to clinch the Cup, but the Chief prevailed 9–7, 4–6, 10–8, 12–10. Thanks to me, when Neale faced off with Barry MacKay in the second reverse singles, the match that would decide the Challenge Cup, it was level pegging again, Australia 2, the United States 2.

My match against Alex was a strange one. How I blew that match is beyond me, suffice to say that I could still be an erratic player in 1959. It's fair to say that I won the match everywhere but on the scoreboard. In the first set I powered ahead to lead 4–0, dropped my bundle, then recovered to take two set points in the 14th game, yet unbelievably I still lost the set. After I won the second set, in the third I took three set points from Alex in the 10th game, and just when I seemed to be in the ascendancy my game fell apart again. Something sadly similar happened in the fourth set when I held another set point in the 18th game, then relinquished that point, and lost the set and the match. My performance was a comedy of errors but without the laughs. I interspersed some terrific ground strokes with some appalling volleying.

The Davis Cup was anyone's when Neale Fraser, the tall, elegant son of a Victorian judge who turned his back on a career in the law or medicine to play tennis, played Barry MacKay in the fifth and deciding match. Before the match, Perry Jones declared, 'We are going to beat Australia 3–2. I am awfully happy and proud.' Perry would have walked off with the Cup then and there, but Neale Fraser thwarted him and his team. Neale beat Barry in four sets and we, not the Yanks, won 3–2. I was off the hook. Losing to Alex Olmedo remains the biggest disappointment in my career. I was down on myself for once again placing Australia in such peril. To his credit, Hop didn't blame me. He knew I'd done my best. He told the press, 'With one more year of experience behind him, Rod would have won.' And it was a nice gesture for Grand Slam winner Donald Budge to find me after my match, shake my hand and say, 'You played a darn good game, you should have won.' I didn't believe Don, but it was a nice gesture. I broke my flight home with a couple of days' rest and recreation in Honolulu. I wanted to analyse another sub-par Davis Cup performance, and I hoped that soaking up the surf and sun on Waikiki would help repair a damaged left shoulder. In fact, it would take six months of treatment before the doc cleared me to play, just in time for the 1960 Australian championships at Milton.

In those years, playing with and against excellent players in tournaments throughout Australia and all over the world, I received a master's degree in tennis. Stronger and fitter than I had ever been, and having experienced different conditions and the high intensity of top-line tennis, my basic game was taking shape.

One advantage of getting stronger was that I could put more top spin on the ball than ever before. Lew Hoad was immensely strong and could roll his whole arm to apply spin, but while I was more powerful now, I still didn't have his strength so I made do by rolling my arm and wrist, and it worked for me. What a good feeling it was, too, when I was timing the ball sweetly. I liked to hit my bread and butter shots, the heavy top-spin forehand and backhand, across the court to my opponent, putting the onus on him to return it and, sure enough, before long the ball was not whistling back at me but coming to me easily. I could keep that up all day, and the older I became, the better I was at dictating play.

I also became adept at the slice, which is when you apply back spin to the ball so it bounces low. To me, the slice is the best approach shot (an approach shot being an aggressive response to a ball coming at you weakly). While top spin makes the ball go faster, a backhand slice slows it down, giving you more time to run to the net to be in a good position to handle your opponent's return. Also, a low-bouncing slice is not easily returned.

I hit my forehand and backhand volley as if delivering a good punch in the nose, a short, stiff jab with no backswing and my wrist firm, utilising the speed from my opponent's ball to blast it back at him. In this, as in all my other shots, my footwork was as much a factor in making the shot as anything I did with my arm and wrist.

I got enormous satisfaction from hitting through the ball, getting my racquet back in plenty of time as soon as I knew whether I'd be receiving a ball to my backhand or forehand, then getting down to the ball, bending my knees, hitting through the ball with the centre of the racquet and following through.

Not being tall, I wasn't built to do a cannonball serve, so I adopted a kicker serve, which enticed a right-hander to his right and so opened up the court for me; a sliced serve to my opponent's backhand (by tossing the ball slightly to the left and hitting it with a snap of my wrist as my arm moved from left to right, giving side spin); and a swinging serve. Serving well is vital. So is returning serve. Having your serve broken is psychologically damaging. I always felt if I could take the first two points and the first two games of every set I was on my way to a win.

I learned not to do anything too strenuous in the hour before a match that could cause me to pull a muscle, so no double knee jumps, for example. I would simply loosen my muscles by stretching and then hit some balls. When the sound of the ball coming off the racquet felt just right to me, I knew I was ready to play. That meant I was middling the ball and my rhythm was okay.

Anticipation – the ability to read your opponent and plan your shot so you know how he will respond to it and be fit enough to then be there in loads of time to deal with whatever he sends your way – began to come naturally. You're a fortunate player if your anticipation is innate.

When I had a form slump, which happens to all tennis players many times in their career, I never panicked or over-intellectualised the problem. Sometimes all it takes for a reversal of fortune is a break from the game; this can be overnight or for a few days, to let your mind put things in perspective. More often, when I was having a losing streak, I went to the practice court and hit a lot of balls slowly, not trying to do too much, concentrating on getting my shots right again, trying once more to find the middle of the racquet, watching the ball and getting my feet moving, bringing my racquet back early enough, following through – checklisting all the things that Charlie and Hop had drilled into me.

I tried to play percentage tennis, cutting down on errors. I wasn't always successful, as my slow starts in some matches, mid-match slumps and resultant losses to lesser ranked players attested. Early on, I was prone to inexplicable rushes of blood that saw me follow a good shot with an appalling one, or muff a winning shot, much like

Les Flanders had done against Ashley Cooper at the 1955 Queensland championships. I got steadier each year, but would remain an erratic, up-and-down player until the early 1960s.

Those readers who know only the modern game of tennis might be surprised to learn that at this stage of my career, I played in whites (made of cotton that, unlike the synthetic clothing of today, became heavy when I sweated), and wore Dunlop OC Volleys (OC standing for 'orthopaedically correct'). Today's shoes provide better traction, support, durability and comfort, but Volleys were as good as anything available back then. They had supple herringbone rubber on the sole, ideal for grass courts, which is what we mostly played on. They were not so good on cement, and would wear out after a set. I wore two pairs of socks, thin ones on the bottom and thicker ones on top, to prevent blisters. I used a wooden racquet, a 14-ounce (397-gram) Dunlop Maxply Fort, which had a small head and not too much flex in the natural gut strings, and a leather grip around a handle that I made thicker by winding tape around it so that it fit my hand perfectly. Oh, and my pre-match diet? Steak and eggs all the way.

I've been asked whether my lack of height was a help or a hindrance. Well, obviously when playing a much taller man I had to be careful how close I came to the net to volley because I could be lobbed, but I think I made up for it. I was short, but I was fast and fit, and when you're in the fifth set on a sweltering day it's a hell of a lot easier to be pushing 68 kilograms around the court than 90.

Because I was light and balanced I was very centred, with good footwork, and able to get back to the middle position after playing a forehand or backhand. Many big guys can't get back into position as quickly and you can keep them on the run.

Chapter 5

Breaking through

IN 1960 I PROGRESSED SMOOTHLY THROUGH THE PRELIMIN-
aries of the Australian national titles at the Milton Courts
in Brisbane, and after beating Roy Emerson in the semi
final – it took five tight sets for me to win – I booked a
showdown with the best player in the world, our Davis Cup
saviour Neale Fraser, in the final. I had made the final at
Wimbledon only to lose, and now I was determined to go
one better and win my first major tournament. Just making
a final was no longer good enough. Adrian Quist harboured
reservations about whether I was up to it. 'Rod Laver gives
me butterflies,' he declared in his column. 'The unpredict-
able Laver fought back from a 5–2 deficit in the fifth set
against Roy Emerson to reach the final of the National
Tennis Titles. I never know what he is thinking. Every time
he swings at the ball one has the feeling it could fly for a

perfect winner or shoot along the ground with the speed of a Bradman drive. But with the casual treatment he applies to the game, his amazing range of shots gives him a slight edge on his opponent.'

I'm proud to say that the 1960 Australian championships men's singles final between Neale Fraser and me is remembered as one of the great matches in Australian tennis history. Many who were at the match say they have never seen a crowd so emotionally involved, with the possible exception of the legendary Lew Hoad–Tony Trabert Davis Cup singles match in 1953 when 17,000 spectators went crazy at Kooyong and most of the nation tuned in on the radio. My match with Neale was a tense and brutal five-setter, played in incendiary January heat in front of 8000 wilting but highly excited fans wearing sun hats and zinc cream on their noses and fanning themselves with their programs. Most were barracking for the local boy, yours truly.

Neale and I made each other venture to places neither of us had been before. It was a match in which all the things that I prided myself on, that Charlie Hollis and Harry Hopman told me would be the making of me – my fitness and stamina, my refusal to be beaten, my array of shots – clicked in . . . in the last three sets, anyway. Neale overwhelmed me 7–5, 6–3 in the first two, and to many my cause must have seemed hopeless. At my flighty, erratic worst, I had been sacrificing accuracy for speed and power in my serves, and committed way too many double faults. However, in the third set I steadied the ship, got my serve back under control and, aware that Neale, who at 26 was five years older than me, was beginning to struggle in the extreme heat, I upped the pace. I won the third set 6–3. Being the champion he was, Neale came back at me hard in the fourth, which, if he'd won it, would have given him the match. It was match point against me in the 10th game of that set but I battled my way out of trouble by scrambling madly to retrieve Neale's shots and level at deuce, then, having snatched back the momentum, I went on to win 8–6.

As we crossed over before the fifth and deciding set, Neale and I, good mates and merciless rivals, stood together for a moment in the shade of the grandstand. (Unbelievably, and shamefully, in those days in amateur tennis there were no chairs for the players at courtside, though plenty for the officials in the hospitality tent.) 'Whew,' said Neale, 'how bloody hot is this!' In the final set, we went hell for leather, and though we were both exhausted, physically and mentally – Neale's legs were actually buckling, like a drunk's – we played some thrilling rallies and each scored with excellent passing shots, and the crowd cheered itself hoarse with every one.

At one stage, Neale lobbed over my head and I raced back and gave the ball an almighty crack with my backhand and it drifted high and wide. Neale volleyed it with his backhand and fluffed the shot. That was the catalyst that swung momentum back my way. Emmo, who was watching in the stand, went to Neale afterwards and said, 'Frase, that ball would have gone out by 15 yards if you hadn't hit it!' Neale saved *six* match points. Afterwards he couldn't remember anything about that set. 'I played in a daze and only vaguely remember some of the calls,' he said. 'I'd completely had it.' In the end, luck was with me and I won the set 8–6. At 21, I was the Australian champion, and only the second Queenslander to achieve that honour.

Adrian Quist, in his match report, seemed happy to change his tune about me: 'I can now understand how Laver, Fraser and Emerson brought the Davis Cup home to Australia. These players have the nerve and courage which are the basic qualities of champions.'

The Australian titles campaign did my bad shoulder no favours, and right afterwards it was back for treatment so I'd be fit enough to be selected for that year's LTAA tour and acquit myself well in Paris, London and New York in the majors.

In the French championships at Roland Garros in June, the area around the bottom of my spine became sore. I lasted until the third round when I was beaten by the formidable Manuel Santana of Spain. Just as I had done against Emerson and Fraser in the Australian championships, I started slowly against Manuel. Slowly? That's an understatement. I lost the first five games in the first set, including the set itself, 6–1. I climbed back into the match but lost in five sets. One reason was that I had gone soft on Manuel. Charlie and Hop, time and again, had ordered me to put a bloke away when I had him at my mercy. I didn't do this against the man they called 'Illustrissimo'. In the second set, with me leading 4–1, Manuel suffered a left ankle sprain. He cried out in pain, sat down, whipped off his shoe and hobbled about gingerly, testing to see if he could continue in the match. I went over to him and commiserated. I should have stamped on his foot. My momentum and concentration were broken. Illustrissimo put his shoe back on and won the next 11 games and the match.

Funny thing about the volatile and biased French crowds. While they'd prefer to be cheering a countryman and giving his foreign opponent merry hell, if there was no Frenchman in the game, they'd always support a Continental player over an Englishman, an American or an Australian. They got right behind Manuel that day. Over the years some players have floundered in the highly charged atmosphere. I have to say I was never too fazed by barracking. My keenness and concentration tended to pick up when I was under pressure and I became doubly determined to win. Anyway, having their favourite down a set tends to take the crowd out of the equation, so I tried to go one-up early. Another trick I picked up to avoid being booed when I came onto the court in a hostile environment was to enter the court at the same time as the local hero, my opponent. They won't boo then, for fear of insulting him, and you can kid yourself that the cheers meant for him are for you.

By Wimbledon one month later, my ailments had healed and my form had returned. I beat Emmo in the quarter final in four sets and Italy's Nicola Pietrangeli in five in the semi, and there, once more, waiting for me in the final was the all-too familiar form of Neale Fraser, bent on revenge. Unlike our war of attrition in the Australian final, this was a percentage match, one of cat and mouse, both of us concentrating on not making mistakes. This mindset suited Neale more than me at this stage of my career, and his superior serving won the match for him 6–4, 3–6, 9–7, 7–5. Bob Mark and I were beaten by Rafael Osuna and Dennis Ralston in the doubles final, which made Darlene Hard's and my win in the mixed doubles a sweet saving grace. There was one funny moment in that match when the elastic in Darlene's pants snapped and she was forced to leave the court for running repairs.

On to the United States nationals at Forest Hills. Following a week-long postponement of the tournament after Hurricane Donna laid waste to large tracts of the US east coast (there were 3.5-metre waves in New York Harbor!), Neale Fraser and I once more fought out the final after beating, respectively, Dennis Ralston and Butch Buchholz in the semis. I was getting heartily sick of seeing Frase's ugly mug on the other side of the net in these big games. What a marvellous rivalry Neale and I had in 1960, and he made it two majors to one when he beat me convincingly 6–4, 6–4, 9–7. He had not dropped a set throughout the tournament.

That year, too, saw the emergence of one of the real mavericks of Australian tennis: big, balding Bob Hewitt, who in his career won all the four majors in men's doubles and mixed doubles and then became a South African citizen. He was unlike any other Australian player. Yes, he was fit and had all the shots, but while he was a pleasant-enough bloke in civvies, on court he was a niggler who liked to upset his opponents with gamesmanship and naked aggression. In a semi final of the Queensland championships at Milton in

November, I teamed with Bob Mark to beat Hewitt and Bob Howe. Hewitt baited Mark relentlessly through the match, and in the dressing rooms afterwards he hurled the contents of a soft drink bottle at Mark, who displayed great self-control in not retaliating.

Hewitt had no such good fortune when he shaped up to Englishman Roger Taylor after an acrimonious match at a Berlin tournament in 1969 and rugged Roger, a handy boxer, knocked him out and split open his eyebrow with a left hook. As Roger told the tale, after he had beaten Hewitt on the court, Hewitt stormed into the locker room swearing and shouting, 'I'm going to fight you! You're a cheat!' When Taylor told Hewitt he was being a sore loser, Hewitt, said Taylor, pushed him into the lockers. 'I thought he was going to hit me, so I hit him first. I can't remember how often I hit him but it was more than once.' Hewitt received six stitches in hospital but made it back in time to play in the doubles. Roger didn't escape unscathed, though. When he belted Bob, he hurt his hand and had to withdraw from the tournament.

Italy faced us in the Davis Cup at White City in December, and we won four matches to one. I was pleased with my form in my 8–6, 6–4, 6–3 straight sets win against the artistic stroke-maker Nicola Pietrangeli in the second singles match. It wasn't as easy a contest as the score indicates, with each of us breaking the other's serve five times in the first set. *The Sydney Morning Herald* sports reporter Alan Clarkson wrote that he didn't think he had ever seen me play better ('His return of service was immaculate, his volleys crisp and well directed and his passing shots, particularly from the backhand, masterful'), and Adrian Quist felt that my triumph showed I was capable of winning any title in tennis. 'The manner in which he subdued Pietrangeli was eloquent testimony to the improvement in his game.'

There was a wonderful sporting gesture from Neale Fraser in the doubles match, when he and Emmo played Pietrangeli and Orlando Sirola. It was set point in the first set when Neale hit a volley which, though it was clearly out, the linesman called in. He was awarded the point but deliberately hit the next ball over the baseline to negate the umpire's error. The Italians, and the fans, cheered him. The Challenge Cup Round was played in a wonderful spirit, and when Nicola beat Neale in the final match to save Italy from a whitewash, the 12,000 capacity crowd cheered him on.

It was after this tie that I received nibbles from American pros to see if I was interested in joining a professional circuit. I thanked them for thinking of me but said no, and begged them not to tell the press they'd been talking to me because I feared the more sensational elements would make a big thing of it for a headline and write whatever they wanted, which would probably be that I was about to defect. The truth was, I still had much to achieve as an amateur. With the Australian championship under my belt, I was determined to also win the French, Wimbledon and United States singles crowns (though I didn't remotely consider I might win them all in a single year) and, besides, I was loving the life of travelling and playing. I didn't need a lot of money and, at just 22 with no responsibilities or girlfriend, and with tennis my only focus in life, I was happy to live on almost nothing a week. We had to exist on the token wages paid us by our sponsors, just a few pounds weekly, plus a small bonus they gave us when we won a tournament. The LTAA paid no expenses for us to compete in the various state championships, nor appearance fees; in my case the Queensland Association contributed a small amount to my hotel expenses. When we were on an LTAA overseas tour, playing the major amateur tournaments, they paid our airfares and accommodation and allowed us expenses of 25 shillings a day. When we played at Wimbledon, they'd buy our lunch. The pay-off for living on the poverty line was to represent Australia against the best amateur players in the world in the iconic tournaments. Speaking for myself, I was happy – and proud – to do that, for a while. Maybe, I thought, at some point in the future when it was time to make myself financially secure, I would reconsider turning professional and make some serious money taking on, for better or worse, the best pro players in the world, including the fearsome Pancho Gonzales and my compatriots Rosewall, Hoad and Sedgman.

Every time I ran into Lew and Ken around the world they advised me to give deep thought to joining them on the professional circuit. They said I would be a great asset to the pros, that it wasn't an easy life constantly travelling and playing a number of times a week and that as an amateur it would take a little time for me to find my feet, as had happened with them, but with my ability I could secure my post-tennis future, and that of my wife and kids. (Not that a wife and kids were on my horizon then!) I told Lew and Muscles that I didn't think I was up to their standard yet, but perhaps there'd come a day . . .

After the 1960 Davis Cup I took stock of my career. The Australian championships aside, I'd had a string of losses after making the finals of major events, and I thought it would be a good idea to go back to the master, Charlie Hollis, and ask him to help me find the edge that would see me win the big matches instead of faltering at the final hurdle. Back at home in Rockhampton, it was as if I was 10 years old again, up at 5am, Charlie putting me through my paces, bellowing, 'Where's that spin? Don't hit flat! I want to see killer instinct!' Right after, I contested the Central Queensland Singles, and beat my old best mate Frank Gorman in the final. To Charlie's approval, Frank's and my friendship was put on the backburner as I ruthlessly blasted him off the court. 'Geez,' happy-go-lucky Frank quipped to Charlie at the end of it, 'what did you do to him? Did you give him a needle?'

In an early doubles match in the 1961 Australian championships at Melbourne's Kooyong I slipped and fell against a scoreboard and badly sprained my left wrist. The court doctor advised me to withdraw from the tournament, but I was the defending champion and I didn't want to relinquish my title without a fight so I toughed it out. Harry Hopman loaned me a ray lamp and with heat treatment, a postponement of my next singles match by 24 hours, and heavy strapping with adhesive tape and flattened cardboard matchboxes to support the top and bottom of my wrist, I was able to carry on. The singles final, however, was a bridge too far that year. I took the first set 6–1 against Roy Emerson, my passing shots and angled volleys working well, but he overpowered me to win the next three 6–3, 7–5, 6–4, and the Australian singles title. I was bitterly disappointed not to win back-to-back Australian championships, but I was delighted for Roy. The confidence he took from the win, his first major tournament victory, took Emmo to a higher level and he became one of the very best players in the world and a thorn in my side for years to come. Bob Mark and I won the doubles final, after which Bob announced he was quitting Australia to settle down with his South African wife in her homeland, leaving me to find a new partner for the major tournaments to come.

My dodgy back and a dose of fever kept me out of the French Championships in '61, but I was recovered and rested by the time Wimbledon rolled around. My form in the championships at Queen's Club in the week before Wimbledon had been sound. I had a good hit out against a 17-year-old Australian named John Newcombe, who was widely tipped to reach the top by those who knew tennis.

Chapter 6

Winning Wimbledon

By 1961 I was an old hand at Wimbledon and the nervousness that consumed me at my first outings there were a thing of the past. I felt confident that if I played well I could win. I looked at the names of the 127 competitors and saw that I had beaten a good number of the seeded players over recent years. If I played at my best now, I should be able to deal with anything in their armoury. To simplify things, I told myself that I had seven matches to win, and if I could do that I would be Wimbledon champion. And the mere fact of surviving the six preliminary matches meant that I would have played myself into good form for the final, should I be lucky enough to qualify. To give myself a better chance, I scratched myself from the mixed doubles that year.

My first match was played in atmospheric London drizzle. I beat the young Russian Tomas Lejus 6–4, 6–1, 6–1, and advanced to the quarters to enjoy another straight sets win, against Chilean Luis Ayala. In my semi final I downed Indian Ramanath Krishnan, who played a slow, methodical game, again in three sets. I was particularly pleased with my speed around the court and my serving. I felt strong and confident and had overcome my injuries.

My opponent in the final was the American Chuck McKinley, a bloke I had handled well in previous encounters. I told myself, 'You can finish this.' Chuck wasn't a big man, about the same size as me. He was incredibly athletic, a pocket dynamo on the court who scrambled magnificently, and he was more powerful than he looked. He had a short fuse, and was infamous for hitting the ball into the crowd when frustrated and berating himself loudly when he fluffed a shot. Chuck would win Wimbledon in 1963, but 1961 was my year. I beat him 6–3, 6–1, 6–4. It's said I was still grinning when Princess Marina presented me with the trophy. I *was* mighty pleased with my performance. I didn't drop a service game in the match and took only 13 minutes to win the first set. I applied pressure from the outset and didn't let up. Charlie Hollis would have been pleased. The match was over in 56 minutes and later the great English player Fred Perry, who had a stopwatch, told me the ball was in play for only 12 minutes. Chuck, who would die of a brain tumour at the tragically young age of 45, was a better player than he showed that day.

At the post-final press conference, I was repeatedly asked whether, with Wimbledon finally won, I would be turning professional and I said that it was not in my plans.

The United States championships were looming and, besides, I had a job to do helping Australia retain the Davis Cup in December.

I spoke to Mum and Dad on the phone straight after the match. The line was crackly and we had trouble hearing each other, but I got the general idea. They were thrilled. Mum, Lois and Trevor and his wife had listened to the final at home gathered around our wireless, while Dad and Bob tuned in at the Gladstone docks. I was sorry none of them could be at Wimbledon to see the match live. It was simply too expensive for them, and I wasn't making any money so I couldn't shout them air tickets. Dad sent a cablegram: 'All thrilled with your win. Love, Mum, Dad and family.'

Winning my matches was child's play compared to performing at the Wimbledon Victory Ball. In those days, the singles winners had to sit in a row at the top table at the black-tie gathering and make a speech (today, a host asks questions, which is much easier). There were about 800 people in attendance, including royalty. It was nerve-racking, to put it mildly. Most terrifying of all for me, a fellow who had never learned to dance, was when I had to take the women's singles winner, who that year was Englishwoman Angela Mortimer Barrett, in my arms and sweep her around the ballroom in the winners' waltz. I stumbled here and there and trod on Angela's feet, and was terribly apologetic to her, and I was relieved and, frankly, delighted, when I was able to scurry back to my seat.

I was more in my element after the ball when I joined other players for a party at Fred Perry's nightclub where we raced mechanical horses on the stage. This old farm boy was always happy on the back of a horse, real or mechanical, and I did pretty well.

Back in Gladstone, where Mum and Dad had now moved, the press laid siege to their home. When reporters asked Dad how he felt, he exclaimed, 'It just won't come in words. I can't explain how I feel. It's terrific! No one can tell me now that Rodney can't play tennis. From what I heard, he was just terrific!' Charlie Hollis in Rockhampton won a pile of money betting on me, and was heard to cry, 'I knew he'd win when he gave that darn fool mixed doubles away!'

I couldn't replicate my Wimbledon success at the United States championships. Just as I had faced my mate Neale Fraser in major tournaments in 1960, in 1961 Roy Emerson was my nemesis. He beat me in the Australian, and he beat me in the final of the US, and his win was especially meritorious because he played shortly after a marathon five-set semi final against Rafael Osuna. No excuses, Emmo was too strong and won in three sets.

Roy and I stopped off in Los Angeles on the way back to Australia to play in the Pacific Southwest Tournament. I'd just arrived back at my hotel room after dining out when there was a knock on my door. It was Emmo and I could tell by his stricken expression that he had bad news. My old friend and tennis rival Frank Gorman, the big, funny bloke with the wide smile and crinkly hair who looked after me in Brisbane when I moved away from home, had been killed when he drove his car into a bridge. I was in a daze. Frank was so full of life, and now he was gone. To that point in my life, I'd not lost anyone important to me. Frank's death put tennis in perspective. I looked forward to being among my family back in Gladstone. I had been on the road for a year and I wanted my loved ones close.

About this time, pro tennis made another bid to sign me, and again I told them, 'Not yet, I want to play Davis Cup and defend my Wimbledon title.' That was true, but I was also mindful that the amount of money that was on offer was small compared to what other professionals were making. It would be a gamble signing on under those terms and I would have to win consistently to make a profit. I also worried whether my recurring back and shoulder problems would stand up to the pro grind. Tony Trabert told reporters he hoped I would turn professional in the future because the troupe needed new blood to complement their roster, which as well as Australians Hoad and Rosewall, Ashley Cooper and Mal Anderson, and the American Pancho Gonzales, now included world stars Alex Olmedo, Luis Ayala, Mike Davies, Andres Gimeno, Pancho Segura, Butch Buchholz, Barry MacKay and Trabert himself. I had to admit, it was a formidable roster, far stronger than the amateur lineup. While basking in my Wimbledon win and my good showings in the other majors in 1960 and '61, I had to ask myself whether I'd have fared so well if I'd had to play Lew, Muscles and the like.

It was a distraction from the job at hand, with the Davis Cup Challenge Round against Italy at Kooyong just seven weeks away, when the pros upped the ante. They now dangled a £15,000, two-year contract in front of me, and added that if I won my share of matches I could earn up to £22,500. That was a considerable amount of money then, but not enough to convince me to abandon the amateurs. Clearly concerned that I would defect, the LTAA acceded to my request that I be allowed to embark on a private tennis tour the following year. A private tour, which could be funded by a promoter, a wealthy tennis supporter or a commercial enterprise, such as the popular Caribbean circuit, would be made up of five tournaments in Mexico City, Barranquilla City in Colombia, Montego Bay in Jamaica, San Juan in Puerto Rico where we toasted our feet on the Caribe Hilton's concrete courts, and Caracas in Venezuela. There was also the option of playing tournaments in St Petersburg and Miami in Florida and Houston, Texas, while we were away. We'd be paid about $300–$400 appearance money and expenses by the various tournament organisers and come home with maybe $2000–$3000 in our pocket. Playing on those tours in those storybook locations with my good mates Roy Emerson, Neale Fraser, Bob Mark and the other Australians remains one of my great memories. We played hard, relaxed away from tennis officialdom, and saw some of the most beautiful and exotic terrain on earth. After I completed my Caribbean jaunt, I confirmed that I would not be turning professional in 1962. My mind was made up. For the time being . . .

I played Roy Emerson in the final of the Queensland tennis championships and once more began slowly and was forced to grimly fight back from two sets down to win, including 6–0 in the third set that turned the tide of the match. We faced off again in the New South Wales singles final, and I again won in five sets. It was a cracker of a match. Emmo broke my serve in the fifth set and looked likely to win the match. Then, as reported by Adrian Quist, 'came the most exciting scene at White City for many years. Emerson at the net was pounding smashes far and wide; Laver was scampering 20 feet behind the baseline retrieving the ball. Desperately, Emerson tried to kill the point, only to see Laver run outside the court area and drift a superb backhand passing shot across the body to score. The shock of losing this point, in my opinion, cost Emerson the match.' Emmo and I were named the singles players for the Davis Cup Challenge Round. He and Neale Fraser would contest the doubles.

Prime Minister Robert Menzies, a great sports fan, was in the crowd that Boxing Day of 1961 when, in 44-degree heat, Emmo played Nicola Pietrangeli and I took on Orlando Sirola – aka Gigante Bueno, the Good Giant – who'd conquered me in my debut Wimbledon singles match five years earlier, in the first singles rubber. Knowing that Orlando was one of the tallest men in world tennis, before our match Hop had Wayne Reid, who was a good player and a future president of the LTAA, stand a metre inside the baseline and bomb serves at me so the ball was coming from the same angle as a Sirola serve. In due course I learned to handle the steep trajectory and was able to return Wayne's serves, and then I started *attacking* them. That practice made playing Sirola less problematic. I also decided to neutralise Orlando's great reach and capitalise on his slower reactions and lack of agility by not hitting wide but drilling the ball at his feet. In our match, that strategy paid off.

During that Davis Cup tie, more than 100 people were treated by St John Ambulance staff after falling ill or fainting in the blistering heat. An announcement was made on the public address system that anyone feeling queasy should put their head between their legs. Some spectators vacated their seats to stand in the shade of the grandstands, craning to see the action on the court. Prime Minister Menzies, Victorian Governor Sir Dallas Brookes and Lady Brookes left their seats in the sun to shelter under a specially set up umbrella. There were no umbrellas out in the middle, unfortunately. It was, literally, an ordeal by fire, and at the end of the first day's play Australia was ahead 2–0. Next day Emmo and Frase won the doubles, then Roy and I each won the return singles, for a 5–0 victory. The Italians were lambasted by the press, who called the tie 'a mismatch worthy of the Roman Colosseum', and by some in the Kooyong crowd, who accused them of 'throwing in the towel'. At times they had seemed dispirited as they won just three of 18 sets in the entire series, but Nicola Pietrangeli redeemed himself in the final reverse singles against me when we had a stirring five-set battle. Wrote Alan Clarkson of my match with Nicola: 'There were some brilliant moments in the 114-minute struggle. Pietrangeli, with artistic touch in his passing shots, and Laver, with his wristy forehands and backhands, brought roars of delight from the 9000-strong gallery.'

At the presentation of the Cup, Australian Governor-General Lord De L'Isle called Nicky's and my match the best he had seen and said Australian tennis was at a high point of its history. 'The ripest fruit is at the top of the tree, and it was even out of reach of Mr Sirola.' Worried that the Italians' lacklustre showing overall may have harmed amateur tennis, captain Hop declared, 'There were one or two early disappointments in this Davis Cup tie, but instead of dwelling on past disappointments our Italian friends should remember that I have a wonderful team and the Australian boys played some wonderful tennis. Our friends will be given a welcome here when they play the kind of tennis they did today.'

Chapter 7

Daring to dream

THE TITLE 'GRAND SLAM' IS A BIT MISLEADING. TO WIN A Grand Slam, as opposed to a single grand slam tournament, is to win *all four* grand slam tournaments in a single calendar year – the Australian in January, the French in June, the All England (aka Wimbledon) in July and the United States championships in September. As 1962 got underway, only Donald Budge (men's singles, 1938), a freckle-faced redhead like me, Maureen Connolly (women's singles, 1953), Frank Sedgman and Ken McGregor (men's doubles, 1951) and Maria Bueno (playing in the women's doubles, three matches with Darlene Hard and one with Christine Truman James, in 1960) had achieved the feat. In the men's singles, which was my focus, the Australians Jack Crawford and Lew Hoad and Englishman Fred Perry had come close. Each won three of the four tournaments in a single year, but faltered at the final hurdle, the United States. The Grand Slam is one of the Holy Grails of tennis and every player who wins the Australian Open wonders if he or she can go on to win the remaining three events to achieve it. I know I dared to dream in 1962.

Winning all four major tournaments in the one year is a daunting quest. The odds are stacked against you and all of your lucky stars must align. You can't afford form fluctuations and have to get your game up to the top level four times over an eight-month period, while also playing in other tournaments in between, and somehow steering clear of injury and illness. Court surfaces vary in Australia, Paris, London and New York, as do climatic conditions, and in my day simply showing up at the tournaments involved an enormous amount of travel. You have to deal with the pressure: the pressure every tournament exacts in its own right, and the pressure that snowballs as you win one tournament after another. Also, and maybe this is the biggest factor of all, you are pitting yourself against elite players, any one of whom can vanquish you on any given day. In my case, I guess it helped my cause that it was in my makeup not to succumb to nerves and pressure. And I looked after myself. The type of bloke I was then, I didn't knock myself around off the court. By my early 20s I was no longer a teetotaller, having learned to enjoy a few friendly and relaxing beers with my fellow players and people I met through the game, but I was nobody's idea of a party animal.

I have always been uncomfortable analysing my game. I know how I played and why I was successful, and have been happy to leave it to others to chronicle my style. Now I'm going to bite the bullet and attempt to give you an idea of how I played the game in 1962, which was a pivotal year in my early career. When in good form at this stage of my development, I had few technical faults, thanks to Charlie and Hop and my endless practice, and from performing those taxing two-on-one drills till I was ready to keel over.

I had a variety of serves, often wide-swinging, which I was able to disguise from opponents. When serving I had learned not to sacrifice accuracy for speed and power. I found that if I put a little bit of top spin or slice on the ball I got more first serves in and didn't have to rely on a weak second serve. I had a feather-light touch on my drop volleys and a backhand drive carrying top spin or controlling slice when the situation called for it. I had worked hard to improve my backhand and make it as natural a stroke for me as my forehand. My wristy ground strokes on both flanks were hit with top spin, as was my attacking lob. My stroke technique was based on quick shoulder turns, true swings and good timing. I was adept at hitting my backhand on the run, which won me many points. At the net I had forcing volleys that I often hit as backhand stroke volleys, and I could hit sharp under spin angles as well. I handled my opponent's low balls well, generally speaking, and loved to smash anything that came at me at waist level or higher. I was difficult to lob because of my fitness and agility. I had also learned to surprise an opponent by doing the opposite of what he expected me to. From observing Lew Hoad I was able to disguise my cross-court backhand; he'd roll his wrist this way and that and make a shot that looked as if it was going straight down the line and I could do this when it mattered, at break point.

I'd improved my court positioning. Till then, opponents with a good return would give me a lot of trouble, so I worked on getting to the net to volley rather than being caught out of position in no-man's land. Being faster and fitter helped all that. I was quick around the court and the strength in my muscular left forearm and wrist gave me power without loss of control even when I was on the run and at full stretch. My speed and strength, especially my forearm and wrist strength, enabled me to hit counter-punch winners after having been forced out of court by my opponent. While once my left forearm resembled Popeye's, it had now come to look like King Kong's. It was 30.5 centimetres around – as big as then heavyweight champion boxer Rocky Marciano's – and my wrist measured 18 centimetres. The American tennis authority Julius Heldman wrote that when '[Laver] got into the zone he went for broke, then he would literally jump and throw his racket at the ball with all the force he could muster, wrist and arms snapping over at the hit.' I won't disagree with that.

Though less so than earlier in my career, it would be fair to say that in 1962 I was still a somewhat flashy player who'd be overwhelmed in the early games and sets of a match, and then have to battle my way back. It wasn't as if I was lackadaisical – I always came to play – but I was too often a mixture of good and bad. I'm still not sure why I lurched from good to bad form, often many times in a single match.

As I matured as a tennis player I learned to sustain my form. By '62 I was getting a little better at starting strongly and controlling my unnecessarily adventurous shots and incorporating percentage tennis into my game.

I could adapt my style to all surfaces and conditions, including clay after I'd made a point of playing on it often and coming to terms with its special challenges, and my fitness and unflustered mindset enabled me to prevail in my share of five-set matches. In addition, I was unflappable on the court, in my mind and my body language. I didn't dwell on it if I played a bad shot; it was instantly in the past. You're not going to be able to win back a lost point no matter how much you obsess about it. All that mattered to me was winning the *next* point. If you can maintain a positive attitude when things aren't going well for you, that can frustrate an opponent. Thanks to Charlie Hollis, and then studying the greats of our game, I had learned how to change my tactics when the going got tough.

I rarely made extended eye contact with or reacted in any way to my opponent. I kept it impersonal and unemotional on the court. There'd be time for congratulations or commiserations or a post-mortem over a beer afterwards. What I was doing by refusing to engage with the other guy was not letting him into my head to break my concentration. Some players tried to play mind games with me, intimidate me, and when they did I'd simply ignore them. If I hit a winner I'd immediately spin around and take up my position for the next point. If my opponent was disputing a call, if I truly didn't know if it was in or out, I'd not get involved and stand implacably at my end of the court. (If my opponent was the victim of an obviously poor umpiring decision, because I never had an interest in winning unfairly, I would speak up on his behalf, yet if the official refused to be swayed I moved on and gave the matter no more thought. The bad and good calls tend to even out.) The only time my robotic demeanour broke was when, if the bloke on the opposite side of the net pulled off a wonderful winner, I'd flash him a little smile and gesture 'too good'. Tennis is a game, not a war, after all.

How a player looks when he comes onto the court is his own business. For myself, the way Mum and Dad had raised me and then the influence of Charlie and Hop made sure I always tried to look the part. I owed it to all of them, my place in the Australian tennis dynasty and the paying fans. On tour it's not always easy to be sartorially splendid. You're travelling light, living out of a suitcase for months at a time. I usually had five shirts and two pairs of shorts and socks, and shoes which I'd keep gleaming white, the laces too. You'd wash your gear on the run at whatever laundromats you could find, or, more often, in your hotel room bathroom sink. When Emmo and I played on clay in Paris, we'd kick our shoes off and get under the shower fully clad and watch that rich red dirt wash down the plughole. Cleaning my teeth, shaving and combing my hair were among the last things I always did before I walked onto the court.

Speaking of shaves, I had a close one at the Australian championships at White City in January 1962. In the third round, former New South Wales junior champion Geoff

Pares, very much the underdog as I'd been seeded No.1, pushed me hard, and I was close to losing. If I had, my year would have been a different beast entirely, but I was lucky to beat Geoff 10–8, 18–16, 7–9, 7–5. The second set was fiercely fought and took 105 minutes to complete. Geoff played well, no doubt about that; I played poorly and made many errors. I had a bad cold, and perhaps this is what made one reporter write that I looked like I was 'sick and tired of tennis'. He was way out of court. I could be injured and out of form, but in all my career I never tired of the game. Then another scribe asked me, 'Do you think you are too casual on the court?' and I replied, quite logically in my opinion, 'If I thought I was, I wouldn't be.'

Midway through the tournament, Australia's tennis writers named me most outstanding personality in Australian tennis in 1961. I was a bit surprised. It had been a good year, but I was hardly a personality boy. I remained the shy country kid I had always been. My horizon extended no further than my next tennis match. Aside from my quip to the reporter about being casual, I was not known for my one-liners or being a larger than life character. I was a friendly, easygoing bloke, a good son, brother and travelling companion to my tennis peers, I had no glamorous girl-friend . . . I didn't have *any* steady girlfriend and never had. I didn't drink much, didn't party, wasn't really interested in music, books or – apart from the odd western – movies. What I did was practise and play tennis. It would take a very special person to bring me out of my shell, and I didn't meet her for a few more years.

In the quarter finals of the Australian championships my form improved and I had a strong straight sets victory over a cramping-up Owen Davidson to join Bob Hewitt, Roy Emerson and Neale Fraser in the semi finals. Roy had beaten 17-year-old John Newcombe, just starting out on his road to glory, who was exhausted after playing a 38-game junior singles match only an hour before. In the semis, Emmo thrashed Frase and I beat Hewitt in a tougher match.

I knew Roy had had a demanding tournament, having played a number of five-set singles and doubles matches, so I attacked him from the outset on a day when a hot wind was sweeping across the court from Sydney Harbour. I had never seen this super-fit man so weary, and believed he should have had an extra day to recover before playing in the final. Still, true to the Australian spirit, and to the teaching of Charlie Hollis and Harry Hopman, I showed him no mercy, and won the first set 8–6. It was a tribute to Emmo's fighting heart that he turned things around totally in the second set and destroyed me 6–0. He was catching me out of position repeatedly with his backhand, just knocking it down the line for winners. Uncharacteristically, in this set I didn't react as quickly as I should have, and he inflicted heavy damage on me. It took me ages to realise I should start hitting more to his forehand. Sometimes in the heat of battle it takes a while for solutions to present themselves. I put that right and got the match back on course in the third set and wrapped up proceedings in four, 8–6, 0–6, 6–4, 6–4. As was his way, Roy refused to make his exhaustion an excuse. 'Rod was just too good,' he told the post-match press conference.

•

Unlike today, the Australian championships were amateur-ish in comparison with the other big overseas tournaments, especially Wimbledon, where players are made to feel appreciated and everything runs like clockwork. In the major Australian tournament, it seemed everything was done haphazardly and on the cheap – little things, like being treated with disdain by officials, the lack of chairs for the players to sit on during breaks in play (not that this was restricted to Australia) and no new practice balls. The balls we had were used and out of shape. The players received little other than glory, and the umpires and linesmen, the ball boys, the attendants, and the LTAA administrators themselves were all pretty much unpaid volunteers. Gate takings and LTAA membership funds paid for the court dressing and upkeep. When we played at the Milton courts in Brisbane it was even worse because some of the people who ran Queensland tennis were, more so than the officials in other states, simply not up to the task.

Although, officially, I maintained my amateur status and continued to turn down offers to become a professional, my growing disenchantment with the amateur set-up had me thinking that a switch in the future, when I had achieved more as an amateur, was on the cards. Early in 1962, the LTAA really put me offside with two of its decisions.

On 14–16 January bushfires raged through Victoria. Outer suburbs of Melbourne and areas of the Dandenong Ranges were turned to cinders. Thirty-three people died and 450 homes were destroyed. So when the International Professional Tennis Players Association (IPTPA) proposed that Lew Hoad and Ken Rosewall play a doubles match against Roy Emerson and me at Kooyong with all the proceeds going to the fire victims, Emmo and I said bring it on. It was a wonderful cause and this was a way we could help ease the suffering of the victims of the calamity – and, undeniably, I was all for playing against the best, whether they were amateurs or pros, and Lew and Muscles were certainly that. All four of us were super keen. So was the public. Unfortunately the LTAA was not. They refused to let Roy and me take part. 'We are sorry that on this occasion it is not practicable to agree to the proposal,' droned LTAA senior vice-president D.M. Frankenberg in fobbing off the plan. 'I hope [our decision] does not put the LTAA in a bad light with the public, but if it does we will just have to accept it. But as the bushfire relief is the main thought behind the plan, it should not matter who plays. The professionals could arrange their own tournament if they want to, but we cannot approve of any plan to bring amateurs and professionals together.' And that was that.

Then the LTAA refused to grant me permission to play in the US Indoor Championships in early February in New York, a tournament that was organised by the US titles referee Billy Talbert, who promised to pay all airfares and $400 appearance money. (Of course, technically, I was not permitted to accept payment, but amateurism wasn't known as 'shamateurism' for nothing. It was common for some amateur champions to accept thousands of dollars from promoters in under-the-table payments to participate in a tournament.) The official reason given for the refusal was that the tournament, though an amateur one, was not on the LTAA schedule. When I persisted and said it was important for me to try my hand at these titles because I would gain valuable experience before the French championships, Wimbledon and the Davis Cup, and surely it was in my, and Australia's, best interests for me to play as often as I could in top-class competition, the LTAA reluctantly relented but said they'd not pay me a single penny in expenses. I found a way to play. I was leaving soon for a long-planned Caribbean tour in March and April so I booked an early flight to the Big Apple, made the semis in Billy's tournament, then caught a flight to the Caribbean.

It was a tough job, but I guess someone had to do it. Along with luxuriating in these tropical climes, Roy Emerson and I played matches in Montego Bay, Baranquilla City, Caracas and San Juan. It was far from a junket. We came up against some of the world's best players, including the United States junior champion Charlie Pasarell and Ham Richardson, who had beaten me in straight sets in my first tilt at the US championships back in 1956. In a semi of the San Juan event against Ham I was able to even the score.

So when I went to Europe to prepare for the French titles and Wimbledon, I had form on the board. After winning the Italian championships' singles on a loose clay surface (beating Emmo) and the doubles (teaming with John Fraser, Neale's brother, to beat Ken Fletcher and John Newcombe), and then taking out the Swiss men's singles title, I arrived at Roland Garros Stadium feeling in winning touch and well-used to slow clay. I had learned that when playing on clay it's best not to try to play winning shots so much – it's harder to do on clay, which is slower than grass – but to simply keep the ball in play, driving my opponents mad by goading them into a rush of blood and letting *them* make the mistakes. Sticking to this strategy, I beat Italy's Michelle Pirro and England's Tony Pickard and another Italian, Sergio Jacobini, in the early matches. My quarter final was against Australian Martin Mulligan, who was living in Italy at the time and was a definite danger because he was more familiar with clay than me. His old mates now called him Martino Mulligano.

The French crowd, with no player of their own to barrack for, got right behind underdog Marty and cheered his every shot, while keeping stonily silent when I won a point. Marty's experience on clay was making him, as I knew it would, a tough opponent and he went ahead two sets to one. In the fourth, he was one point away from trashing my dream of a Grand Slam. I was behind four games to five and serving at 30–40. My first serve went into the net. The crowd was screaming for me to fluff the second so their adopted hero would win. I spun the ball to Marty's backhand and sprinted in to the net behind it. I'd considered staying back at the baseline, but Marty had been sending his backhand return down the line for winners so, to surprise him, I raced up with a backhand volley to the open court, cut off his return and won the point for deuce and then held my serve for 5–5. A reprieve. Marty's serve. His look of deadly intent left me in no doubt that he was planning to finish me off, and that would have suited the vociferous French crowd just fine.

At 8–8, he served and I hit a deep approach shot that Marty believed was out. The linesman disagreed, and called it in. It was genuinely too close for me to call from where I stood. In such stand-offs in those pre-Hawkeye days there was only one result. It was in. All hell broke loose. Marty was a mild-mannered, friendly bloke, but when the call went against him he totally lost his composure. He began yelling at the linesman and then the umpire. He called them 'blind' and 'idiots' and, I'm afraid, much worse. It was a shocking moment. I had never experienced anything like Marty's rage. Then it got worse. Marty drilled a high-speed ball at the wall. It narrowly missed the linesman's head. Perhaps this bloke's eyesight *was* faulty, because he didn't duck. The match referee rushed onto the court and the four of them stood shouting abuse and gesticulating. The linesman ruefully rubbed his noggin. Then the crowd roared again, only this time, upset with his behaviour, they were jeering at Marty. They hurled insults, whistled and stamped their feet at him. I stood still and expressionless at the other end of the court, waiting for the tumult to subside. When it eventually did, after many minutes, and the game recommenced, poor Marty fell apart. He was emotionally spent. I won eight of the last 10 games and progressed to the semi final.

It never worried me unduly if my opponent blew up and started arguing with the umpire and throwing his racquet around. The more furious my opponent became the cooler I tended to be. I'd encountered it a lot before Marty Mulligan. Warren Woodcock, Bob Hewitt and Bob Mark, unlike most Australian players, all had short fuses and could be undisciplined. I'd think that if the other bloke was so busy being angry he couldn't possibly be concentrating on the match. I've found that in the great majority of cases, when your opponent loses his temper over an annoyance such as a line call that goes against him, you benefit, as I did against Marty Mulligan. Exceptions were Pancho Gonzales and, later, John McEnroe and Jimmy Connors, who thrived on discord so much that, if they were behind in a match, they were not above creating a stink to rattle their opponent. I suppose it was up to the opponent whether he let it get under his skin or rose above it.

Across the net from me in my semi was Neale Fraser. In the fifth set he was serving at 5–4 and all but had me beaten. Frase had the best serve in world tennis. Inexplicably, he didn't follow his serve to the net and I returned a winner. With that shot I snatched the initiative and won the next three games and a place in the final. Against? Who else but Roy Emerson. These French championships were becoming like old home week. Once again, as I had through the tournament, I started slowly and Emmo took the lead. He had me almost dead and buried at two sets to one and leading 3–0 in the fourth. That's when he abandoned his normal attacking game and, most unlike Emmo, shut up shop and tried to hang on for the win. As with Frase, this was the signal for me to go for broke and claim the momentum that had been all his. I won in five, taking the final sets 9–7, 6–2. The Australian and the French titles were mine. Now for Wimbledon, where I was seeded No.1 and Emmo No.2.

I won the Queen's Club tournament in the immediate lead-up to Wimbledon, and considered that a good thing, not a jinx as many did. In the past almost invariably the fellow who won at Queen's fell short of the Wimbledon title.

As the previous year's Wimbledon winner, in 1962 I had the honour of opening the great tournament on centre court before the Duchess of Kent and 15,000 in the grandstands on a sunny London summer's day. I think the occasion got the better of my first round opponent, Naresh Kumar of India, and I won in three sets. Although I made too many mistakes for my liking, I also had straight sets wins in subsequent matches against Tony Pickard, Whitney Reed and Pierre Darmon. Of the eight players who made the Wimbledon quarter finals that year, six – the Fraser brothers Neale and John, Martin Mulligan (who beat Emmo, who was suffering a bruised toe on his right foot . . . bizarrely, he had chased a ball up into the stands during a mixed doubles match and his foot slid into the grooves on a bench seat and he twisted his big toe!), Ken Fletcher, Bob Hewitt and me – were Australian.

I made a point during any tournament in which I competed of watching the key match-ups, checking on the form of my rivals, hopefully picking up something I could use against them. That was certainly the case at Wimbledon. There wasn't much for the players to do at a tournament in those pre–computer, iPod and iPad days, other than play cards and watch the tennis. The Wimbledon organisers were always looking for ways to make us feel special, collecting us in Bentleys and Rolls-Royces from our hotels in the morning and dropping us home at night, and they fed us, including the scrumptious strawberries and cream Wimbledon is renowned for. At least once a day before our matches, even though I knew there was a good chance I'd be playing him in the Wimbledon semis or the final, Emmo and I would go to the Queen's Club and have a hit together.

My opponent in the quarter final was Manuel Santana, who had vanquished me in the final of the French championship two years earlier. He was a tough, talented and scrupulously fair player and our match was probably the best of the men's singles that year. I suffered some really bad line calls, every player does, and on a couple of occasions when they were crucial calls I confess that I struggled to keep my emotions in check. Manuel and Andres Gimeno were probably the best players Spain ever had, at least until Rafael Nadal came along. The son of a ground-keeper at Madrid Tennis Club, Manuel's playing on clay made him a master of forehand and backhand top spin. He won a long, long first set 16–14, and had me down 5–1 in the second but I scratched and clawed my way back to snatch it off him 9–7. Luck was also with me. A number of my returns hit the net and popped over. Tennis is as much a mental game as a physical one, and with Manuel suffering the misfortune of losing a set that he should have won, coupled with my outrageously lucky winners, served to sap his spirit, and I won the last two sets 6–2, 6–2.

Now Neale Fraser stood between me and the final. Honours in the first set were evenly shared, and I sneaked home 10–8. Then, early in the second set, Neale fell heavily and was thrown off his game, and with my backhand passing shot working well, I won 6–1. He fought back and we went at it hammer and tongs until I won the third set 7–5.

In this, my fourth consecutive Wimbledon final (I'd won one and lost two), I played my Roland Garros rival Martin Mulligan in the final, and this time there were no fireworks. I won the first set 6–2 in 16 minutes. I think this, and, possibly, the immense occasion, took its toll on Marty. With my game coming together crisply, I was able to keep him out of the match in the remaining two sets, which I won 6–2, 6–1 in 52 minutes, to become only the fourth Australian after Sir Norman Brookes, Gerald Patterson and Lew Hoad to win Wimbledon twice. Marty was not disgraced and at one point he had the normally sedate crowd cheering him on when he gallantly saved four big smashes I sent his way.

Without being stupidly complacent, I had gone out there on the court refusing to accept the possibility that Marty would beat me. Looking at photos of the match, I'm certainly wearing a grim and determined expression. As much as anything, I was trying to make sure I started well and played good enough tennis from then on to keep Marty at bay. I was desperate to avoid suffering a let-down, as I had in the past, often against Roy Emerson and Neale Fraser, right after I'd played a good match. Nothing to do with being over-confident – in fact I could never work out why I had these form slumps. When I played like that Charlie Hollis would say to me, 'Where were you in that set? What happened? You looked like you were out to lunch.' Suddenly the serve I'd had on a string in the previous match – or the previous set in this very match! – would start going out. Suddenly my footwork would be imprecise. Suddenly I'd be on my heels. Suddenly I'd be behind, and be forced to scramble to win, or I would be beaten. I was not going to let any of that happen in the Wimbledon final.

Nothing compares to winning your first Wimbledon, yet *every* Wimbledon title is very, very special. And making it sweeter for me as I bowed to the Queen when she presented me with the magnificent trophy, and worried whether I'd make a fool of myself dancing with women's winner Karen Hantze Susman of the US at that night's Wimbledon Victory Ball (I'd been taking lessons to avert the disaster of 1961 when I bungled the light fantastic with Angela Mortimer Barrett), was the fact it had hit me with some force that now I had only to win the United States championship to achieve the coveted Grand Slam. Afterwards, Marty Mulligan was gracious in defeat, and to the spectators he expressed his distress at letting down the fans who had come to the Wimbledon final expecting a classic encounter. He kindly said he had never seen me play better, and feared he must have offended me for me to inflict such a severe defeat on him. It was a classy performance from a bloke who was hurting. In turn I said that Martin had given me a much harder match than the scores indicated.

I made a point all through my career of not basking in a victory. I felt that to do so, apart from it not being in my nature, was to disrespect my opponent and to tempt bad karma. 'Rooster one day, feather duster the next' is an old but true saying. As Rudyard Kipling proclaims in his inspirational poem 'If' (which, fittingly, is at the players' entrance at Wimbledon), 'If you can meet with Triumph and Disaster and treat those two imposters just the same . . . you'll be a man, my son.'

Some publications also seemed intent on helping me keep my head in proportion. They observed that I was lucky not to be in the professional ranks because I wouldn't have things so easy against Gonzales, Sedgman, Hoad and Rosewall. There was an element of truth in that, and I knew it, and I looked forward to the day when I would be able to prove myself against the top pros. Publicly, I could only riposte that I could do no more than beat the man on the other side of the net, which was also true. The pro-favouring and America-centric *Time* magazine, in the edition of 13 July 1962, which came out right after Wimbledon, didn't like my chances of taking my place alongside their beloved Donald Budge – in fact, there were sections of the article that made me wonder whether the writer knew anything about me or had even seen me play. The journalist first claimed that I had had it easy in the amateurs because anyone who was good enough to make me 'work up a sweat' had defected to the professionals. He carped that early on when I was starting out as a 'B-team scrub on the great Down Under squads' I had regularly taken my 'lumps' at the hands of Hoad, Rosewall and Ashley Cooper. Even after these guys had turned pro, noted *Time*, I had lost twice in the finals at Wimbledon and twice at Forest Hills, but this year 'the Rocket [was] finally off the pad.' I had swept the Australian and French singles titles, and at Wimbledon I had needed only 53 minutes to crush my unseeded countryman Martin Mulligan, for my third national championship of the year. And now, only the US championship in September stood between me and a Grand Slam of amateur tennis, a feat accomplished only once before, by America's own Don Budge in 1938.

In the writer's view I would probably fail and if by some miracle I pulled off the Slam it would be some kind of unfair fluke. 'Short (5ft 8in), and bowlegged, Rod Laver is not in the same bracket with Don Budge.' According to the magazine I was temperamental, easily thrown off stride by the bad breaks of a match and lacked the power of a Hoad or the dexterity of a Rosewall. Instead, I relied on guile and 'a unique ability to re-set his wrist in mid-stroke – just before contact with the ball – that permits him to hit the ball flat, give it top-spin, or impart a low-bouncing under-spin.' At Wimbledon last week, the article went on, everything had worked, and the ball acted 'as if it had corners.' Then, after this faint praise, the journalist attempted to end on a more generous note by quoting Australian team manager Alf Chave. 'No one could have lived with Laver [in the final]. Mulligan's only chance would have been to go out and buy a rifle.'

•

Because of my habit of pulling wins from seemingly certain defeats, I was known back then as 'Lucky' Laver. I always thought that was a bit simplistic, because you have to put yourself in a position where you can take advantage of the breaks that come your way. A victory is a victory, whether you blow your opponent away or come from behind to win.

One time when I didn't argue with the 'Lucky' moniker was on 27 July, just 20 days after my Wimbledon win, when I was flying from London to Amsterdam to contest the Dutch championships. One moment I was dozing peacefully and the next I was jolted awake when the Pan Am 707 lurched, dipped violently, slowed, then levelled out. When descending out of the clouds to land, the skipper had narrowly averted a mid-air collision with a Dutch fighter plane by accelerating straight up, then rolling and levelling out. Apart from when I stand up to go to the loo, I have always worn my seatbelt at all times when I'm flying and thank goodness I did that day, because those passengers who weren't belted in were catapulted out of their seats. Many suffered spinal damage, head wounds and broken bones. Heads went through the overhead lockers and there was hair on the ceiling. People were screaming and crying. A number in the first class cabin had glass cuts because they'd been served drinks only two minutes earlier, and the dive tossed the glasses everywhere and smashed them. To calm the passengers, the pilot announced that there had simply been a mishap with the controls and that all was well. We didn't find out till the next day what had really happened. Of the 79 people onboard, 26 were hospitalised on landing in Amsterdam, 14 with bad injuries. I wasn't hurt, just suffered a bit of shock – as much from the realisation that I could have been killed in a mid-air collision as from the buffeting and the awful sight of the injured – but, thank God, nothing serious and nothing that would prevent me playing tennis the same day. For the next three weeks, Pan Am kept calling me to ask if I was experiencing delayed trauma. I was fine.

I almost didn't make it to Amsterdam, but I won those Dutch championships, adding them to the list that, to that point in 1962, already included the Australian, French and Wimbledon men's singles titles, as well as the German, Italian and British Hard Court singles titles. All up that year, as well as the majors, I would win another 17 titles, including the 'clay court triple' of Paris, Hamburg and Rome, a feat that only Lew Hoad had managed before me, in 1956. Now a confession: one of the few finals I lost that year was the Alpine Lands Open Tournament at Kitzbuhel, high in the Austrian Alps. I tend not to make excuses when I lose, but this event was staged on the day after my 24th birthday – and having decided by now that I liked both the taste of beer and sharing a drink with friends, I celebrated a little too enthusiastically and, there's no way of getting around it, I was feeling a little dusty when I went onto the court.

Chapter 8

My first
Grand Slam

MY RESULTS ALL YEAR QUALIFIED ME TO BE THE TOP SEED at the United States championships. The persistent offers from the pro ranks were pleasant, if unsettling, distractions from my preparation to win the US tournament and the Grand Slam. Truth to tell, I was certainly keen to win the Slam, though far from obsessed about it. 'Philosophical' best describes my state of mind when considering the prospect. If I achieved it, great. If not, the sun would still rise tomorrow.

Through Ken Rosewall, the IPTPA (the professionals' governing body) made no secret that I was top of its wish list, and with a war chest of £67,000 they were also targeting Roy Emerson, Swede Jan Eric Lundquist, Mexico's Rafael Osuna, Manuel Santana of Spain, and Germany's Willie Bungert and Christian Kuhnke. I told them once more that I'd be making no decision about whether I would or wouldn't turn pro until after the US titles and Australia's Davis Cup defence in December. The ageing professional Pancho Gonzales also offered me a minimum $50,000 and a maximum $100,000 to take him on in a one-year head-to-head pro tour at venues all over the world. I turned him down for the same reason that I'd said no to the IPTPA, and, more than that, I had reservations about dealing with the temperamental Gonzales.

I hoped coming out and stating that I was not interested in becoming a professional just yet would earn me some peace. No such luck. The approaches from the professionals kept coming, as did persistent queries from reporters pressing me about what my future held. The press even got on the blower to my father in Gladstone. Dad played a straight bat, giving nothing away even though we had discussed the pros and cons of turning professional many times. 'We would like Rod to stay amateur, but it's up to him to use his own discretion,' he said. 'Actually, it doesn't worry the family in the least one way or the other. We'll leave him to make his own decision. After the excellent year he's had it wouldn't surprise me if a big money offer was made to him, and it would be a big thing for a young fellow not used to a lot of money to turn down a big pro offer. Rod has a pretty true idea of everything. We hope to have him home for a week after the American tournaments and we'll have a family discussion then.'

At Forest Hills I was raring to go. I played forceful, precise tennis and had straight sets wins against Elezer Davidman of Israel, Eduardo Zuleta of Ecuador, Bodo Nitache of

Germany, and my old Davis Cup opponent, Tony Palafox of Mexico. By taking me to four sets, including a 13–11 second set, American Frank Froehling, who had a booming serve and forehand but a suspect backhand that I preyed on, gave me the contest I probably needed at that stage in the quarter finals.

I was honoured, halfway through the tournament, to be contacted by the great Donald Budge, who, as one who had achieved a Grand Slam and knew better than anyone the pressures involved, suggested that I might benefit by joining him for a day and a night at a secluded resort in upstate New York where we could relax away from the championship hubbub, have a gentle hit-up together and shoot the breeze. We did all that, and had a meal and saw a movie. It was the ideal way to decompress. I was a bit surprised a few weeks later when I heard that Don had been putting it about that he and I had played a deadly serious match and *I had nearly beaten him*. I thought, 'What!' Don was 47 and a decade and a half past his prime, and our 'deadly serious match' was a series of innocuous taps to each other across the net. Don was a bit like that. I think he had trouble existing out of the limelight after his career ended, and anyone having a conversation with him knew very quickly and in copious detail all the great things he'd achieved in tennis. People would see him coming and say, 'Here comes the Grand Slammer.' I promised myself that if I did manage to win the US title, I'd never give anyone a reason to say that about me.

After I'd accounted for Rafael Osuna 6–1, 6–3, 6–4 in the semi, I readied myself to play the final against the man

I knew in my heart was always going to be there to try to foil my Grand Slam: Roy Emerson. I could not help harking back to when Ken Rosewall deprived his great mate Lew Hoad of a Grand Slam at the United States titles, and wondered whether Emmo would do a Muscles on me. I knew that he'd be trying to.

The evening before the final, the Tennis Writers' Association of America staged a dinner to honour Sir Norman Brookes, one of Australia's finest players who in his career between 1898 and 1920 claimed all the major titles, a stalwart of our Davis Cup side and president of the LTAA from 1926–55. When he was presented with the Immortal Tennis Award for the lasting impact he had made on our sport, he spoke eloquently, and never more so than when he said he wanted an end to the amateur–professional divide so the world's best players in either camp could play against each other. 'I only hope I will be with you long enough to see an open championship,' said Sir Norman. Happily, he was. He passed away on 28 September 1968, at age 90, exactly 20 days after the inaugural US Open championship final. There were other awards doled out that night. Pancho Gonzales was given a Presidential Citation by the People-to-People Sports Committee for being the 'Tennis Ambassador of the United States', and I won 'World's Most Popular Tennis Player', which mystified me a bit because I was one of the more introverted blokes on the circuit.

Next day, against Roy Emerson, my strategy was to avoid my usual slow start and attack with my power game from the outset, to try to overwhelm Emmo and put him away in three sets because his superior fitness could be decisive if the match went to five. What was it Harry Hopman said? The fittest bloke will normally win the fifth set, so I wanted to end the match before then. In the first set I broke Roy's serve and won the first two games, always my objective in any match to get off to a good start and put pressure on my opponent, and claimed the first set 6–2. My service and drives were going exactly where I wanted them to, and this was instrumental in me winning the second set 6–4.

Then, as I knew he would, Roy rallied and began attacking me ferociously. I wilted under his accurate serves and volleys and made errors, and he won the set 7–5. His passing shots were always good and the grass court – Forest Hills was still grass in those days – was bouncy and suited him. I *had* to win the fourth. I just couldn't risk the match going to a fifth set, when I'd become a sitting duck for Roy. I took the ascendancy and unleashed every shot I knew and found myself leading 40–15 and serving for the match. There's no other way to account for what I did next. When I served and ran into the net to deal with Emmo's sitter of a forehand volley return, I had the wrong grip and I smashed Roy's return . . . right into the net. Such setbacks have the potential to change the course of a match. I reined in my emotions, took stock, settled down, and thought of nothing but getting my first serve in. I did that, and Roy returned. I volleyed deep to his forehand. His passing shot went long down the line. I had won the match in four sets, 6–2, 6–4, 5–7, 6–4.

The Grand Slam was mine. In my jubilation I threw my racquet high into the air then ran with my arms out-stretched to hug Emmo, who was waiting for me at the net with a big grin, as happy for me as he was no doubt disappointed for himself. As we walked off the court, Don Budge rushed over and shook my hand. 'Welcome to the club!' he boomed, and I think he may even have meant it. He was certainly generous when he told reporters who invited him to compare us as players, 'I'm glad I never had to play such a fine left-hander with all the shots. And I must praise Rod's and Roy's sportsmanship. I think some of our boys and other players could learn from them.'

I was swamped by back-slappers and when reporters asked me how it felt to be the best player in the world, I told them I wouldn't know because there were guys named Hoad, Rosewall, Sedgman, Gonzales, Trabert and Segura whom I hadn't beaten, because I hadn't played them. I also knew that making up the 128 players in the major amateur tour-naments were fellows who were not really up to standard, young blokes with a tennis racquet who travelled the world entering tournaments and rarely lasting a round.

There was no official dinner, no victory waltz, at Forest Hills. I was much happier to front up at the bar at the club-house there and shout anyone who wanted to have a drink with me. I know one bloke who'd earned his beer was Emmo.

Once more, the Australian media besieged Mum and Dad, and my mother offered one reporter the following gem: 'Success hasn't changed Rod. He still calls me Mum.' I don't know what else I could have called her.

I played in the Pacific Southwest tournament at the Los Angeles Tennis Club on my way home to Australia after the United States championships in New York. In the crowd and at the various functions were a number of celebrities who were serious tennis devotees, and seemed as much in awe of the players as we were of them. There were some big names I'd never thought I'd ever meet in my life, such as my childhood cowboy hero John Wayne, who shot up the open air picture show in Rocky where I was a front row regular, Charlton Heston, Burt Lancaster, Kirk Douglas, Lloyd Bridges, Dinah Shore . . . These stars could handle a racquet and had courts in their backyards, and Kirk and Charlton invited me and some of the other players to their homes for Sunday tennis days and barbecues.

When reporters told me that a wax likeness of myself was being sculpted to stand beside Don Bradman's in the Sports Hall of Fame section of Madame Tussaud's wax museum in London, I turned bright red and ducked for cover. When I finally saw it, I had to admit the dummy wasn't a bad likeness . . . they'd taken enormous trouble to get my facial features, legs and bulging left forearm right, and in the end I was proud to be included in such exalted company as Bradman, not to mention Madame Tussaud's galleries of kings, queens, emperors, movie actors, rock stars and serial killers.

When I landed at Rockhampton airport on 27 September, I saw through the plane window a crowd of more than 1000 people crammed five deep by the terminal. There were TV crews and photographers milling about. I wondered who they were there to see. When I disembarked, and there were Mum and Dad, my sister Lois and my brothers and friends, I realised they were there to see me. Amid all the hugs, kisses and back slaps, and cries of 'Good on you, Rocket Rod!' and 'Welcome home, digger!', Mayor Pilbeam, resplendent in his heavy chain, officially welcomed me home and presented me with a two-metre-long replica tennis racquet and the keys to the city. (Not that I've ever known what you're supposed to actually do with such keys!) When I was called upon to say a few words, I told the people of Rocky the truth, that I took strength from knowing that they were supporting me from afar, and this gave me confidence in big matches. I said that winning Wimbledon and the Australian title and representing Australia in the Davis Cup was a dream come true and every day I thanked my lucky stars. Claude Farmer, who had bought the Marlborough property from Dad, piped up and said if it wasn't for him I might still be out at Langdale ring-barking trees.

On the Saturday, there was a procession in my honour. I was plonked in a convertible sports car alongside Mayor Pilbeam and driven down East Street escorted by police on their motorbikes, the City Band and a tribe of local junior and senior tennis players in their whites holding their racquets high as we made our way to a civic reception at City Hall. Thousands of people lined East Street, cheering and clapping. I was truly overwhelmed. From there, I was whisked to the Criterion Hotel to be guest of honour at a luncheon hosted by the Central Queensland Tennis Association. You'd think I'd be better by now at public speaking, but my shyness took over and after mumbling a few words of thanks, I sat down with relief to a hearty meal. That night I was feted at the local speedway and did a lap of honour on the back of the motorbike of Queensland speedway champion Ivan Mauger. Days later I saddled up for the Queensland Hard Court Titles and beat Emmo in straight sets in the final, then teamed with him to down Wimbledon runners-up Fred Stolle and Bob Hewitt, who'd returned briefly from South Africa, in the doubles final.

By the time I returned to Australia, I had all but decided to turn professional as soon as the Davis Cup was done and dusted. Frank Sedgman and Ken Rosewall, who were acting on behalf of the IPTPA (Muscles was the secretary and treasurer), had made me a very good offer, upping the ante from what I'd been offered before the Grand Slam win. Still, I tossed and turned over my decision. One day I'd think becoming pro and guaranteeing my financial future was a no-brainer at my stage of life, and then I'd convince myself that I loved playing in those fabulous major tournaments at Roland Garros, Wimbledon and Forest Hills too much ever to say goodbye to all that. Money was definitely a factor making professionalism tempting, though. I wanted to secure my future, to be able to buy a home and perhaps settle down one day, make some investments. And my family wasn't flush with funds. Mum and Dad had helped all they could, buying my racquets, balls, shoes and clothes, and dropping everything and driving me to tournaments when I was a kid. Somehow, they made all that happen. And these days I was always welcome to stay with them when I was touring in Queensland. They asked for nothing, and were perfectly happy with their life, their home and town, but I wanted to repay them by making them financially secure, perhaps buy them a better car. Whatever contortions I was going through in my head, publicly I didn't let on how I was feeling or give any indication of what I might do. I sounded out Frank and Ken, as well as Lew and Ashley Cooper, about what life would be like on the pro circuit, but the only people I told what was really in my heart were my parents and brothers, when I took some rest and recreation in Gladstone after returning from America and we talked long into the night about the importance of making the right decision.

I left Gladstone knowing I was going to turn pro. Having now achieved all there was to achieve in the amateurs it became obvious that I had to take on new challenges if I wasn't to stagnate. And didn't I owe it to myself and my family to profit from my talent? I'd been warned that it was inevitable that I would struggle at first on the professional circuit, every newcomer did, but if I ended up making it there was the chance to sock away a lot of money. That trip home to see the family, to fish and water-ski a bit with Bob and Trev, and to stay, as in the old days, with the Shepherd family for a week or two, cleared my head, brought me down to earth and put tennis, and life after tennis, in perspective.

I decided I wanted to play against the best players and also save some money. When I retired from tennis, I didn't want to be forced to put my name on someone else's sports store in Rocky, or trade in on my reputation by selling life insurance, or run a pub like many Australian champions in all sports ended up doing. LTAA president Norman Strange declared that he was resigned to losing me. 'If Rod Laver turns professional, we wish him well. It is a personal decision Rod has to make, and we don't want to come into the picture. Rod has given Australia years of great service to amateur tennis and the LTAA is grateful. His loss would be regrettable but not tragic. There are many fine young players waiting to step into the Davis Cup squad. That is why Australia is the envy of the tennis world.' It was comforting to hear Norman's conciliatory words. I had a feeling that Harry Hopman, an amateur to his bootstraps, might not be so understanding if I turned my back on the system that had made me and took the professional plunge.

I was under no illusion that LTAA chiefs Esca Stephens and T.E. Robinson were not furious at the prospect of my defection, and I also knew that these men held down lucrative jobs in private enterprise that enabled them to be tennis administrators in an honorary capacity, so what they felt didn't concern me. Frankly, it wasn't in the interests of certain amateur officials for professionalism to succeed. It might put at risk all those free trips to Paris, London and New York where they were treated like kings, and the luxury accommodation and transportation they enjoyed. I also suspect that many of the journalists who criticised us did so because they didn't want their all-expenses-paid junkets to Europe and America to end either. The journos at the Brisbane *Courier-Mail* seemed to feel that if I defected I would be betraying the great game of tennis by making money out of the sport I loved. They demanded that I be omitted from the Davis Cup squad unless I came out and unequivocally said I wouldn't be joining the pros. If I played while *intending* to leave the amateurs, they said, I would be 'cheating'. Thankfully, the LTAA countered that unless I had officially joined the pro ranks I was still eligible to play Davis Cup.

There was an element of hypocrisy in the media's criticism. It seemed to me that they were demanding that I stay an amateur and continue living on the smell of an oily rag while they were raking in a good salary for being journalists, and could afford to pay off a car and a home and have a family. I had a lot of glory but no money, and glory and $5 will get you a kilo of sausages. Even when I received a trophy, a firm handshake and a £15 voucher for winning Wimbledon, it wasn't 15 quid in cash, it was a voucher that could be redeemed by buying Wimbledon-approved products.

In the lead-up to the Challenge Round tie against Mexico, I suffered a post–Grand Slam form slump. It was, perhaps, inevitable. I had played so much high-pressure tennis all year long and with the Grand Slam in my kitbag, without ever meaning to, I relaxed mentally, and naturally my body followed suit. John Newcombe, who was one of the young up-and-comers mentioned by Norman Strange as waiting to step into my shoes, beat me in the South Australian titles final, and I was taken to the wire in the third round of the Victorian singles championship by the man who would go on to be Newk's doubles partner and a champion in his own right: Tony Roche. Tony, from the little town of Tarcutta in New South Wales, was another in the long line of boys from the bush – including Roy Emerson from Blackbutt, Queensland, Mal Anderson from Queensland's Theodore, and yours truly – who rose to the top of Australian tennis in that era. Nor should I fail to mention the great women players Margaret (Court) Smith and Evonne (Goolagong) Cawley who hailed from Albury and Barellan respectively.

On 27 December, Australia retained the Davis Cup when Emmo and I beat Rafael Osuna and Tony Palafox in the doubles to give Australia an unbeatable 3–0 lead in the tie, which was held at the Milton courts. The day before, I'd downed Rafael in the opening singles and Emmo had beaten Tony. Looking back on those days, it seems another age. When it rained during the tournament, Hop made us all wear spikes, but our opponents, who rarely had use for them in bone-dry Mexico, had brought none. So Hop went out and bought a set of spiked shoes for Tony Palafox and gave his own pair to Rafael Osuna. Can you imagine such sportsmanship today?

When it was all over and we'd enjoyed a 5–0 whitewash, Hop, our captain, knowing now that I was all but certain to turn professional after the Davis Cup dinner in two days' time, indulged in a little unsubtle emotional blackmail to try to shame me into changing my mind. He chose the Cup presentation ceremony to declare that he was far less optimistic than Norman Strange about the state of Australian tennis without me. 'Without Rod Laver, Australia will not be nearly as dominant in world tennis. If Mexico makes the Challenge Cup tie next year and we're without Laver and

Neale Fraser [who was retiring] they'll give us a very tough fight. Our prospects as a tennis nation are not bright. In the past there have always been young players pushing the established stars for their Cup places. That is not so now,' he grumbled, totally contradicting Strange. 'We had players like Fletcher, Hewitt and Mulligan. What's happened to them? The young players we do have need a terrific amount of work and I'll not be around to supervise them. I suppose we'll just have to look around for a new singles player and a new doubles partner for Roy Emerson.'

On 30 December 1962, I turned professional, signing a contract accepting their offer of a guarantee (against prize money and 22 percent of gate takings when I won and 17 percent if I lost) of US$110,000 for three years, playing 11 months of every year and travelling wherever in the world the tournaments were. It would be par for the course to play matches, as we did in my first year as a professional, on 28 straight nights, shuttling between England, France, Italy and Germany. I was a good catch for the pros because at that time they had an ageing roster of players, and having the Grand Slam winner in the troupe would be good for business.

There was an element of risk involved. That $110,000 was all on trust. There was nothing in escrow, there was no squillionaire backer guaranteeing payment, or even a guaranteed promoter to make sure the money would be available and that I'd be paid my share. We'd be relying on gate takings and sponsorship, and they were by no means done deals. It would be up to me and my fellow tennis gypsies to whip up the public's enthusiasm to come and see our matches with our playing skills and marketing hype. Lew and Ken wanted me on board so badly they pledged to make up the difference if I didn't make my $110,000 in the three years. I thanked them, but would never have accepted their offer. I wanted no safety net.

The media was there in Brisbane to photograph me signing the professional contract, flanked by the treasurer and the vice-president of the IPTPA, Muscles Rosewall and Barry MacKay. I told the reporters, 'It took me a long time to make up my mind just what to do. I have decided to play professional tennis and I am convinced it is the correct course for me to take. It will, of course, make me financially secure. I consider my new career a challenge. I don't expect to set the world on fire because I will be playing against some of the best players in the world, but I'm sure I'll do well.'

I know for a fact that Hop, my great coach and mentor, was disappointed, perhaps even felt betrayed, that I'd defected to what he considered the dark side. He never said a word to my face. I could understand how he felt. He had devoted so much of himself to Australian amateur tennis for so long, and in fairly recent times he had seen so many of his 'fine young men' turn professional, among them Lew and Muscles, Frank Sedgman, Ken McGregor, Mal Anderson, Ashley Cooper . . . and now me. His fears about Australia becoming less of a force in the Davis Cup proved justified, in 1963 at least, although I suspect that was because our opposition that year was better than in

1962 rather than my not being available. The United States wrested the Cup from Australia (represented by Emerson, Fraser and the tyro John Newcombe) 3–2. As it happened, Australia brought the Cup back home in 1964 and retained it until 1967. But by then Hop had departed the scene. He went to America and coached the young John McEnroe and Vitas Gerulaitis at Port Washington on Long Island, New York. I heard from Mac in years to come that he benefited enormously from Hop's coaching and that Hop would say to him when coaching a particular shot, 'John, you can do it! If Laver can, you can! You've got the same mechanics.'

Soon after my announcement, I received a letter from the All England Club (Wimbledon) telling me that, as with every amateur who turned professional, the honorary membership with privileges that had been bestowed upon me automatically when I won the men's singles title had been revoked, and that consequently I was no longer entitled to wear my purple- and green-striped Wimbledon winner's tie. In their eyes, too, professional was a dirty word and by becoming one I was a treacherous pariah.

I played a straight bat, giving little away. Eight years later, when the dust had settled, I took the opportunity to express my feelings of frustration when a reporter from *Sports Illustrated* magazine asked me whether it had been a difficult decision to leave amateur tennis and my anger bubbled up. I took issue with the Australian tennis chiefs accusing me of turning pro for selfish reasons. Who were they to talk, I wanted to know? I told the journo that if I ran my business the way the Lawn Tennis Association of Australia ran its business I'd be bankrupt. In my experience, the LTAA's idea of caring for Davis Cup tennis players was paying our air fare and $5 a day, and if we went overseas we were forced to live like nomads. I left the *Sports Illustrated* correspondent in no doubt that we travelled on a shoestring and added that when we returned home their attitude to me had been, 'Good show, Rod, you're our boy, here's $5, go buy some ice cream.' It was an open secret that amateurism was phony because there was big money to be made on the side. It was a fact, I pointed out, that Roy Emerson didn't turn pro until he was 32 because he thought he could make more money as an amateur. A lot of players, and I made it clear I wasn't talking about Emmo, were 'shamateurs' who bargained around, made agreements with promoters, went through the back door, demanding, say, $1500 to play in a tournament. Everybody knew that's how it was done, but nobody said it, because they all had something on each other. I was pretty upset and gave the LTAA both barrels in this interview. I revealed that maybe six or eight players were clearing $500 a week and some European players wouldn't get out of bed for less than $1000. This was an uncharacteristic outburst on my part, but it felt good to get things off my chest that I'd been keeping to myself for years. There was no chance to dwell on my decision. It was straight into it. My professional baptism of fire would come early. The following weekend I would embark on a national professional tour, playing against Lew Hoad and Ken Rosewall.

Chapter 9

The gypsy years

Professional tennis has been played in the United States since 1926, and it's always been considered the bastard and, by some, much reviled offspring of amateur tennis. Ostensibly, the basic difference between professionalism and amateurism was that professionals played for money and amateurs for glory and basic expenses. Until 1926, amateur tennis, administered by the national amateur tennis associations and the London-based International Lawn Tennis Federation (ILTF) was the only game in town. The amateur establishment ran the great national tournaments in Australia, at Wimbledon, in Paris and New York, as well as the Davis Cup and the Wightman Cup, for which British and American women competed. The ILTF and its satellites also policed the laws of amateurism, which included that no player could receive prize money or play against anyone who had. Although the amateurs crowed that all that was at stake in their tournaments was glory, only the naive imagined that the better players were not receiving under-the-table rewards.

Enter in 1926 the 44-year-old American entrepreneur Charles C. 'Cash and Carry' Pyle, whose expertise was in managing theatres, sports agenting and promoting American football. He had been mulling over organising a competition in which his players would compete for money, but he knew his scheme would be stillborn if he could not attract champions. Nobody was going to fork out their hard-earned dollars to see second-raters play. The best male players in the world at that time were the Americans Bill Tilden and Vincent Richards, and Suzanne Lenglen of France and Mary Browne and Helen Wills of the United States were the foremost women. Pyle made them all offers to play a series of pro matches, singles, doubles and mixed doubles, across North America and Canada. Richards, Lenglen and Browne took the bait, and Pyle completed his troupe of six by signing the capable Paul Feret of France, and Americans Harvey Snodgrass and Howard Kinsey. Some 13,000 curious fans attended Pyle's first event, at Madison Square Garden, on 9 October 1926.

With Richards and Lenglen the marquee players, the caravan then played tournaments in Toronto, Baltimore, Boston and Philadelphia. The gallant little troupe endured bizarre playing conditions: ice, snow and floods, unreliable transport, flea pit accommodation and rip-off-merchant promoters. Adding insult to injury, the players were ostracised by their former amateur masters, which led Richards to furiously declare that he would rather align himself with 'honest professionals' than 'sham amateurs.' A 910-kilogram linoleum and canvas tennis court surface followed the troupe on the back of a truck, and Pyle paid a pair of clowns to amuse fans during breaks in play. Before each event, the players barnstormed the local media to whip up interest and entice people to their matches. By all reports, the punters were more than satisfied by the fare provided. Said one, 'I had never seen tennis of this grade, and two minutes after they started playing I was unconscious whether they were pros, amateurs, or royalty! I didn't care. I was simply carried away by the wonderful tennis. That was all.'

It didn't last. Pyle dissolved his tour in February 1927, cancelling a proposed European jaunt after Lenglen, who he claimed wanted more money and had been disloyally sounding out rival promoters who had jumped on his pro bandwagon, flounced off. He knew that without her, the tour would fail. Cash and Carry Pyle's pioneering pro tour lasted just a few months, and the riches he had promised his players didn't eventuate, but it was the blueprint for all the professional tennis troupes that followed over the years, right up to Jack Kramer in the 1950s and, later, the Association of Tennis Professionals (ATP) and the International Lawn Tennis Players Association (ILTPA). (In 1977, 'Lawn' was dropped from the title.)

Like Pyle, Jack Kramer, who was a champion American player turned professional promoter, knew from the outset that he needed standout competitors playing deadly serious tennis on his circuit if fans were going to part with their hard-earned, so he signed the charisma machine Pancho Gonzales and, in 1953, Frank Sedgman, who the year before had won the French, Wimbledon and the United States titles, and his doubles partner, fellow Aussie Ken McGregor. With them on board, he aggressively pursued and recruited other amateur stars who wanted to profit financially from their talent. In that category were Ken Rosewall, who joined Kramer in 1957, and Lew Hoad, who switched in '58. (I have an indelible memory of me as a 19-year-old watching Gonzales play Rosewall in one of Ken's first pro matches, at Kooyong. Jack Kramer had rounded up all the juniors playing at the tournament and hustled us off to witness this master class.) In 1960, Kramer bowed out, and in the vacuum the players took affairs into their own hands by forming the International Professional Tennis Players Association (IPTPA), based in Los Angeles. This meant that an elected group of players acted on behalf of professional players throughout the world, and worked with organisations promoting and conducting pro tournaments, tours, matches and exhibitions as well as administering the finances.

In the '50s and early '60s, when I joined, a stream of champion players defected from the amateur to the professional ranks, to the point where, although the pros carried the stigma of being mercenaries, undeniably the best players were in the pro ranks. This made professional tennis viable. I was sure that I'd made the right decision.

As in the days of Pyle and Kramer, my job, like that of my fellow professionals, would be to travel the world like a gypsy playing in tournaments staged by various promoters who relied on gate takings and whatever sponsorship could be scraped together to advertise the event, pay us prize money, cover expenses and boost their own bank account. Promoters commonly ended up in the red.

It was a fact of professional tennis that it took a new-comer, fresh from the amateurs, time to find his feet. It was no easy thing to get used to the endless travel, to play against hardened professionals competing for money at one-night stands many times a week, sometimes on established indoor and outdoor grass, clay and concrete courts such as at Madison Square Garden and Longwood Cricket Club, but also on makeshift surfaces hastily thrown down and marked up in community halls, school gyms, theatres and concert halls, ice rinks and barns. In South America and Spain we played in bullrings. While our motto was 'Put up the money and we'll play on broken glass', in some ways broken glass might have been easier to play on than some of the surfaces we confronted. For instance, a canvas court stretched over an ice rink presented some particular chal-lenges. For a start, it wasn't a good idea to slide or run off the canvas to try to retrieve your opponent's shot because you'd end up in the ice. And, despite the boards and canvas over the ice, your feet would freeze and you'd be numb from the ankles down unless you wore a couple of pairs of thick woollen socks.

It also took time for newcomers to adjust to the standard of play. When Jack Kramer, who was America's top amateur, first switched he was regularly thrashed by seasoned pro

Bobby Riggs before he found his feet. In turn, Pancho Gonzales struggled against Kramer at the beginning, then Lew and Muscles were outgunned by Pancho for a year or so until they acclimatised to the grind. When, at 24, I became the new kid on the pro block at the beginning of 1963, Lew and Muscles, who were still only 28 but hardened professionals, licked their lips.

My matches against Hoad and Rosewall on Saturday 5 January and Sunday 6 January 1963 caught the public's imagination, and at White City in Sydney's Rushcutters Bay, the venue for the matches on that first weekend of our Australian tour, all 8000 seats were snapped up quickly. The only time White City seats had moved faster was for the Hoad–Gonzales pro clashes in 1958. The NSW Lawn Tennis Association (the state affiliate of the LTAA), which owned White City and was not prepared to do the professional interlopers any favours, had no qualms pocketing the £3000 the pros paid them to rent the grand old courts.

Sure, Lew and I had had practice hits when I was a junior and played exhibitions while we were on the road for Dunlop and he was yet to turn professional, but this would be the first time I had ever faced him in a real match. I didn't realise this proud man had been training hard right through Christmas to be in top form for our match. I learned later that he'd told Ken Rosewall, 'I'm going to show that little shit Rocket that I can still play this game.'

In the match I reverted to my usual big-match tactic of starting fast and taking the initiative, and it worked. I won the first set 8–6 and was serving well and reeling out my array of shots. The ball was coming off my racquet sweetly. I was feeling good, and believed I would win. Sections of the crowd thought so, too. 'Get stuck into him, Rod. You can beat him easily!' came one raucous cry from the grandstand. Well, it turned out that I couldn't. In the second set, Lew's awesome power game clicked and, displaying frightening concentration with no glimmer of friendship evident in his steely features, he took that set and the next two to win the match. Frankly, I was amazed by Lew's power. He treated my serves with disdain, and held his. My volleying fell away under his pressure. His pinpoint-placed, heavily top-spun backhand was virtually unplayable. It was a sharp learning curve for me. I was shell-shocked, but put on a brave face and after the match told reporters that I thought I played well enough but had to tighten up some shots, while Lew remarked in something of a backhanded compliment that 'Rod was better than I thought he would be. He's going to be a tough proposition.' I certainly didn't disgrace myself, and the big crowd, few of whom had left the grandstands by the time we finished our match at midnight, gave me a standing ovation at the end of the match. My £1200 share of the £6000 gate would come in handy too. Yet I hadn't been prepared for the vast gulf between the amateur and professional standard of play, and it was a gap I would have to work hard to bridge if my switch was not to prove a disaster.

Muscles Rosewall continued my tennis education next day at White City when he walloped me in straight sets, 6–3, 6–4, 6–4 in front of 6500 people. I was stiff and sore after my marathon match with Lew, but no excuses. It was my worst defeat in three years. 'I thought it would be tough in the professionals,' I opined after the match, 'but the play is about 50 percent better than in the amateurs.' Ken, a brutally honest man, made no bones about the challenge facing me if I was to succeed as a professional player. I thought he was being a little harsh, yet I knew where he was coming from when he said, 'Laver's contract demands that he be in the best physical condition, and that he concentrate entirely on tennis. I think he has spent too much time recently playing golf. He had better stick to tennis from now on, if he wants to realise his possibilities.'

The Sydney Morning Herald's Alan Clarkson wrote perceptively that even though I was struggling hard to adapt to the rigours of professional tennis and was still out of my depth, the quality of my matches was still superior to what was being offered by the amateurs. While pro tennis lacked the drama and suspense of the great Davis Cup clashes, it was high-standard tennis, and that was what the public wanted. 'Here was Laver, fresh from Grand Slam and Davis Cup victories, and acknowledged as the most outstanding amateur player in the world. And Rosewall handled him with amazing ease . . . Rosewall hit his groundstrokes with micrometer-like accuracy, and the harder Laver tried, the more proficient Rosewall's passing shots became.' I fought as hard as I could and tried everything I knew to win even though it was obvious that the match was a lost cause in the third set. There was no point gilding the lily. Ken's victory, as Lew's had been, was comprehensive. Most tennis writers agreed that my shot-making and intensity was good but needed to improve and that on the strength of these early matches the jury was still out on whether I would succeed as a professional. Clarkson wrote: 'Yesterday's match showed Laver has much to learn before he can hope to match Hoad and Rosewall. He came off the court yesterday knowing his easy days in tennis are finished.'

All too true. I played Lew Hoad eight times during that Australian tour and he won every match. I played Ken 13 times and could beat him just twice. The beatings continued when we played in New Zealand. I won't deny that I was demoralised: the reputation I had trained and played so hard to forge was being called into question, and at times I wondered if I would ever make it as a pro. Sometimes, despite my illustrious amateur record, I even questioned whether I'd chosen the wrong sport. Maybe I should just skulk off and find another line of work. But quitting was not in my makeup and I soldiered on, determined to learn, toughen up and improve to the point where I could serve up Ken and Lew a little of their own medicine. I made two immediate adjustments to my game. I began using a shorter backswing to compensate for the faster wooden floors of the indoor courts we often played on, and I tried to move forward to meet the ball rather than letting it come to me. Ken Rosewall told me the changes had improved my tennis by a point a game. He and Lew remained staunch supporters, even while punishing me on the court.

I had a mountain to scale if I was going to make it as a pro, and I started climbing when I faced off against Rosewall, Luis Ayala, Andres Gimeno, Barry MacKay and Butch

Buchholz in the US World Series of Professional Tennis staged in February and March, with its total prize money of $112,500. Lew Hoad would have been there but had been struck down again by the chronic back ailment that would end his career a couple of years later. The six of us piled into two station wagons and motored through the ice and snow to our matches in Boston, Philadelphia, Richmond, Baltimore, Albany, Montreal, Toronto, Detroit and smaller towns. I said my prayers more than once as our vehicles slid and broadsided on the treacherous ice that covered the 230-kilometre route from Ithaca in New York State to Albany. My old Davis Cup adversary and now mate, Barry MacKay, turned to me with a big grin and said, 'Rocket, welcome to pro tennis!' It crossed my mind that normally at this time of the year I'd be playing on a private amateur tour in the Caribbean, and I wondered what in hell I had got myself into.

My first match at Boston Garden ice rink was against Barry. Playing him after being beaten up by Lew and Muscles, I felt as if I had suddenly taken my head out of a cement mixer. Not that I beat Barry. Far from it. Using a block and tackle, the ice rink staff stretched our marked-up canvas court over the wooden boards that covered the rink. I could feel the loose and bumpy wooden boards moving beneath my feet. When Barry served he aimed for the cracks and bumps and the ball shot along the ground or over my head. I couldn't pick it. Barry's serves were hard to handle at the best of times, so I had no chance as they careened off the uneven surface.

Yet slowly, surely, in those first months, I became pro-hardened and notched eight wins and seven losses in that series, behind Ken, who won 12 and lost three. I finished square with Butch Buchholz, and ahead of Barry, Andres and Luis. The highlight of that first pro series for me was when I played Ken at Madison Square Garden and beat him in 39 minutes, 6–0, 6–3. That was the night I first allowed myself to believe I had a future, perhaps a bright one, as a pro. Summing up how my game had changed since turning pro, I was finding that no situation my opponent put me in fazed me too much, no shot he played was anything I couldn't handle. On the backhand I could hit strong, flat shots, or top spin, or sliced shots across court and down the line, or check and play a top-spin lob or a drop shot. I had pretty good control with my forehand. At the net my reflexes were sharp and my volleys went where I aimed them. My serve and overheads were reliable and strong, although I could have used more power on my serve. I could scramble but mostly I tried to get out of trouble by attacking the ball. Sometimes things were going so well that I felt I could have played with a broom handle and won.

The way the professional circuit operated was that the promoter of an event and the players split gate takings about 50–50 (occasionally other deals were done, depending on the circumstances). The promoter hired the venue, wooed sponsors, and stumped up for advertising and promotion. Our share went towards prize money and our travel, accommodation and food costs. (Thank goodness hot dogs were cheap!) We learned which promoters put on good tournaments (that is, with good publicity, enthusiastic crowds, a playable venue, sponsor support and worthwhile prize money), such as Pat Hughes in London, Hank Quinn in Bermuda and Jimmy Van Alen in Newport, Rhode Island, and favoured them. Even so, it was not unusual to turn up ready to play and find only a handful of people in the bleachers. In such cases, neither the promoter, nor we players, got paid, and the best the hapless entrepreneur could offer us after we'd played ourselves to a standstill was his apologies. When we identified a crooked or incompetent promoter we'd make sure we didn't get dudded twice. There was another time, at the Spectrum in Philadelphia, when we were forced to abandon our matches midway through the tournament because we had overrun our time and the arena had to be dismantled to allow an ice skating show to be staged that night.

Typically, a ticket costing $5–$15 would buy a spectator a seat to see the curtain-raiser – matches played by some of the troupe's lesser lights (or 'donkeys', as they were cruelly known) – then there'd be a doubles match featuring the 'stars' such as Sedg, Lew, Muscles and a little later myself and, when he signed on with us, Pancho Gonzales. Then we'd play each other in singles.

We truly were a bunch of gypsies – the amateur establishment preferred to brand us outlaws – hustling across the globe, putting on a good show for the paying customers, moving on to do it all again in another town, another country, next day. Typically, we finished playing at midnight or 1am, got to bed in our $15 a night Holiday Inn or Howard Johnson hotel room at 3, and by 7 were up again to grab a hot dog or a burger at a greasy spoon, cram into our two 1963 Ford Mercury station wagons and be on the road to our next destination. The canvas court would have been rolled up and trucked, like a circus tent, to our next venue, where we'd catch up on some sleep, raise a bit of interest among the locals with a radio or TV interview that our promotions man, the former fine American player Tony Trabert, had set up, get the feel of whatever surface we'd be playing on, and then go to work.

We notched up a lot of air miles, in America and around the world. At first I suffered jet lag, flying from time zone to time zone day after day with no chance to acclimatise. Through trial and error, I found that my confused body clock responded better to a brisk hit out on a local court as soon as possible after landing, rather than crashing at my hotel and trying to sleep my way back to something approaching normality.

By mid-year when the six of us flew to the island of Bermuda off the coast of New York for our next tournament, I had displaced Buchholz as No.2 ranked pro. Hank Quinn, the promoter of this event, was typical of the promoters who staged the pro events. Larger than life, always dressed in a candy-striped jacket and dapper straw hat with two carrots attached, he saw no reason why he should pay for publicists, ticket sellers, MCs, party organisers and someone to be in charge of the linesmen and ball boys: he did it all himself. Hank, who also coached at Davis Cup and junior level, made a killing, as the tournament was played under clear blue skies and every day was sold out.

And the carrots? 'People always ask me that,' he once said. 'It starts the conversation and pretty soon I have a new tennis pupil. Besides, it wouldn't do to have a cabbage up there.' Well, as one who *had* worn wet cabbage leaves in his hat to keep cool when playing in the Queensland heat as a youngster, I beg to disagree.

It was a further sign that I was making progress when I played Lew, who was back on deck, in the semi finals of the Adler tournament, and beat him for the first time, and in straight sets 6–4, 6–3, 6–4. Though Lew was in continual pain from his bad back, he was a fighter and overcoming him was always a win to savour. Muscles Rosewall beat me in the final, but I was now occupying the rung just below him in the pro ranking ladder. By mid-year I had tallied 25 wins and suffered 16 losses, while Ken had won 31 matches out of 41.

•

The dynamic of our troupe changed dramatically when Pancho Gonzales, then aged 35, emerged from retirement in September 1963 to join our group. I had first laid eyes on him back in 1957 when he and Rosewall played a pro match in Rockhampton. I never dreamed that one day it would be me facing him. I had been a teenager and he had been nearing 30, and he was so regal on the court, he *prowled* it like a panther. He was tall and lithe, had a handsome, ever-glowering face and his black hair was prematurely tinged with grey. Best of all, he was a masterly tennis player. It was a treat and a privilege to see him play in my hometown.

He was born in Los Angeles to Mexican parents in 1928, a heritage that made him *persona non grata* in Los Angeles' upper class tennis enclaves, and I believe that this was the genesis of the giant chip he carried on his shoulders in years to come. In 1948 he won the United States championships at age 20 after being ranked 17th in the US, and he won it again the following year. He was the scourge of Australian Davis Cup teams before he turned pro. Although his iconoclastic mix of charm, menace and unabashed devotion to looking after No.1 tended to make Pancho respected more than liked, his talent was undeniable. 'Gonzales is the greatest natural athlete tennis has ever known,' said one of his sworn enemies, Tony Trabert. 'The way he can move that 6ft 3in frame of his around the court is almost unbelievable. He's just like a big cat . . . Pancho's reflexes and reactions are God-given talents. He can be moving in one direction and in the split second it takes him to see that the ball is hit to his weak side, he's able to throw his physical mechanism in reverse and get to the ball in time to reach it with his racquet.' Like many women, legendary women's player Gussie Moran was smitten by the smoldering Gonzales: '[Watching him on the court] is like watching a god patrolling his personal heaven.' Bud Collins, one of the finest tennis writers and commentators, said simply, 'If I had to choose a tennis player to play for my life, I'd choose Pancho Gonzales.'

Riding horses was one of the many delights of growing up in the Queensland bush. This time I managed to stay mounted.

My brother Bob, me, my mother Melba, father Roy and brother Trevor in a family portrait from the early 1940s, before my sister Lois was born. Mum and Dad were strict and never had much money, but to them nothing was too much trouble to help us achieve our dreams.

In 1942, Bob, me and Trevor (front) posed in the backyard with our father and aunts Florrie and Emily. Extended family was always dropping in for a natter and perhaps a hit-up on the home court.

Dad drove me, aged 10 (at right in white), and my cousin Victor Roffey to Brisbane in the family rattletrap to compete in my first junior titles. I seem keener about the trip than Victor.

I owe my parents (pictured here dining out in the 1950s) an enormous debt. Without their sacrifices and drive I could never have become an elite tennis player.

Floods and drought come with the territory if you live in the Queensland bush. When the main street of Rockhampton was inundated, as it sometimes was, it was all hands to the pumps.

I was always a better tennis player than a student. For some reason I was allowed to hold the class sign when Park Avenue Primary's Grade VIII posed for the school photograph.

Both my coaches, Charlie Hollis and Harry Hopman, believed in the value of drills to attain winning tennis form. If you performed a stroke correctly at training, again and again, chances were you would be able to replicate it in a match.

Frank Gorman was my friend and tennis rival, a funny, forthright young man who looked after me when I left home to work with Dunlop. Tragically, Frank's life was cut short.

It was a blessing growing up by the waterways around Rockhampton. All my life I've returned to fish and go boating there.

Looking the part. I was so proud of my official Davis Cup jacket when I was chosen in the Australian team.

The redoubtable Charlie Hollis, my first coach, in his army days. Charlie, an eccentric loner who travelled Australia dispensing tennis wisdom and technique to young players, was the making of me.

Harry Hopman (at Wimbledon in 1954) was my coach, mentor, Davis Cup captain and a stalwart of amateur tennis. A prickly customer with a big heart, he insisted on the highest standards of behaviour on and off the court, and was one of the reasons behind Australia's golden age of tennis in the 1950s and '60s.

After early misgivings – he thought I was too scrawny – Hop took me under his wing and instilled in me a killer instinct and a determination never to give up.

In 1956, Harry invited young champion Bob Mark and me to travel with him to Paris, London and New York for a baptism of fire in the major tournaments. He and Bob seem to have lost their appetite at the prospect of eating the breakfast I'm serving up.

Lew Hoad (playing against the United States in the Davis Cup Challenge Round at White City in 1954) was my hero, an irresistible mix of sublime skill and raw power. Lew dealt me some heavy defeats when I first turned pro. (Gelatin silver photograph purchased by NPG in 2003.)

DOUGLAS MILLER/KEYSTONE/GETTY IMAGES

BOB THOMAS/GETTY IMAGES

Frank Sedgman (pictured after winning Wimbledon in 1952) typified the Australian breed of tennis player in the golden years. He was modest, fair and prepared to fight to the death to win a match.

Roy Emerson (left, after beating fellow Aussie Fred Stolle in the Wimbledon final of 1965) was one of my fiercest rivals…and best mates. We gave each other no quarter in many classic finals but always got together as friends afterwards.

POPPERFOTO/GETTY IMAGES

There was never an easy match against Ken Rosewall (pictured in 1954), my most persistent nemesis who in his long career won eight grand slam singles tournaments. I played against him in the amateur, professional and open eras, and any win over 'Muscles' was well earned. Some of our encounters have been ranked by pundits as among the most competitive and exciting ever played.

ERN MCQUILLAN/NATIONAL LIBRARY OF AUSTRALIA, VN3562066

Tony Roche (below) was a scrapper from Tarcutta who never took a backward step on the court and figured in some controversial matches against me.

DENVER POST VIA GETTY IMAGES

In the 1950s, the doubles team of Ken Rosewall and Lew Hoad (above) triumphed in the major tournaments and Davis Cup. Ironically, Ken thwarted Lew's Grand Slam attempt when he defeated his mate in the US titles final in 1956, after Lew had won the Australian, the French and at Wimbledon.

POPPERFOTO/GETTY IMAGES

Neale Fraser (pictured here after beating me in the 1960 Wimbledon final) took over as Australia's Davis Cup captain and led the so-called Dad's Army team, that included John Newcombe, Ken Rosewall and myself, to victory in 1973.

Right: Until I won my first Grand Slam in 1962, the great American champion Donald Budge was the only one to have achieved the feat. On 10 September 1962, after I downed Roy Emerson in the final of the US championships in Forest Hills (below) to wrap up the Grand Slam, Don was one of the first to congratulate me.

The tennis players of Rockhampton donned their whites to take part in a street parade to welcome me home after I won my first Grand Slam in 1962.

I almost burst with pride when I beat Martin Mulligan to win the 1962 Wimbledon singles title and was presented with the trophy by Queen Elizabeth II. By now a Wimbledon veteran, I had perfected my bow and was no longer a bundle of nerves.

This page and opposite: days at the office in my long career.

Pros on tour. We were gypsies, travelling the world playing for promoters of varying ability and integrity. Here, Butch Bucholz, Lew Hoad, Luis Ayala, yours truly and Frank Sedgman pose with promoters to publicise an upcoming tournament in the United States.

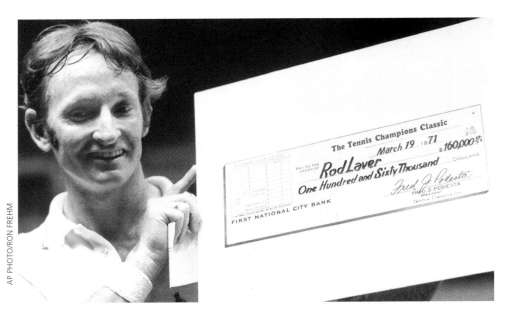

When I turned pro in 1963 I lost match after match to Lew and Muscles, but I persevered and improved, learned to adapt my game to the rigors of the professional circuit, and the wins soon flowed. After a couple of years, I (pictured here in Madison Square Garden, New York) was the top-ranked pro and the highest earner.

Pancho first became a pro in 1949 when he toured the United States playing against Jack Kramer and Bobby Riggs. That pair ran the show and after a bit, Pancho's stormy temperament led to his partners cutting him adrift. He opened a sports store for a time, then in 1954 he rejoined Kramer's new pro troupe. For four years, Pancho suffered at the hands of Kramer, on the court and financially. In 1958, Pancho asked Kramer to increase his cut of the gross takings of his matches by 5 percent. Kramer refused. Pancho sued him. He also dredged up the iniquity of playing a series of matches against Tony Trabert in which Trabert was paid more than Pancho whether he won or lost. Trabert received $100,000 and Pancho a measly $15,000. Kramer won the lawsuit. Pancho, disgruntled, soldiered on. When, in 1961, Kramer ceded control of his professional tennis operation to the players' association, the IPTPA, with Trabert as acting promoter, Pancho feuded with the organisation and quit. He sulked for two years before he returned to our circuit in 1963. Time away hadn't mellowed him.

I'd heard unsettling stories about Pancho from Hoad and Rosewall and the others, but being someone who thinks well of a person until they prove themselves a bastard, I kept an open mind. As it turned out, nothing could have prepared me for Gonzales. When I was introduced to him, he refused to acknowledge me. Then when I beat him in our first match, he was so angry he refused to shake hands afterwards, just brushing me aside. A couple of weeks later, we played each other again in a semi final at White Plains, and I thought I'd teach this old-timer a lesson. I started the match on fire and won the first set 6–0. 'Take that, you bastard!' I was leading 3–1 in the second, and was thinking I had Pancho on toast. That was the first and the last time I made that mistake. He came from behind to win that semi, then beat Rosewall in the final.

Pancho, nicknamed Gorgo, was one of a kind. On his day he could be kind, friendly and generous – it's said that his smile could warm New York in December – or, if he chose, he could be rude, seal you in a block of ice. The American player Ted Schroeder once summed up Pancho well: 'We hardly ever spoke a civil word to one another, but we were friends. He was a very prideful man, not proud, prideful. When you understood that, you understood him.' To me, Pancho was a prickly and aloof loner who, despite his achievements, seemed to be at war with the world. He flew into rages against opponents, umpires and linesmen, spectators, photographers and reporters. The racquets he flung into the crowd and at officials could have done serious damage if they'd connected, and some came close. Once, Pancho left the court to confront a fellow who had been heckling him. He charged into the crowd and stood menacingly, fists clenched, in front of the fan who, when he stood up, was a good head taller than the formidably built Pancho. Pancho gulped and returned to the court with his tail between his legs. We loved that.

I believe Pancho felt it helped his game to have this siege mentality, to think of us all as the enemy, to actually hate us. I can see that mindset paying dividends one-off, in a final perhaps, but to work yourself into a fury against the same blokes night after night after night takes some doing. He could not bear to be bested on the court and was prepared to do whatever it took to get the upper hand. Unlike many of us, the angrier he got the better he played. He terrified opponents, and he knew it. He was a master of gamesmanship and sometimes threw a tantrum – or his racquet – not because he was genuinely upset but simply to shred the concentration and confidence of his opponent. Another tactic, when his opponent was on a roll, was to feign an injury or a problem with his gear to stall for time. When he wasn't shouting and trash-talking me he was grizzling and moaning – though my experience of this came in handy later when our son Rick was born and my wife Mary asked me if I minded his bawling. 'Why would I? I'm used to it,' I replied. 'I've been listening to Gonzales for five years.'

There was just no figuring Pancho. He was a force of nature and a law unto himself. None of us was spared his histrionics. We learned to accept the blow-ups as part and parcel of playing against him. The training and hardline upbringing of the Australian players, particularly, conditioned most of us to stay icily composed when Pancho was exploding on the other side of the net. In my matches against him, my credo of not making eye contact or reacting in any way to his ploys stood me in good stead. Some players, however, worked themselves up into a state of nervous paralysis when they went onto the court against him and, just as he intended, they were easy prey.

While Pancho's tantrums and tirades on the court were often calculated to upset his opponent and make him lose the match, or to intimidate umpires and linesmen into giving him a better deal, when he lost his cool for real, look out. He shouted and swore, put his fist through walls and lockers, and tore up dressing rooms. I never saw him punch anyone, but I have no doubt he was capable of doing so. In Bogota, he and I had a big run-in. I ended up winning the match, and the $100 (yes, $100!) prize money. He was so enraged at losing that, once more, he wouldn't shake hands with me at the net. Then, in the dressing room, he angrily accused me of being a bad sport. To any sportsman, let alone a redhead from Rocky, them's fighting words. I vehemently disagreed, and yelled at him, 'That's it! Pancho, I'm tired of your crap! I give up on you, Gonzales! You wrote the book on bad sportsmanship.' Pancho wouldn't back down and kept accusing me of poor sportsmanship and soon we were shouting at each other. This wasn't his usual mind game. He had really convinced himself that I'd cheated and he was *enraged*. I thought we would come to blows, which wouldn't have been a smart move on my part because in spite of my childhood boxing training I was no fighter and Pancho was much bigger, and angrier, than me. Dennis Ralston and Fred Stolle, who were in the dressing room with us, hastily left. Happily, our argument blew itself out. An hour later Pancho and I were having a friendly hand of gin rummy together.

At Wembley one year I was playing Pancho and he was serving for the match. He rolled a beauty down my backhand side and he thought there would be no way I could return it, so he relaxed. But I went hard for it, rolling my wrist over the top of it and hitting a whistling bloody backhand down the line that beat him all ends up. He was so infuriated that I'd broken his serve and got back into the match that he wielded his racquet like an axe, attacked the wires that were holding the net up and smashed his Spalding to pieces.

Sometimes Pancho's antics backfired on him. Once, when we were playing in the final at the Seventh Regiment Armory courts in New York, by the third set I was getting the better of him. He tried a ploy. He screamed at me that I was quick-serving him. I said, right across the net, 'Well, if you're not ready just put your hand up, and I'll wait. I'm happy for you to let me know when you're ready. But, Panch, it's your responsibility to be ready.' I wasn't being cute about it. I had no interest in taking an unfair advantage. He kept griping about my quick serves and started waving his racquet menacingly in my direction. My dander was up. I shot back at him, 'I know what you're trying to do and it's not going to work. You'll never take my mind off beating you. And after what's been happening, there's no way I'll be losing to you today.' And much later, after he'd been abusing me in our match in Melbourne in January 1968, I couldn't help verballing him as nastily and loudly as he was haranguing me. The crowd was shocked to see usually mild-mannered me respond in this way.

Although, in a match, his opponent was the enemy, after-wards in the dressing room and on the road he would deign to be friendly with players who could beat him. However, if he felt you were no match for him and consequently didn't respect you, he would treat you with contempt. He wouldn't even lower himself to talk to you. Not a word. One fellow he was careful never to pick on, though, was Lew Hoad. Lew intimidated Pancho not through angry words, just by being himself. A friendly, fun-loving but steely and very, very strong man, Lew exuded self-confidence and, without even trying, the aura of one not to be messed with. He wasn't scared of anything, and people tend not to take liberties with those who betray no fear. Pancho and Lew had a fierce but sporting rivalry on the court, and off it there was mutual respect. Any win for Pancho was sweet; a win against Lew was like Christmas. The same went for Lew.

What really cheesed off Ken Rosewall and me, in particular, was that in spite of the fact that we were better players than Pancho at this stage of his career, he was the undisputed star of our troupe, the guy whose name was in big type on the posters and the one the media rushed to interview. More than any of us, he was the guy who put bums on seats. Crowds were prepared to forgive and forget his appalling on-court behaviour. He was larger than life, the ultimate showman. 'Without Pancho, you guys would be out of business,' promoters and journalists repeatedly told us. It was disheartening to think that fans turned up to see Pancho's tantrums rather than our skills.

On the court or off it, there was always a problem brewing with Pancho. It made good sense for the players to be available to the media to promote matches, yet even though the press fawned over him, Pancho rarely played ball with them, and his refusal to talk to reporters hurt us at the ticket office. We all travelled together, Pancho travelled alone. He didn't get involved in the workings of the IPTPA like the rest of us. He refused to join, so attended no meetings nor abided by its rules. He played only when he felt like it. Many times, to no avail, we were forced to lay down the law to him. 'Pancho, we would love you to be with us, but you can't just play whenever you feel like it. If you're not going to be part of the IPTPA and play when we need you, then we don't want you.'

So, in 1963, in a desperate bid to get him onboard, we made a regulation that unless you were a member of our organisation, you could not play in our tournaments. Pancho responded by suing us, and that was one of the scariest things that ever happened to me. Pancho claimed our edict was a violation of America's anti-trust laws and he set his attorney onto us. All the guys in our troupe were subpoenaed one afternoon at the Los Angeles Tennis Club. Pancho was suing us for $250,000. If he won, where on earth would we find a quarter of a million dollars? My respect for the bloke, never all that high, was nonexistent when he did that. All we were trying to do was have a solid organisation to help administer the game and ensure all of our livelihoods, including his. Suddenly there I was in a very different kind of court than I was used to. I was terrified when I took the witness stand and my brain turned to mush when Pancho's lawyer started grilling me about dates and facts. In the end, the judge affirmed Pancho's right in a free enterprise system not to join us and to negotiate his own fees with any organisation. The judge ruled that we didn't have to pay him $250,000, but we were still up for $7000 in court costs. Bottom line: Pancho continued to play with us, but where and when he chose. The best spin I can put on his lawsuit was that his alleged earlier persecution by Kramer, Riggs and Trabert had made him mean and determined to be master of his own fate.

But, gee, the bloke could play. Pancho had the best serving action I have seen. He rolled up and uncoiled, had that wonderful arch. He moved the ball wherever he wanted. His accuracy was such that when we played on canvas he could hit the seam of the canvas every time and the ball would fly in all directions. He could play a power game, a speed game, or a soft and delicate game. He had excellent anticipation, and he was smart. He worked out ways to win. Once he was playing Lew Hoad in a best of 100 series and Lew was ahead 40–21, beating him regularly with his backhand returns of serve that powered the ball right into the back corners of the court. Pancho would be forced to get the ball back over the net with his chip backhand and Lew would smash his innocuous return away. To counter that, Pancho developed a flat backhand that sent the ball down the line or across the court at mighty speed, which stymied Lew. Gonzales started to catch him up. Lew came to me with an exasperated grin on his face and said, 'That bloody Pancho!' He had his share of wins against me as well. I was much younger than him, much fitter and in form, yet on his day, such as when he trounced me in the final of the Alan King Tennis Classic in Las Vegas, he could give anyone in the world a hiding.

Even though Pancho was bloody impossible and undoubtedly a troubled soul, the more I got to know him I saw that for all his tantrums he was a kind man at heart and possessed a nobility that matched his talent. Never was that nobility more in evidence than later in his life when he faced a cruel illness with courage and dignity. Looking back today, with Pancho long gone, I retain affection for that beautiful, crazy man.

Chapter 10

If it's Tuesday . . . this must be Khartoum

WHEN I MADE THE FINAL OF THE PRO WORLD TOURNAMENT at Forest Hills' West Side stadium in September 1963, my reservations about turning professional were well in the past. I was now used to the travel, the challenging – sometimes bizarre – venues, and the unrelentingly excellent standard of my opponents. In fact, I was enjoying it all and thriving on it. I also made the final of the Bermuda pro event by beating Pancho Segura and Butch Buchholz, who had become seriously dispirited at slipping down the pro rankings after my arrival, only to be downed by, you guessed it, Ken Rosewall in the final.

I scarcely had time to draw breath and buy Muscles a congratulatory beer when we were bundled onto a plane for a hectic program in South Africa. Because South Africa hosted no major amateur grand slam event, the fans appreciated us visiting their country and came out to see us in droves. In one match, against Alex Olmedo, my nose inexplicably began to bleed. Blood dripped all over my shirt. I looked like I'd been shot in the head. Play was halted and Alex applied cold compresses to my face and neck until the bleeding stopped and we were able to resume. There could have been more blood shed when the car in which Tony Trabert and Butch Buchholz were travelling to their match in Pretoria swerved to avoid a head-on collision, blew two tyres and spun out of control. The car skidded to a stop with its occupants unscathed.

In South Africa I began to feel that after spending six months as the new boy in the troupe, the pampered amateur, the Mr Grand Slam winner, the fellow everyone enjoyed beating the most, I had become accepted by my fellow pros as one of them. If there were any lingering doubts about me, they were put to rest when I played on through the South African tour despite influenza and stomach pains that, when I had a chance to see a doctor, were diagnosed as appendicitis. With antibiotics, I carried on, refusing to leave the tour short-handed. I knew many of the fans were keen to see the bloke who had won all the previous year's grand slam events. I got over the shakes and fever, but for weeks, I felt weak. Somehow I still managed to beat Tony Trabert and Alex Olmedo to win our tournament in Cape Town. Afterwards, Tony addressed the boys: 'Rod is a pro in every sense of the word as he never let us down nor complained or made excuses for playing below par.' I appreciated that.

It was a point of honour among pros that we played while injured or ill. Lew Hoad battled on for years with his back injury, and there wasn't one of us who didn't defy a doctor's orders not to play – at various times I played with a gashed hand, a bad back, a sprained ankle, the flu, tennis elbow, extreme headaches and, in South Africa, appendicitis. Our schedule was so relentless, we never had a chance to heal until the annual four-week break at the end of the year. Another incentive was that if we didn't play we would make no money. And, perhaps even more than that, to no-show at an event after we'd been advertised as a participant would have been a breach of faith with the people who had bought tickets expecting to see us. They would have justifiably felt cheated and not bother to turn up next time we rolled into their city, and as the organiser of any travelling troupe of sportsmen or entertainers knows, positive word of mouth and repeat business are all important.

At the end of my first year as a pro, I'd made $50,000 and was entrenched as No.2 on the circuit. Muscles Rosewall held the top spot, and it was gratifying that two Australians led the rankings and were making the lion's share of the money. I returned home to spend Christmas 1963 with Mum and Dad, Lois, Bob and Trev, and bask in the broiling Queensland sunshine and champagne waters. I also checked in to Gladstone Hospital and emerged minus my pesky appendix. When I had rung the doc on a Friday and told him I needed to have my appendix out he said he was going fishing on the weekend but could perform the operation on

Monday. It was a success, and afterwards he sent me a bill for £5. How times have changed.

My recuperation proceeded without complications and I was whacking a squash ball within two weeks. It was so good to be home after a year spent constantly on the move. Friendly people stopped me in the street to say g'day. They treated me as if I was a local, not some superstar tennis player, which is how I liked it. When I hit up with my family, or played in charity tennis matches at the little town of Brooklands, south of Rockhampton, where the soil on the court was as red as my hair, folk came from all around to cheer. The Central Queensland Tennis Association told me that they were planning to name after me their swish new aluminium and glass-plated pavilion with shaded verandah at the Tennis Centre at Rockhampton's Victoria Park, right beside the courts where Charlie Hollis had put me through my paces 15 years earlier. I unveiled a plaque at the opening ceremony and was also invited to plant the first tree in a new park and place the winner's sash on a horse at the Callaghan Park races. I was feeling rested, recuperated and very special indeed when, in late January, all too soon, I rejoined the pro circuit.

The 1964 tour kicked off in Australia, and our troupe comprised Ken Rosewall, Lew Hoad, Pancho Gonzales and me. We played various combinations of each other in Western Australia, Victoria and New South Wales, and finally Queensland, where terrific crowds came to see the local boy. Some 1600 turned up to watch us in Rocky. Even little outback Roma had 900 spectators packing into the local court to see us. Lew and I stayed with Mum and Dad in Gladstone when we were in their neck of the woods. Then it was across the ditch to New Zealand for more matches and then back to the US to play in all the tournaments there.

At one stage that year, Muscles and I travelled together, sharing the driving in a station wagon. We were averaging 400 kilometres a night and once, when we drove from Houston, Texas, to Little Rock, Arkansas, we covered 633 kilometres. What days they were. By the end of those trips, there wasn't too much we didn't know about each other. It was an easy camaraderie we all shared, which ended abruptly when we faced each other on the court. We were aware that there were still plenty of people out there who believed that pro matches were fixed. Lew Hoad told me that he had played a hard-fought five-setter against Ken Rosewall in Tokyo and the capacity crowd of 8000 went wild as the two tennis greats pushed themselves to the limit. Afterwards, a member of the press congratulated Lew and Ken for making their match look so real. Lew nearly belted him. Consequently we made it our mission to bust a gut for every point every time we went onto the court to put paid to such ridiculous accusations.

After the US tournaments, we played in La Paz in Bolivia, Khartoum in the Sudan, Paris, Munich, South Africa and the UK, then returned to appear in more cities and towns of America. We crossed time zone after time zone in cars, buses, boats, trains and planes. To hype our matches in St Louis, Missouri, the local authorities allowed Ken, Butch,

Pancho and me to play an exhibition match in the main street which, it turned out, wasn't all that remarkable considering some of the surfaces we had to play on. Sometimes I thought we were showmen as much as tennis players.

Whatever we thought of Pancho Gonzales' tantrums and bloody-minded selfishness, none of us doubted his great heart. In one match in particular he epitomised the never-give-up, try-your-best-at-all-times spirit of our pro troupe. He was playing Ken Rosewall in a semi final of the French International Tennis Championships in Paris in mid-1964 when, early on, he pulled a muscle in his leg. Ken asked him if he wanted to forfeit but Pancho wouldn't hear of that. He played on through the pain, running hard for every shot, and Ken, who doesn't know the meaning of 'mercy', let alone 'take it easy', ran him around all over the court. The torturers of the Spanish Inquisition could not have inflicted more agony. Pancho didn't buckle. He battled on and on, and it took Ken five sets to finish him off. Only as he limped off the court when it was all over did he let on how incapacitated he was, and the crowd, and Ken Rosewall and all of his fellow players watching, cheered and clapped. As if all that wasn't enough, an ordinary mortal would have pulled out of the play-off for third place the following day. Not Pancho. He not only showed up, he beat Andres Gimeno 6–2, 6–2 in less than an hour.

In the final, Ken was up against me, and won in four sets. I played Ken again in London just weeks later in the final of the Indoor Professional Tennis Championships that they held on a platform constructed above the Empire Pool at

Wembley. This was a novel setting for a memorable match, which, for me, was further evidence that I was bridging the gap between Ken and me. We were at each other's throats from the first point. It was a war between mates. Each of us punished the other's mistakes, and lifted each other to new heights. At two sets each, I was down 5–4 and he was serving for the match. I then thought, 'What have I got to lose?' I threw caution to the winds. I broke Ken's serve and then broke him again at 6–6, and won the set 8–6, and with it the match. Some have said this was the best match Ken and I ever played, and they may be right. Fred Stolle, a man whose opinion I respect, said that match was one of the best he had ever witnessed.

The day after that epic encounter I nearly choked on my cornflakes when I picked up one of the London newspapers and read that, being the top-ranked pro at age 26 with £35,000 worth of earnings to date, I was surely the world's most eligible sporting bachelor. Following up on the 'scoop', a reporter from Sydney's *Sun-Herald* called to grill me about my love life. I told him the truth: my love life was nonexistent, just a date, a kiss goodnight, then back on the plane. I simply had never had the chance to form a serious relationship because, I said, 'I've never been in the one city for more than a month at a time since I was 17. I never get a chance to really know a girl. I have occasional dates, but seldom more than two with the same girl. I might be in, say, Chicago for one night with the tennis troupe. I'll go out with a girl after I've played my match. But when I return to Chicago to play again a year later, I ring her up and it goes,

"Oh hello, Dolly, this is Rod. What say you and I get out and hit the town?" Then a deep voice comes on the other end of the line and says, "Sorry, buddy, my wife is going to be tied up tonight . . . by the neck!" It's amazing how many girls I know who got married last year.'

The *Sun-Herald* article, published on 27 September 1964, ran under the embarrassing heading, 'Tennis Star the Girls Can't Meet: He's Lonesome with £35,000: Rod Tells'. Nevertheless, it offered a snapshot of my life and career at that time, and it's worth reprising it here:

> Rod expects his social life to improve a little when he returns to Australia at the end of November. 'A few of my old contacts down there haven't got hitched yet. I'm looking forward to coming home.' To see Rod Laver off the tennis court is to see the antithesis of everyone's idea of a gay and wealthy young bachelor. He travels the world with only two suits and a meagre supply of sports clothes. He rarely goes to nightclubs, spends much of his solitary hours sitting alone in a hotel room. 'My only real possession is a portable record player and a few Frank Sinatra LPs,' he told the *Sun-Herald* this week. 'I'd go nuts if I didn't have my record player for company while I'm stuck in some hotel room by myself. You can't relax in a big tournament until someone beats you and lately I've been ending up in the final most of the time. So I can't join in the big parties with the boys who get knocked out in the first couple of rounds. Pro tennis in some ways can be more fun for

the perpetual losers. They can start *playing* as soon as they are beaten because they haven't got the big match to worry about tomorrow.'

When Australians next see Laver in action against Rosewall they will see a standard of tennis that is near perfection. The names Rosewall and Laver in tennis now rank with Pele in soccer and Lindrum in billiards. The young Australian pair play the game as it has never been played by even the greatest players of the past. Their match at Wembley last week was described by the London press as the greatest game of tennis ever played in England. Laver said, 'Winning that one was the biggest kick of my life. We are playing a calibre of tennis now that leaves me in awe just thinking about it. To beat Ken Rosewall, the No.1 player, well, it was a tremendous feeling.'

He is more confident and sure of himself. 'I know where I'm going and what I want, now that I'm a professional,' he said. 'As an amateur I didn't really know what I was doing in tennis or where it was getting me. But today I'm more in love with tennis than I ever was. This game is my whole life now and I've got no plans of giving it up. I know it's robbing me of a really good social life, but I don't care. I'm getting enough kicks out of tennis to make up for anything.'

That pretty much summed up me in those days.

With Lew Hoad's bad back limiting his appearances, Ken Rosewall was probably the fellow I was closest to in those days. He was the perfect person to travel with. He never got into any strife, and was quiet and reserved, the total pro. He was a bit like me, in that he was on tour to play tennis and make money. He wasn't much of a one for partying or sightseeing. If he said, 'Meet you in the hotel lobby at 3,' he would be there at two minutes to. He was Mr Consistent on and off the court. And as one who was famous for minding his money, he was the ideal troupe secretary and treasurer.

In 1964, Ken and I each won seven important pro titles, but I was able to beat Muscles in 15 of our 19 matches. I was a far, far better player by this stage than I'd been when I turned professional. The grind of constant playing against tried-and-true champions and the endless travel had strengthened my mind and body, and my shot-making was consistently precise. There's no doubt that playing for money rather than a trophy also toughened me up and honed my killer instinct. Whereas before my form could fluctuate, now I was steadier, more controlled. I was more tactically astute, and I could steel myself to play at a high level no matter who I was up against, a Muscles or a Hoad, a Gimeno, a MacKay, a Segura or a Gonzales, and no matter whether I was playing at a sold-out Madison Square Garden or on a wonky makeshift court plonked on an ice rink in Timbuktu in front of 100 spectators.

By the end of 1964, in just less than 24 months, I had already earned more than my three-year $110,000 guarantee. I had also edged ahead of Ken Rosewall to be the top-ranked pro. Turning professional, for all its challenges, was looking like an excellent decision. Of course I had pangs of regret when I read the results from the Australian, Wimbledon, French and US amateur titles . . . but those tournaments were not my world anymore.

It was in my bones to shy away from publicity – I hated being the focus of attention – yet when the media sought interviews, I always obliged, because if I was in the papers, then I was promoting our tours, and a positive article could attract a good crowd to our next event. In late 1964, soon after I became the world's No.1 professional, I explained to a reporter how things were for me. It was a snapshot of that time in my career. I said I'd learned a lot since turning professional. Pros, I said, couldn't afford to play a bad game. While amateurs needed only to win the match, what mattered in the pros was how many points you won by because this determined your seeding for the next tournament . . . I was a better player today, and harder mentally. For my first professional match at White City early in 1963, my opponent Lew Hoad had trained for weeks to be at his top against me. Lew left me in no doubt that the pros jealously defended their reputations. 'The whole group descends on a newcomer like eagles on lambs back home in central Queensland.' Lew and I had played until midnight; the next day I was so stiff I couldn't run and Ken Rosewall took less than an hour to beat me. My education had begun and it took me months to settle down. I turned the corner, and then came that night at Madison Square Garden when I beat Ken in

39 minutes – winning the first six games in only 13 minutes while losing only nine points.

Each year's pro tour started in Australia and, once more in 1965, it was good to spend time with my family in Gladstone when we swung through Queensland. The lads were all determined to play our best tennis because we knew our tour was being white-anted by the LTAA, which had programmed its events to clash with ours. We had a point to prove: that our matches were legit and, into the bargain, we were better players than the amateurs. All we wanted was for the fans to come to our tournaments and compare the fare we served up with that of the amateurs. To the LTAA's consternation, the crowds did flock to see us and we rewarded them with some classic matches. By now, Lew was a shadow of his former self, but he continued to give it his all. As Pancho had when he pulled his leg muscle against Muscles, Lew played through intense pain to treat the crowds to some fabulous tennis. At Milton, I had to be at full-stretch to beat him in a frenetic semi final. He kept coming at me, and the power of his serves and volleys was awesome. Pancho, too, gave me no quarter in our semi final in Adelaide. He was at his snarling best, or worst, at acrimonious odds with me, the umpire and linesmen, and the crowd. Throughout our marathon first set, which I won 20–18, he fussed and stalled and bickered, trying to break my rhythm and concentration. He accused *me* of stalling and trying to upset him. I won that tournament, and won in Perth as well, while Ken and Pancho came out on top in Brisbane and Sydney, respectively.

There was never a dull moment in that crazy time. We certainly knew we were alive. In Reston, a suburb of Washington DC, the court was not quite ready. In fact, the court was still a construction site, by and large, and the building dust was so thick in the air we were gagging. The dressing sheds hadn't been built so we changed in our cars. After our matches, showers had to wait.

Just as we arrived in Khartoum in the Sudan in Africa, serious rioting broke out. Nothing to do with us, I hasten to add. The Communists and the Muslims were at logger-heads, with the latter about to form a government. Soldiers armed with machine guns and surly attitudes were every-where in town, and at the tennis courts. We prided ourselves on playing anywhere, but this time I was thinking it might have been a good idea to pull the plug. A further discourage-ment was the prize money on offer – a princely $1000, to be split between four of us. The promoter was at his wits' end. He had been unable to publicise the tournament because the government had shut down the newspapers and radio stations. He optimistically estimated that perhaps 150 people might show up. When we told him that we expected to play in front of many more than that, he and his friends hit the phones and soon word spread through Khartoum that there was a tennis tournament on. When we arrived at the rough-hewn grass court in the oppressive heat of late afternoon, 1000 fans were there to greet us. Because this court was not equipped with lights, when twilight fell at 6 we players, and the crowd, all pulled up stakes and relocated to another court, a concrete one with lights, where we continued play.

All was going well until a horde of bugs, attracted by the lights, descended on us like something out of a Biblical plague. Thousands of bugs were hurtling through the air, careening into us and making it impossible to play. I decided I would never complain about Australia's blowflies again. The fans, being battered and eaten alive themselves by the insects, were happy enough that we called it quits. Needless to say, with just $1000 to divvy up, we did not have a slap-up meal and luxury accommodation for the remainder of our stay in Khartoum.

La Paz in Bolivia is approximately 3660 metres above sea level, and this brought particular problems. The lack of oxygen at that altitude exhausts you, no matter how fit you are. The altitude also brings on nosebleeds. And the balls flew like pigeons in the thin air. Tap a ball and it'd zoom out of the court and up and away. We had to stick skewers through the balls to deflate them so they'd behave. And the prize that we literally shed blood for? A watch. That said, I tried as hard at La Paz and Khartoum and all those other whistlestops as I did at Wimbledon and the Australian and United States championships in my amateur years. It was the same with all of us. I never saw a pro give less than the very best he was capable of. I never saw anyone throw a match, or go easy on an opponent. There were matches against the 'donkeys' – in which I was in sufficient control to practise shots and rectify weaknesses, although doing so often led to me losing the match. There were no slouches among us; we were all champions.

There'd be times when we played in venues, perhaps a basketball court or gymnasium, with low ceiling beams and you had to adjust by lobbing over and through the rafters. Sometimes we'd smash a light bulb or even dislodge a piece of the ceiling wood, which would come crashing down on us or the spectators. Forget about playing on grass, clay and concrete – we were the best roof rafters players in the world, and of us all, Pancho Segura was the champ. I got fairly adept at it too and one night during a game in Utica, New York, I beat Andres Gimeno with a rafter shot that wandered among the beams as if directed by radar. As I was trying to negotiate the ceiling beams at Utica back then in those gypsy days, did I think about the glory days of full-page press stories, huge crowds, glistening trophies and limos at Wimbledon? Occasionally . . . then I put such thoughts out of my head and kept hitting for the rafters. The hardships we shared made us proud of our skills and perseverance. They certainly ensured we were more determined to make a go of it.

One time we all had to get from a tournament in Hungary to another in West Berlin. Remember that there were two Berlins then, West and East, and East Berlin was under Communist control. We decided to take the train rather than hire cars, and were a tad concerned when we saw a soldier manning a machine gun perched on top of our carriage. Of course, we ended up on the wrong, or Communist, side of Checkpoint Charlie, the entry point between the two Berlins. First we tried to leave the train and catch a cab to West Berlin but were halted and made to get back on. I was the designated bag man, and I was juggling five suitcases on a trolley. Well, the train took off again and after our papers were checked we travelled all of 200 metres down the track before we were shunted off and made to get on another locomotive that progressed a further 200 metres. Two more 200-metre train trips and three more passport and bag checks, and we were in West Berlin. It took us 90 minutes to travel 800 metres.

It wasn't all fun and games, though. For a moment in 1964, it looked like the professional circuit would cease to exist. The US Pro Championships had been a staple of the United States pro circuit since Cash and Carry Pyle's day beginning in 1926, but when we played them at Forest Hills in '63, attendance was poor, the promoters went broke and the troupe – including Muscles who won the final, and me, the runner-up – received no money. So for a while it seemed we might not be playing in the States. Then, a guardian angel in the form of Ed Hickey, a public relations man for the New England Merchants National Bank and, most significantly, a tennis fanatic, persuaded his bank to stump up $10,000 to allow the US Pro Championships to be staged at Longwood, the second oldest tennis club in America. With the bank on board, it was easier to attract sponsors, and the tournament went ahead to good attendances and a tidy profit. I beat a food-poison-affected Rosewall in the semi and then Gonzales in the final, which was played in the rain. We were back from the brink and on our way again.

There simply were no easy matches. Of all the places to play Lew Hoad, a bloke who could really put you to the test, a court laid on a platform erected atop an ice rink in Altringham, England, with condensation dripping from the ceiling and drenching the 'court', would hardly be my first choice, but this was the pro circuit, and so there Lew and I were, slipping all over the place, finding it nigh-impossible to make our shots under the treacherous conditions and doing our best to keep the punters happy. We could so easily have broken a leg. I reckon it would have been safer to don skates and play on the ice rink. With neither of us able to achieve the purchase to hit home winners, the score was soon 20 games each. What a time for my jockstrap to break with a loud *snap!* But that's exactly what happened. After some running repairs, we resumed this most bizarre of games until, at 27 games all, we called it quits because the court, wet and slippery at first, had become a pond. That was the longest set I ever played.

Again in England, on this occasion in Nottingham, I was facing Frank Sedgman. A short time into our match it occurred to each of us that we were hitting an extraordinary number of passing shots. Frank was passing me again and again and I was doing the same to him. What was going on? We called a halt and had someone measure the court and our suspicions proved correct. Whoever had marked up the court had made it a metre wider than regulation. No wonder we couldn't get to each other's shots. There was not the time to have the court realigned, so we made do, just stood at the baseline and whacked the ball back to each other till one of us prevailed. The show had to go on.

And on . . . At the World Professional Championships at Wembley I beat Pancho, despite his usual shenanigans, to win my second successive title there. By now Pancho had become the showman of the tour and would often have the crowd in stitches as he carried on like a music hall villain. Ken Rosewall and I were the straight men, concentrating on playing our best tennis and leaving the histrionics to Pancho and his fellow Latin firebrand Pancho Segura. We were all back in the United States again in May 1965 for the Manhattan Tournament at the Seventh Regiment Armory. We were without two of our stalwarts. Lew had bowed out to have an operation on his foot, and Frank Sedgman, who was 38, was taking a well-deserved break back home in Australia. The cynical New Yorkers who had been led astray by the amateur brigade's propaganda voted with their feet and on the first night only 200 of them were in attendance. It took a glowing account of the night's play in the sports pages of next morning's *The New York Times* to convince the locals that pro tennis was on the level, played at a standard that put the amateurs to shame, and we were worth their money. After the *Times*' recommendation, crowds picked up and by the end of the tournament we were playing to packed houses.

It was always a pleasure to play in South Africa, and even more so in 1965, my third year on the pro circuit, when my travelling companions and opponents were Rosewall, Hoad, Sedgman, Buchholz, Gimeno, Ayala and Olmedo. Don Black was a real character. He was the father of Byron and Wayne Black, who formed one of the finest doubles teams of the

'90s. When I was in Rhodesia, as it was known then (today it's Zimbabwe), I stayed with Don on his 50-acre farm. Some whites made life intolerable for the black population of Rhodesia. Don was not one of them. He was a kind and friendly man who hired as many black people as he could afford to give them work and wages. They built three grass tennis courts on his land and he encouraged them to play on them. What I'll never forget about Rhodesia are the magnificent jacaranda trees that lined the streets. It breaks my heart to see what happened to that country once Robert Mugabe took control. I met Prime Minister Ian Smith, who was being hammered by the pro-black forces, and he looked at me sadly after we'd spent some together and said, 'See, I'm not such a bad bloke after all, am I?' But I was saddened by the poverty I saw. Too many African kids we met were malnourished. Most of the ball boys had no shoes, a few wore just one. Their T-shirts and pants were in tatters. At the end of our African tour Butch Buchholz and I took our suitcases to a park and gave the children all our shirts, shorts, hats and shoes.

Promoters are usually unconventional characters. It's the nature of the beast. A minority of the promoters we ran into reminded me of the old carnival barkers who stood outside sideshows when the circus came to Rockhampton when I was boy, shysters with loud voices and louder jackets who promised us gullible locals the world and gave us an atlas. The show these charlatans claimed we were going to see bore little resemblance to what we actually witnessed after we'd paid our 10 pence entry fee and filed into the tent. Not that there were two-headed sheep or half-men-half-women on the pro tour. But there *were* shifty fellows who wouldn't pay us what they'd promised to entice us to their hall, ice rink or hastily assembled court in the backblocks.

Happily, to balance the ledger, there were straight arrows, and in the US one was Jimmy Van Alen, the events promoter of the Newport Casino, who was a true tennis visionary. Jimmy decked himself out in a white wide-brimmed planter's hat, a Technicolor tie and bright suede shoes. He signed us up to play a tournament there in late 1965 under his revolutionary new Van Alen Streamlined Scoring System (VASSS). The matches would be played based on table-tennis rules, the winner the first to reach 31 points, and at the end of the round robin, after all the players had played each other, our points would be tallied and the winner would be the one who'd accumulated the most. Jimmy believed VASSS would ensure more exciting rallies and make tennis a speedier and therefore more spectator- and television-friendly game. We were sceptical but went along for the ride.

Born in Newport, Rhode Island, in 1902, Cambridge University-educated Jimmy had been a musician, poet, publisher and civic leader and was renowned for his annual 24 December readings of ''Twas the Night Before Christmas' to local children at his Newport home, which Van Alen had purchased from the poem's author, Clement Clarke Moore. Jimmy also found time to be a national real tennis (or court tennis) singles and doubles champion. (Real tennis is the ancient game on which modern tennis was based.) He is best remembered today not for VASSS, which didn't survive the test of time, but for founding the International Tennis Hall of Fame and Museum at the Newport Casino in 1954, for introducing night tennis and electric scoreboards, and for inventing the tie break. In the old days, it was not unusual for a set to drag on for hours, with scores like 32–30 not uncommon. Though most elements of VASSS were pooh-poohed, such as playing for $5 a point and penalising big servers by making them stand a metre behind the baseline, even his critics conceded that the tie break, which would be played when the score reached 6–6 in a set, was a damn good idea. In the tie breaker the first player to get five points – the original VASSS tie break was best of nine points, so both players had match point at four points-all – would be the winner of the set. This was later increased to the best of 12, or the first to seven points with a two point lead, and that arrangement remains in place today.

We were the guinea pigs, the first to play tennis under Jimmy's VASSS. Our grand old game had never experienced anything like Van Alen's events at Newport. Jimmy rang a large antique ship's bell to signify the end of each match, and although he had rigged up powerful lights to enable night play, they were useless when the thick evening fog rolled in off Narragansett Bay. The pea souper was made even more impenetrable by the thick pall of smoke from the fireworks Jimmy ignited each night in a bid to make the four day and night tournament an even grander event.

Despite Jimmy's best efforts to explain them to us, none of us really understood the rules of the VASSS system, so confusion reigned. We didn't know if we were winning or losing, especially when the electric scoreboard was engulfed by fog. Pancho, true to form, became angry. He moaned and shouted and sacked a linesman, and when he was soundly beaten by Andres Gimeno, he exploded, 'It's bad enough playing in the fog let alone worrying about this fool system!' In another match, he had a meltdown and hit the ball clear out of the stadium, which prompted Jimmy Van Alen to come onto the court to remonstrate with him. 'I don't think that's a nice thing to do,' said Jimmy. 'Oh no!' hollered Pancho. 'Well if you don't like it, I'll leave.' Knowing the volatile star was his top drawcard and best chance of turning a profit from the tournament, Jimmy backed down and left the court. Pancho, however, was not placated. He finished the match, then made good his threat. He marched into the dressing room, collected his belongings and stormed out of the arena even though there was a doubles match, featuring him, scheduled next. Pancho was perfectly happy to leave his partner stranded, even though this would cost him prize money and disappoint the spectators. Pancho's wife saved the day when she physically restrained him from departing and dragged him back onto the court.

I had a lot of time for Jimmy Van Alen, and I ended up winning that tournament with 93 points, ahead of Muscles on 90, but, frankly, apart from the tie break, the VASSS system was ridiculous and unworkable. It was adopted by some organisers of professional tournaments, but fizzled out after a couple of years, and today the tie break is its sole remaining remnant.

Chapter 11

Love match

By the end of 1965, the record books showed that, for the first time, I had beaten Ken Rosewall more often than he beat me. Ken and Lew had been right. If I survived my initiation, I would do okay as a pro. But better than my No.1 ranking, better than prize money – by far – was something else that befell me in '65. I met the love of my life. It had always been just tennis and me. Tennis was my everything. I was fixated on playing my best and being the best. I likened my life at that time to floating around on a great big wave. Sure, I'd been on dates on my travels, and met and had fun with some wonderful girls, then I was off next day on a plane to somewhere and our paths would never again cross. Being honest, I guess part of it too was that I simply had never met anybody I really cared for. Then into my life came Mary Benson and everything changed.

We met at a charity benefit tennis day at Jack Kramer's tennis club at Palos Verdes, south-west of Los Angeles. I was immediately attracted to Mary. She was a dark-haired beauty, green-eyed, slim, and her deep tan gave her away as a beach lover. She was there to watch some swimming events, and only knew I was a tennis player because I was carrying a racquet. We chatted and I couldn't believe how easy it was to have a conversation with her, despite her being 10 years older than me. Until Mary, my usual state when meeting women was tongue-tied and edgy. She was interested and interesting, funny and smart, with a warm personality. I hung on her every word and could not stop gazing at her. She reckoned that I was attracted to her because 'I was so tanned and he was red-headed, fair-skinned and freckled!'

Being with Mary felt natural and right. I'd never had feelings like this about a woman. We'd just met, yet seemed like old friends. Before too long we knew all about each other. I told her about my tennis career, and filled her in on my growing-up years in rural Queensland. I regaled her with tales about my parents and brothers. When she could get a word in, she told me that she had been raised in Sycamore, Illinois, where her dad was a grocer. She married young and gave birth to three children, Ron, Steve and Ann Marie. Her marriage ended and, after the divorce, Mary brought up the children at her home in Corona Del Mar, a town close to Newport Beach, California, where she worked as a book-keeper before becoming a very, very good accountant. She was an active, outdoors woman who snow-skied, swam and enjoyed the beach with her children. She was also a lover of art, antiques and beautiful things in general. That evening, she later told me, she went home and told the kids that she'd met a champion tennis player. 'Oh,' they said, 'Pancho Gonzales?' She replied, 'No, he was an Australian.'

We dated, and played tennis together. Her children liked me, and I thought they were tremendous kids. She came to tournaments with me that year, such as to South Africa, where she went on her first wildlife safari, and to Australia in February 1966, where she charmed Mum and Dad and my brothers. Always curious about other countries and cultures, Mary revelled in the weird and glorious land Down Under.

Mary and I stayed for a short time with my old tennis mate Jim Shepherd's family in Moorooka, a suburb of Brisbane . . . and the years peeled away. I had often been a guest there when younger and on tour and we all played crazy games on their court and generally had a lot of fun, and the Shepherds' hospitality had not lessened over time. I told Mary about the day when Lew Hoad and I were having dinner and Lew, as he did on occasion, dropped the F-word. Mrs Shepherd turned white with shock. I thought there would be trouble, but no, whatever she was feeling about Lew's blunder, she kept it to herself.

I was aware that a few players on the tour were surprised that I was in a relationship with a woman considerably older than me. We didn't care. We were having too much fun together. We even had a laugh, after we were engaged, when we saw the front page of the local *Daily Pilot* newspaper with its banner headline that read: 'Australian National Hero to Wed Corona Del Mar Divorcee'.

Mary and I were married in San Francisco on 20 June 1966, in St Luke's Presbyterian Church in the suburb of San Rafael. I nearly didn't make it. I was committed to playing in a tournament in St Louis, Missouri, half a continent away. The doubles and singles finals were scheduled for 19 June so, if I qualified, that would give me next to no time to make the trip to San Francisco and be there late that evening in time to catch my breath, have a sound sleep, and then attend a wedding rehearsal before the wedding breakfast and the ceremony in the afternoon. I did make both finals, and lost each time. I could always focus on my tennis and banish everything else from my mind, but if I was preoccupied by the pending nuptials perhaps I could be forgiven.

Lew Hoad, who of course I'd invited to my wedding despite him beating me in the tournament, and I collected our rental car and drove to the airport to catch our early evening flight. Halfway there, the car spluttered and died. A quick look at the petrol gauge told us why. By the time we had jogged to a gas station, refuelled and driven to the airport, our plane was long gone, and we had to cool our heels for four hours until the next flight to San Francisco. I was panic-stricken, afraid Mary would be left stranded at the altar. Typically, Lew's solution was for us to have a few calming beers while we waited for our plane, but it was a Sunday night and no bars were open. I sat there sweating.

At last we boarded the flight and arrived in San Francisco at 3am on my wedding day. We sprinted to the all-night rental car counter, and it was there, while I searched in my bag for my driver's licence, that I discovered that in my panic I had left on the plane my licence and $3000 worth of air tickets and vouchers for our upcoming tour of Europe and Africa. I dashed across the tarmac to try to retrieve them just as the plane was being towed to its hangar. After much arguing and pleading on my part, the flight staff allowed me to reboard the plane and retrieve my papers, which, thank heavens, were still on my seat. Back to the car rental office, into the car . . . and I fell into bed at 5am, a scant four hours before the wedding breakfast.

After all that, I arrived at St Luke's right on time for our 5pm wedding. At the altar, I turned to see Mary walking up the aisle, looking like a dream in an eggshell silk and cotton embossed, embroidered empire-style gown with a fabric Chanel bow in her hair.

There at the church to help us celebrate our wedding were many of my mates from the pro circuit, including Lew Hoad and Ken Rosewall, Mal Anderson and Barry MacKay. My best man was former Sydneysider Kevin Sullivan, a one-time tennis player who was now managing Jack Kramer's Los Serranos Golf Club in Chino, California. My younger sister Lois, the only member of my family who was able to attend, was Mary's maid of honour. When we emerged from the church in a shower of confetti, the fellows, with Lew and Muscles prominent, formed a guard of honour by holding aloft their tennis racquets. We were engulfed in goodwill. It was sad that Mary's children didn't come, yet we made up for lost time, and to this day they have been both family and friends. Sometimes kids don't take kindly to a new man in their mother's life. I never wanted to replace their dad, just be a good husband to Mary, and create a happy and financially secure life for us all.

Mum and Dad had known for some time that Mary was the girl for me and that we'd be getting married at some stage and they gave us their love and blessings. I assumed that they probably wouldn't be able to come to our wedding because they were elderly now and a big, pricey trip to the United States would be a bit daunting for them, and in fact, caught up in my tennis and the wedding preparations, I forgot to tell them that we had set a date. So when Mum was doorstopped by the *Australian Women's Weekly*, our wedding was news to her. When the reporter dropped the bombshell that her youngest son was now a married man, Mum put on a good show of playing it cool: 'The wedding is a surprise . . . because Rod is so casual, but we had a fair idea it was happening. Mary is very attractive, quite tall, with dark hair, and a very nice girl. My husband and I are happy for them. We feel that if Rod is not marrying an Australian girl, we are delighted he is marrying Mary. We came to know her when she stayed with us in Gladstone for about a fortnight last February. Rod said Mary would be back and forth as usual for tennis tournaments. So we will see just as much of Rod, but will have the additional pleasure of seeing Mary, too.'

Mary's and my eagerly awaited week-long honeymoon didn't happen because another pro tournament had been slotted into my schedule without warning, and I was expected to be there. So we had one day together before I packed my kitbag and set off again. Mary had heard about tennis widows and now she was one. She was under no illusions that we'd be living a normal life. In the year we'd been an item, Mary had come to know what she was in for by marrying an itinerant professional tennis player. We'd grabbed what time we could cobble together between tournaments. It wasn't much. It was just the way it was, and would always be until I retired from tennis and could live like regular people. She knew we would have long periods apart and she accepted that. She was not the kind of woman to stay home pining. Her plate was full. She had a burgeoning career, and the teenage children kept her focused. She had a large circle of friends and as a devoted snow-skier often holidayed at Aspen, and in Austria and Switzerland. We compromised. She learned to play a little tennis, and I took cross country skiing lessons and became quite reasonable at it – until I realised that one slip on the snow could put me out of tennis and onto the breadline.

Mary was a staunch ally. She was my confidante and booster as well as my wife. When she came to a tournament with me, be it Wimbledon or some tiny event in a small town, she took it upon herself to make sure my dietary needs were met. She once explained, 'Feeding Rod is a full-time job. The care and feeding of touring athletes is something someone should write a book about. Rod puts away a lot of food. I wouldn't dream of eating each time he does. He eats plain food – steaks, vegetables, lots of greens. Then he needs sweets – ice cream, pies – for energy. He tries to eat a large meal before a match. This may mean having dinner at 8 or 9am and breakfast at 8pm.'

We bought a larger home in Corona Del Mar, near Newport Beach, big enough for the five of us. Mary managed my money, running the household and investing wisely in shares and property. She proved herself an astute and hard-headed financial manager. She also opened negotiations with the International Management Group (IMG), American Mark McCormack's management organisation, which boosted the earnings of celebrities and such elite sportsmen as golfers Gary Player, Jack Nicklaus and Arnold Palmer. She suggested that as the No.1 pro tennis player and a Grand Slam winner as an amateur, I would surely be a marketable client and a magnet for sponsors. Mark turned us down because he didn't feel that tennis was popular or lucrative enough for him to get involved in. He would change his mind.

•

By the end of that momentous year, 1966, the pro troupe had slogged and slugged our way through Australia and New Zealand, the United States, France, Italy, South Africa, Kampala and Abidjan in Africa, Portugal and England. Mary joined me on some of these adventures, but always she had responsibilities at home and when she wasn't with me I missed her so very badly. Thanks to winning 13 out of 18 matches against Ken Rosewall and 17 major tournaments such as the Don Budge Masters, and the French,

Johannesburg, Milan and Wembley Pro titles, I retained my No.1 ranking.

The travelling pros were back in Australia in January 1967, and this time our troupe's ranks were bolstered by my old Australian rival Fred Stolle and the American Dennis Ralston, two wonderful players. In their first professional year Fred and Dennis suffered much the same fate that I had in mine. Up against tougher, more determined players than they'd been used to opposing as amateurs, they lost more matches than they won until their game and temperament were forged in the fires of life on the road.

We could always count on a Pancho Gonzales blow-up, and this time it came when, after attending his son's wedding in Los Angeles, he travelled to Australia solo, and when he arrived at Brisbane airport and there was nobody there to greet him he spat the dummy. When we reminded him that he had not bothered to tell any of us when, or where, or even *if*, he'd be landing, he was unfazed. He truly expected us to *know*.

The big crowds we drew right through Australia – even in Queensland, which was being battered by Cyclone Dinah with its ferocious winds and torrential rain – was heartening. We responded by showing the fans some fine tennis.

Back in the Americas we began our tour in New York playing on rubber stretched over wood at the poorly lit Seventh Regiment Armory on Park Avenue. It was during the semi final of this tournament that I had my big blow-up with Pancho Gonzales when he accused me of quick-serving him. He had niggled me through the first set, which

I won 7–5, then, to put me off my game so he could win the second set, he revved his bad behaviour into overdrive. What a match, a frantic affair with both of us scrambling to return each other's serves and volleys, which were flying like bullets off the rubber surface. In the second set it was 6–6, 7–7, 8–8, 9–9, and Pancho toughed it out to win 16–14. One set apiece. In the third set it was clear that Pancho, who was nearing 40 years of age, was running out of puff after that taxing second set so, naturally, he threw a tantrum to try to disrupt my concentration. I was leading 6–5 and serving for the set and the match when he began screaming at me across the net. When I called him on it, he pulled his head in. I held serve to win the third set 7–5 and then the fourth 6–2. After the match I shook Pancho's hand and he grinned, probably pleasantly surprised by my flash of temper, and we each said, 'Well done.'

After New York it was on to Puerto Rico, Miami Beach, Orlando and Boston Garden. Then Europe. The delights of our perpetual world tour were never so apparent as in April 1967 when we played a series of tournaments in the picturesque French cities of Lille, Bersancon, Lyon, Marseilles, Toulouse, Bordeaux and Rammes. We were well received and the locals' hospitality didn't stop at the tennis venue. Mary joined me in France and we had rarely feasted so well on such delicious food. Maybe there *was* more to eating than steak and eggs. The countryside was green and rolling, and Mary and I enjoyed it together.

Despite the delights of France, a pall descended on us when news came that Lew Hoad, who was undergoing treatment for his back injury and was not on the tour, was retiring from tennis at the comparatively young age of 33. After his magnificent early years when Lew was the best tennis player in the world, his bad back had derailed the last years of his career. Now he and his wife Jenny, who as Jenny Staley had been a formidable tennis player in her own right, were going to establish a tennis *campo* near the town of Fuengirola on Spain's Costa Brava. I could picture Lew there taking shade from the blazing sun under an olive tree, drinking deeply of an icy beer and enchanting his guests with stories of his mighty career. When I was a kid Lew was my idol, and nothing I'd seen travelling the world with him, playing with him and against him, had knocked him from that pedestal.

The surfaces we played on continued to surprise us. We were the first to stage matches on Astroturf that had been laid over cement (it made the ball bounce as erratically as a Mexican jumping bean), at a tournament at the Los Angeles Tennis Club, then we tried our hand playing on carpet that had been sprayed with an acrylic solution to slow down the surface at the Madison Square Garden Invitation Pro Tournament in New York. By now Fred Stolle and Dennis Ralston had weathered the storm and were stringing together some impressive wins.

Remembering those times, it was another age. When we turned up at Jimmy Van Alen's Newport Casino VASSS tournament in 1967, he had organised for proceedings to be televised, but unlike today when the play is beamed live straight into your living room, back then the film, 30-minute reels of footage at a time, had to be unloaded from the camera, placed in a light-proof container, and flown by helicopter to the TV station to be put to air.

When we played the Wembley tournament in 1967, one very interested spectator was Herman David, chairman of the All England Tennis Club. Afterwards he told us he had been hugely impressed by the high quality of all our matches and by the 10,000-strong crowd's enjoyment of it. He said to me, 'This is crazy. Why do I have to come to Wembley Empire Pool to watch you guys play?' Yet, knowing how opposed to our existence the tennis establishment was, it was still a surprise when the All England Club invited the eight leading professionals to play a tournament on Wimbledon's hallowed centre court on 25–28 August, just two weeks after the Wimbledon championships. It was a breaching of the establishment's most formidable bastion.

We didn't know it then, but Herman David and certain others in the amateur game had long been keen to end the professional–amateur division, because they realised that the existence of tennis depended on the best players from each group facing off, not being quarantined from each other. There was also a growing realisation that players were simply no longer prepared to be paid peanuts and treated like monkeys. Glory did not pay the bills, and this was evidenced by the burgeoning number of amateurs who were turning in their club ties and defecting to the pro ranks. Our Wimbledon matches would be broadcast on national television in colour and the prize money would be a record $35,000. The professionals selected to play were Ken Rosewall, Andres

Gimeno, Butch Buchholz, Dennis Ralston, Fred Stolle, Pancho Gonzales, myself . . . and Lew Hoad, who came out of retirement in Spain to play again on the court where he had enjoyed, and provided, so many glorious moments.

We played the first round matches to half-empty stands. Obviously there was still a stigma attached to professionalism in England. For many Brits, it wasn't the done thing to support the mercenaries. I know for a fact that there were many in the establishment who fervently hoped our tournament would be a fizzer. Gimeno beat Ralston, Rosewall downed Buchholz, and I beat Stolle to make it through to the semi finals. In the remaining first round match, the old lions Gonzales and Hoad went at it. Both were rusty, not having played for some months, but were soon taking it to each other as if they had never been away. Pancho won the first set 6–3. In the second set Lew mustered one great effort and hit Pancho with everything but the kitchen sink. He had Pancho huffing and blowing as he ran him all over the court. Lew took the set 11–9. In the decider, Lew recovered from 0–40 down, breaking Pancho's serve twice, and, predictably, Pancho got up to his old tricks. You'd have thought he'd played Lew Hoad too often not to know that the Australian had nerves of steel and chewed up tantrum-chuckers for breakfast. At match point, Lew caught Pancho totally out of position. He won the set 8–6 to vanquish his fiercest rival. Pancho lost his temper and hit the ball so far out that I reckon it landed in the grounds of Buckingham Palace. Not finished yet, he hurled his racquet at the ground. Looking up, he saw Lew at the net, grinning and offering his hand. Pancho melted and congratulated Lew on a grand performance.

After that epic match was reported in the newspapers, the grandstands were packed for the semis. Londoners saw that what we were serving up was the best tennis in the world and responded by beating a path to Wimbledon. Bone-tired, Lew was fittingly put to the sword 6–2, 6–2 by his great mate and 1956 Grand Slam nemesis Ken Rosewall. After I beat Andres 6–4, 6–4, I booked my place to play Ken in the final, and we were watched by a standing-room-only throng. Muscles and I had played each other so often in recent years that neither of us felt that old Wimbledon final tension, just a determination to win. That said, the centre court at this magnificent ground was just as daunting as I remembered it. This day we brought out the best in each other, and the crowd appreciated our efforts. My returns, backhands and serves were all going like clockwork, and I won the first two sets 6–2, 6–2. Ken rallied in the third set and he kept passing me. In a flash, he was leading 5–2 and serving for the set. Somehow I hung on and broke him, surviving three set points, and came out a 12–10 winner, which gave me the match in straight sets. It was an honour to win the first pro tournament ever to be held at Wimbledon. I hoped it would not be five years before I played here again. I followed up my Wimbledon win to snatch the London Professional Indoor Tournament at Wembley for the fourth year in a row, again beating Ken. This was one of the richer tournaments and I pocketed $2500.

We played pretty much nonstop for what remained of 1967 and into 1968. It was a constant round of boarding and disembarking planes and trains, rattling down the highway in our second-hand station wagons or beat-up Thunderbirds, and checking in and out of hotels the quality of which varied from flea-pit to ordinary. There was rain, ice and snow. There were heatwaves. In '67, I won 19 professional titles, including the four most important: the US, the Wembley Pro, the Wimbledon Pro and the French Pro championships. A good year.

Chapter 12

The open tennis revolution

IT'S ONE OF SPORT'S GREAT IRONIES THAT THE MAN WHO brokered the reconciliation of warring tennis factions knew practically nothing about the sport. Dave Dixon was the catalyst for open tennis (all tennis players, whether they were designated amateur or professional, playing against each other in the great tournaments) which became a reality at the British Hard Court Championships at West Hants Club in Bournemouth, England, on 22 April 1968.

Early in 1967, Dixon, who had been a professional golfer, was the chairman of a proposed new Superdome in New Orleans and he was on the hunt for sports that could be played in his pride and joy. There'd be football and baseball on weekends, they were naturals, but he needed to stage events during the week to make his arena viable and turn a profit. Someone suggested tennis tournaments to him, which made Dixon wonder if there was still such a thing as a pro tennis circuit. Racking his brain, he seemed to recall reading occasional small items in the sports pages about blokes named Gonzales, Rosewall and Laver who played tennis against each other in the United States and around the world. He assigned his secretary to do some sleuthing. Even in those pre-Google days it didn't take her long to track down our ragtag, and frankly floundering, organisation, the IPTPA, and discover that we were playing a series of matches at the Racquet and Riding Club in Binghampton, New York, that very week. Dixon booked his flight.

From the first game of the first match of pro tennis he ever saw, Dixon was hooked. He reported back to his colleagues, 'Where have those guys been? They're fantastic athletes, and nobody knows about them. I got to Binghampton and hardly anybody in the city could tell me where the tournament was. No publicity, no posters. Finally I found them hidden out at a private club, and I sat on uncomfortable wooden bleachers to watch.' He figured that with a little streamlining of our fly-by-the-seat-of-our-pants set-up and some effective marketing of players and the brand of tennis we could turn on, we could draw crowds to his stadium. Then he went one better. He would not only stage our matches, he would run our circuit. So he contacted his old friend, the sports-loving Texan oil tycoon Lamar Hunt, and convinced him that in the right hands – theirs – tennis could be as lucrative as football, basketball, baseball and hockey. With Hunt as his partner, Dixon flew to London where we were playing a tournament and offered us contracts to join his fledgling

World Championship Tennis (WCT) organisation. Basically, we would receive guarantees against prize money to play in WCT-promoted tournaments.

Great minds, it's often said, think alike. And just as Dave Dixon was tabling his offer to us, another American, George MacCall, who had been the United States Davis Cup captain from 1965 to '67, established his own pro tennis outfit, the National Tennis League (NTL), and knocked on our door with an offer similar to Dixon and Hunt's. Because it didn't take old hardheads like us two minutes to realise that Dixon, though he was pleasant and intelligent, would not have known a backhand from a backside, Ken Rosewall, Pancho Gonzales, Fred Stolle, Andres Gimeno and I aligned ourselves with MacCall. I received a guarantee of $10,000 per month for nine months of the year plus travel expenses, and we were soon joined by Roy Emerson, who had finally departed the amateur game. MacCall also signed a women's troupe comprising Billie Jean King, Ann Jones, Francoise Durr and Rosie Casals. The IPTPA was wound up, and it was a relief to be able to concentrate on tennis instead of managing and promoting our tours. To make the most of our newfound wealth, Muscles and I invested in an office building in Elizabeth Street, Brisbane.

The MacCall and Podesta NTL crew played their first tournament in Sao Paulo in March 1967 and were due to play in Los Angeles on 7 April, but when Martin Luther King Jr was assassinated on 4 April and the United States was plunged into profound shock and mourning, the matches were postponed. We returned to LA in June, and then played to fair-sized crowds in Buenos Aires, Bogota and Florida. Roy Emerson took to professional tennis quickly, proving himself the exception to the rule that an amateur took some months, maybe years, to match it with the professionals. Unlike myself, and Pancho, Lew and Ken before me, Roy won his share of matches from the start. He and his wife Joy made their home not far from Mary and me in Newport Beach.

Our fellow pros Butch Buchholz, Dennis Ralston and the Frenchman Pierre Barthes found more to like in Dixon and Hunt's bid than Rosewall, Gonzales, Segura and myself and said goodbye to us to align with World Championship Tennis. Part of the reason some of our team moved to WCT was that they were upset that at NTL the top-ranked players took a bigger cut of earnings than the lower rated players, the so-called donkeys. Not surprisingly, Pancho Gonzales, Ken Rosewall, Fred Stolle, Andres Gimeno, Pancho Segura and I figured we'd earned the right to be paid more and so had opposed the evening out of the payment structure.

To bolster its roster the WCT plundered the best amateur players by offering record guarantees. When I turned pro in 1963, I made a leap into the unknown; there were high hopes and good intentions but no financial guarantees. The pay of the new generation of professionals was backed by Hunt's millions. Hunt's WCT troupe – John Newcombe, Tony Roche, Cliff Drysdale, Roger Taylor and Niki Pilic, along with Buchholz, Ralston and Barthes – became better known as the Handsome Eight, because of the matinee idol appearance of its players. (Rochey confessed amazement at being called 'handsome'. Resembling a boxer or rugby player more than a movie star, he had strong and rugged good looks and would never have been mistaken for a romantic lead. When he was asked where he was ranked in beauty in the Handsome Eight, he replied, 'Fourteenth.')

In WCT, Butch Buchholz took the role of an elder statesman who helped the new boys deal with the rigours of professionalism. He summed it up for all veterans of the pro circuit when he said, 'As long as the building doesn't blow up, nothing can shake me. I'm a veteran of the Texas death march. My first year as a pro, 1961, somebody – and it must have been a fugitive from the Texas Rangers – scheduled us throughout the state on a tour that meant about 500 miles a day driving. We were in towns that no one has heard of yet, playing the worst buildings and courts, for short money. Every night I wanted to quit and go home, try to get reinstated as an amateur. I was only 20. But I was a pro and I stuck it out. These kids now don't know what a tough tour is like.'

After the defection of these elite players (Newcombe, Taylor and Pilic were in the final four at Wimbledon in '67, and Newk won the championship) the amateur ranks were threadbare and suddenly amateurism's showpiece events – Wimbledon, the Australian, French, and US titles, and the Davis Cup – were doomed to be lacklustre tournaments contested by unknowns.

Open tennis took the professionals by surprise. I never thought I would see it in my playing career. I was resigned to exclusion from the grand slam tournaments and the Davis

Cup. Our professional game was stumbling and bumbling along, the money wasn't too bad, and although the players spoke of open tennis, we thought of it as a pipe dream that might be realised in the distant future. I admit that when Lew Hoad and I returned to Wimbledon in 1965 as the guest of our promoter Pat Hughes while we were in London playing a tournament, I was thrilled to be back in those hallowed surroundings. It struck me that I missed the old joint and wanted to play there again. There was no point in grumbling. We'd made our bed and would lie in it. We'd all enjoyed the prestige of playing in the grand slam events earlier in our career, now we were making a living playing the game we loved. There are worse fates.

Despite mutterings of 'sacrilege' from some die-hard traditionalists, the British Lawn Tennis Association, some of whose most influential members, including Herman David, had been keen to allow pros to participate at Wimbledon since our grand showing there in September the year before, voted that in 1968 the British Hard Court Championships at Bournemouth in April and Wimbledon would be open events, including the best eight pros. Fortress Establishment had been breached, and soon the organisers of the Australian, French and United States as well as those of some lesser tournaments caved in. Most Australian officials, such as Davis Cup captain and still-influential coach Harry Hopman and Big Bill Edwards, the staunchly traditional president of the Lawn Tennis Association of Australia, two men who had loomed large in my formative years, remained bitterly opposed to change. Hop, I believe, never got over his sense of betrayal when, after developing generations of great Australian players, they abandoned the amateur system of which he was a pillar to turn pro. I could understand that. But change was upon us, and trying to resist it was as futile as trying to stop the waves from breaking on Bondi Beach. In due course, even Bill Edwards realised that further opposition to a new open era was pointless once the British welcomed the professionals, and he softened towards the concept and then gave it the green light. Explaining his change of attitude, he shrugged. 'Australia wants open tennis. It was going to come anyway, and now we have to do what we can to help it. The next Australian championships, to be held at Milton, Brisbane, are certain to be open.'

There were inevitable teething problems that took time to iron out, such as when the ILTF decreed that professionals could only compete against amateurs in 12 designated tournaments, including the French titles and Wimbledon. Now this was unfair because the ILTF decision allowed amateur players to make money from *all* tournaments by designating them as 'registered players', which discriminated against us, who were still banned from many events. All this was soon resolved. By and large, tennis was united, the time of segregation was over. From now on, all tennis players could compete in privately promoted tournaments as well as the grand slam events, although not the Davis Cup. After five years as an outlaw, I was back in the fold.

My old mate in Australia, the wise and influential Adrian Quist, gave open tennis a big tick in his newspaper column when he mused that while Britain did not have the world's leading players, it was in the vanguard when it came to tennis common sense. This was because the decision-makers at the British Lawn Tennis Association had voted for an open Wimbledon, which meant that Ken Rosewall, Fred Stolle, myself and our pro colleagues would be allowed to step onto Wimbledon's hallowed courts in 1968. Adrian called the breakthrough the greatest step forward since tennis shorts superseded long trousers. He couldn't understand why the British decision was being resented in some quarters. Possibly referring to Australia, he insisted that it was immaterial if some countries resented the move because Wimbledon was the most important championship and any player wanting to make it on the world stage had to play there. Nations holding fast to amateurism were doomed to be second-raters. Making the amateur defenders' stance more ludicrous was the open knowledge that they had engaged in under the table payments to their players for years. 'It's like a breath of fresh air to know there is one country which has become sick and tired of all the hypocrisy. Finally, it had the courage to throw open the doors to open tennis.'

Dave Dixon didn't hang around our game long. Due in no small part to his dearth of tennis knowledge, WCT lost nearly $100,000 in its first three months, and Hunt bought him out and benched him. Before long Dixon began new ventures in different sports. Under Hunt's sole stewardship, WCT thrived and prospered. Yet Dixon's boldness played its part in ushering in open tennis, and despite some missteps, such as playing his matches in four 10-minute quarters and sounding a hooter, football style, to signify the end of a session, some of his innovations, such as coloured clothing and more professional sponsorship and marketing, propelled tennis into a new, modern age. Pro tennis, *all* tennis, owes a debt to Dave Dixon. Thanks largely to him, interest in tennis boomed all around the world, as did the money coming into the game, and the broadcasting of it reached unheard-of heights of sophistication. In the not too distant future, the leading money winners on the tennis circuit were earning as much as, or more than, the champions of golf and football and basketball.

The British Hard Court Championships at Bournemouth was a landmark tournament. The program's lead article began, 'Yes, open tennis has come at last and Bournemouth has been entrusted with the task of a world-shaking launching!' The pros were there in force, but unfortunately only British amateurs took part, after the organisers were tardy in issuing invitations to amateurs in other countries. Of the eight top seeds, seven were professionals, with amateur Bobby Wilson grabbing the eighth spot. I was seeded No.1 and Rosewall No.2.

Open tennis officially began in the first match when British amateur John Clifton served to Australian professional Owen Davidson. Despite the program's purple prose, only 100 people and a dog were on hand to be shaken. Those tennis traditionalists who rugged up to take themselves along that wet, chilly day cheered when Clifton took the first point with a resounding smash . . . then the pros had the last laugh when Davo won the match 6–2, 6–3, 4–6, 8–6.

The pressure on the professional players was enormous, and some of that pressure was self-inflicted. Unfortunately, a couple of pros had been crowing that we would destroy the poor amateurs and suddenly the onus was on all of us to prove that we were as good as we said we were and not hot-air merchants. Also, we were not used to playing five-set matches, and our lack of familiarity with playing on grass and in the open air with its sunlight and shade, wind, heat and cold after years of matches indoors on synthetic courts under lights and in controlled mild temperatures put us behind the eight ball when compared to the amateurs. The establishment rubbed its hands in gleeful anticipation of our inability to hold our own against their boys.

When he took to the court on the first day, an out-of-sorts and nervous-looking Fred Stolle only narrowly defeated the young and little-known Englishman Peter Curtis, and the next day Fred was again taken to the wire by another British no-name, Keith Wooldridge. Fred's frustrations bubbled over when he faced the media. 'We're the ones with the reputations to lose. The amateurs can be loose. They're playing for expenses and they're sure of those. If they lose it means nothing. If I lose, it disgraces my profession.'

Another to hold the amateur flag high at Bournemouth was a 24-year-old British left-hander with a cherubic face and masses of blond curls named Mark Cox. No one envied him when he was drawn to play the mighty Gonzales in the second round, and when Pancho won the first set 6–0, Cox looked a shot bird. But he was not fazed and battled on. He began to move the ball – and his opponent – around the court, and Pancho, nearly 40 years old now and not having played a five-set match in years, began to wilt. So of course he blew up to unsettle the Englishman, but Cox was mentally tough and wouldn't be put off his game. He won 0–6, 6–2, 4–6, 6–3, 6–3. To Cox went the honour of being the first amateur to beat a professional – indeed, the most illustrious professional – and his triumph was on the front page of every newspaper the next day. Tickets to the championships were suddenly impossible to obtain and we played in front of full stands. Gonzales took his beating well, and I can report that the lockers in the dressing room remained un-punched. In fact, he was philosophical about his defeat: 'Somebody had to be the first to lose, so it might as well be me. This open tennis is a whole new world.'

And so it was . . . We pros were all fine players and match-hardened, but we had become used to playing against each other in our insular little travelling troupe and while we knew each other's game backwards, we had little knowledge of the style of the amateurs. And our matches were the best of three sets, not the infinitely more gruelling five. Importantly, too, the amateurs prized our scalps highly. When he beat Pancho, Mark Cox became an establishment hero. Next day he dealt Roy Emerson a terrible beating, 6–0, 6–1, 7–5. This after Emmo had easily downed Cox when both were amateurs just a few months earlier. I think that result at Bournemouth showed the pressure the pros were under.

To the disappointment of many, the gutsy giant killer Cox's good fortune ran out when I downed him in three sets in the semi, which qualified me to play Ken Rosewall in the final. Phew, I thought, enough of the craziness, at last things are back to normal. I played well, hitting finely into the corners, but Ken played better. He was made for those slow clay courts, and he was always in exactly the right place to return smack on the lines. He won 3–6, 6–2, 6–0, 6–3, and squirrelled away $2142 prize money.

We were all looking forward to the greater stage of Wimbledon. Even the hard-to-impress Gonzales could not conceal his excitement at the prospect of playing there, and he made it clear he was one pro who was not daunted by having to play under unfamiliar conditions. 'It will be good to be back at the home of tennis . . . and good to play on grass in daylight. I was getting sick of all those indoor matches on makeshift courts under lights and wreathed in smoke.'

But first, before Wimbledon, there was the inaugural French Open. In late May, the MacCall group, some free-lance pros (not including the Handsome Eight, who were struggling to survive in the US at that stage) and a number of amateurs converged on the red clay of Paris' Roland Garros Stadium. It was an unforgettable experience, and not just because of the tennis. Paris was paralysed by anti-de Gaulle Government riots by students and supporters of the far left, and a general strike involving 11 million workers. Instead of delicious cooking smells, the evocative strains of accordions and the pungent but not unpleasant aroma of Gauloise and Gitane cigarettes, there was the stink of tear gas in the air and sirens shrieked day and night. The hospitals were hard-pressed to treat the many injured. We players and our partners were warned to refrain from sightseeing to avoid getting caught up in any of the violent clashes between the police and the demonstrators and strikers that had trans-formed the beautiful and romantic Latin Quarter of the city into a battleground. We stayed in a little hotel just off the Champs-Élysées that was popular with tennis players. Once or twice we'd venture out to a restaurant for dinner and suddenly there'd be a mob of people charging down the street, and there'd be cops and a pitched brawl and we'd take refuge in a shop or anywhere handy. It was scary.

From a tennis point of view, there was one positive result. With nobody at work, there were excellent attendances at Roland Garros. Because there was no petrol to be had for love or money, and so no cars or buses, people walked from their homes all over Paris to see us play. The matches must have been a welcome distraction from the civil strife. Pancho Gonzales stormed into the quarter finals, where he met Roy Emerson. Although the crowd had cheered on local boy Pierre Darmon when Pancho thrashed him in the fourth round, they were well and truly in Pancho's corner when he played Roy. They gave him a standing ovation fit for a conquering monarch when he came onto the court, and Pancho thrived on the applause and channelled it to beat Roy in five sets. Some in the crowd wept for joy. I played amateur Ion Tiriac and he was so keen to beat me that he literally threw himself around the court and badly skinned his knees in the process. His adrenalin, and a strong clay court game, saw him take the first two sets from me. I steadied the ship and won the next three, including the fifth 6–0, for a hard-fought victory. Ion and I came off the court caked in red dirt.

After Ken Rosewall beat Andres Gimeno and I downed Pancho in our semi finals, once more, for what seemed the millionth time, Muscles and I faced each other in the French final, some 15 years after he had last won it. Of all my rivalries, with Neale Fraser and Emmo, with Pancho, the rivalry that defined my career was with Ken. Over the course of our tennis lives, as professionals and then in the open era, according to what set of figures you believe, I beat him in 80 of 147 matches or 79 out of 150. I can tell you that, no matter what the score, every one of those matches was a battle in which we took each other to the limit of our skills and physical and mental strength. He was incredibly competitive. We both knew each other's game thoroughly and the only way I could ever beat Kenny was to have a very good day. He anticipated my shots so uncannily that my only option was to hit them so bloody well that his uncanny anticipation and tireless road-runner legs were no use to him.

I've long maintained that Ken is the least appreciated player in tennis history. He never received the kudos he deserved because, after he signed with Jack Kramer in 1956 when he was 21 (right after he thwarted Lew Hoad's Grand Slam bid at the United States championships), he spent his best years in the relative anonymity of the pro circuit. Early on, he was regularly beaten by the troupe's kingpin, Pancho Gonzales, until, like me, Ken stuck it out and became a far better player than he had ever been. In time, he overcame Pancho and assumed leadership of the group, but very few people were aware of his progression. The public didn't know because pro match results were rarely reported in the media. Ken, too, for all his talent, was doomed to be in the shadow of, at first, Lew Hoad, and then Pancho. Lew and Pancho were handsome Adonises with gigantic personalities to match their talent. Ken – like me, I suppose – is small and was not blessed with movie star looks. He was, and remains, a quiet, clean-living bloke who probably still has the first pound note he ever earned. But has there ever been a quicker, steadier, more competitive tennis player? I can't think of too many. Certainly, in my day, he was the player that every guy on the circuit had the most trouble with.

Fred Stolle certainly subscribed to that sentiment. He was once quoted as saying, 'No, Laver doesn't worry me. If the Rocket is hitting his shots there's no chance for me, true enough. But there's always the chance that he'll be a bit off and then you're right in the match. Rosewall was *never* off. The pressure was on you every second because you knew when you hit a bad shot, he'd make you pay for it without fail. He's got you crazy serving because his return is so good. You knew if you missed the first serve you might as well forget the point because Muscles would murder the second ball. You were pressing so hard to serve well on the first ball that you would usually miss it, and you were at the mercy of what he would do to the second. I'd rather play Laver any day than Rosewall.'

Just the year before, in the final of a pro tournament in Berkeley, California, in a best of three sets match on clay, I was ahead in the third set 5–4, 40–0: triple match point. I was serving for the match. Ken, as ever, was not rattled. He simply hit three searing backhand returns to claw back to deuce, then he hit two more to win the game, and he won the next two games as well, to take the match. I was shocked. How on earth could that have happened to me? Easy. My opponent was Muscles Rosewall. Sadly, Ken didn't receive his winner's pay for his mighty effort, nor me my runner-up's cheque. The crowd was so small, there simply was no money to pay us. We would just have to settle, the mortified promoter informed us, for applause. That night, after I shouted Ken dinner, the least I could do, I lay in bed and analysed where I had gone wrong. I concluded that my error had been, when I felt safe at triple match point, serving every one of those five balls to the same place, and Ken simply got into a groove and dealt with each ball the same. I should have mixed it up. I just didn't believe that he could keep hitting winner after winner and treating my serves with such disdain. I was a fool. If you give an opponent enough chances at the same kind of ball, he'll eat it up, and if that opponent is Ken Rosewall, he'll have you for dinner – and breakfast.

So my recent record against Ken on clay, at Berkeley and at Bournemouth, was not good. Which gave me something more to prove at the French Open of 1968. Ken's best days were behind him when open tennis began, but even when, at age 35 the following year, 1969, he made uncharacteristic mistakes and had some losing runs, his sublime skills never deserted him and his reflexes remained sharp. He was a formidable opponent for anyone for as long as he played the game. As I learned to my cost in that French Open final.

Ken, relishing the slow pace of the clay court, was placing his shots perfectly. He took the first two sets 6–3, 6–1. I clawed back into the match and won the third set after I was able to run Ken around a little, and he seemed to grow weary. I couldn't go on with it though: he found his second wind, regained his touch, and won the fourth set decisively, 6–2. Ken was the first winner of a grand slam tournament in the open era. While I never enjoyed being beaten, I couldn't think of anyone I'd rather lose to than him.

Just days after the French Open we all reconvened in Boston for the US Professional, and this time, for the first time, the MacCall players and the Handsome Eight went head to head. It was good to spend some time with John Newcombe, Tony Roche and Mal Anderson over a beer or four before things got serious on the court. Tony beat Muscles in their first round match, which had the Handsome Eight believing that maybe they did have a future as a pro troupe. Newcombe beat his great doubles partner Rochey in the semi, which set him up for the final against me. After many rain delays we finally made it onto the court, where I accounted for Newk 6–4, 6–4, 9–7. It was wonderful to once more be playing against men of the calibre of John and Tony.

Newk was young – at 24 he was six years my junior – but he had developed into a formidable player. He had a devastating serve, volley and forehand, and was strong and fit and mentally tough. He had won both Wimbledon and the US championships the year before, in '67, and had been a pillar of the Australian Davis Cup team since 1963. He was handsome and dashing and, like Pancho Gonzales, a poster boy for female fans. We would have many more tense and exciting matches.

Around this time, I was buttonholed by a reporter who asked me the deep and meaningful question: 'Who is Rod Laver?' It didn't take me long to come up with an answer: 'I have no superstitions, I'm not very religious, I love my wife, and I worry about money.'

•

There was palpable excitement in the air at the All England Club, Wimbledon, that year, despite the incessant drizzle and a rail strike that kept many fans away. The more progressive elements in the British tennis establishment had been instrumental in establishing open tennis, and now amateurs and pros were rubbing shoulders on Wimbledon's historic courts. It was an amnesty ceremony as much as a tennis tournament. Before Mary and I set out for the first day's play, I took enormous satisfaction from dragging my old purple and green Wimbledon tie out of my suitcase, the tie that had been unceremoniously yanked from my neck when I turned pro in 1963, and putting it on. I was not the only former Wimbledon champion taking my tie out of mothballs.

That Wimbledon was a splendid reunion for all the ostracised professionals. There was Frank Sedgman, 40 years old now, on a sentimental journey to try to achieve again what he had in 1952 and become Wimbledon champion. Lew Hoad, who was 34 and who'd won Wimbledon in 1956–57, had once more wrenched himself away from his tennis *campo* in Spain to join in the tournament. It would be Lew's swan song in a grand slam event. Remarkably, Donald Budge, the first Grand Slam winner, 52 years young, had come to play in the senior men's doubles. Wimbledon ties sprouted like daffodils in spring, and no matter how much we'd been vilified by the establishment, never let anyone tell you that we did not wear those ties with pride.

Tennis writer Phil Wilkins heralded my Wimbledon return by saying that after six years in the professional wilderness, playing on a variety of eccentric surfaces from music halls to ice rinks, I was back at 'regal' Wimbledon. 'The Rocket is a little fellow – not quite 5ft 10, he claims – but is more explosive in power than [far bigger] men. His left arm is that of a harpoonist of Ben Boyd days, gnarled with sinew and noticeably thicker than his right. He is blue-eyed, remarkably placid and seems to channel his copperhead temperament into the brutality of his game . . . His face is blotched in red and brown sun blisters.' Phil kindly reasoned that I was able to make difficult shots spontaneously and with a minimum of fuss because of my years of dedicated practise and full-on competition. Plus, he claimed, I had a 'natural genius that defies definition'. I don't know about the latter, but experience definitely played a role.

The veteran pros were ranked according to their victories in years gone by and so were seeded far too high, and they fell like nine-pins to younger, fitter amateur players. Pancho, Lew, Niki Pilic, Andres Gimeno, Dennis Ralston and Butch Buchholz all made early exits. Both Dennis and Butch made the quarter finals, which was a good effort because they were seeded nine and 10; I accounted for Dennis and Tony Roche downed Butch. Alex Metreveli of the USSR was a little abashed at vanquishing Pancho. 'I read about him as a child. Gonzales is the one tennis player whose name is known all over my country.' Contributing to Pilic's downfall was that, as a pro, he hadn't played outdoors for years – and his match against American Herbie Fitzgibbon was played in a roaring gale. At one point in the match, Pilic cried out, 'Why we have to play in such weather this tennis . . . *why?*'

In all, 11 professionals were eliminated by an amateur opponent. Harry Hopman turned a blind eye to the fact that the two men's finalists were pros, and one of the women's, and that all of the pros who were beaten were veterans or part-timers except for Andres Gimeno, and gloated over the professionals' disappointing showing: 'The big thing is that this Wimbledon has put an end to all the bull about pro tennis that has been going on for the past 15 years.'

On my way to the final against Tony Roche, I beat the Americans Gene Scott, Stan Smith and Marty Riessen,

Briton Mark Cox – the young bloke who had covered himself in glory at Bournemouth – then two more Americans in Dennis Ralston and the young African American Arthur Ashe, whom I played in the semi final. Arthur was a fine man and a fine player who carried a heavier load than most. As America's No.1 rated amateur player he was the stalwart of the US Davis Cup team and carried the nation's hopes at the grand slam tournaments. And that wasn't his only burden. As a high-achieving black man, he was the champion of African Americans and so was under pressure from black organisations seeking to promote equality to wage a political battle for the cause. Others could concentrate on playing, but with Arthur, who took his responsibilities seriously, it was always about more than the tennis. In 1988, Arthur would contract HIV from a blood transfusion he received during heart bypass surgery. He died of AIDS-related pneumonia in 1993, and in recognition of his tennis career and courageous work in civil rights and promoting awareness of HIV-AIDS, President Bill Clinton posthumously awarded Arthur the Presidential Medal of Freedom.

Rochey was playing to win his first Wimbledon, and me my third, and we were both keen to get our hands on not just the famed trophy but the £2000 winner's prize money. We were neck and neck in the opening games until I broke Tony's serve and went on to win the match 6–3, 6–4, 6–2. As I was handed the silverware after the match, I had a sense of deja vu. Although I'd been in the professional wilderness for five years, in some ways I had never really been away.

I possibly should never have played at Wimbledon in '68.

In one of my US Pro tournament matches in Boston shortly before, I slipped on a rain-affected court and severely sprained my left wrist. I so badly wanted to be there at that historic Wimbledon that I did some rough running repairs. To support my wrist I took the plywood from a box of redhead matches and, after we found a convenient surreptitious location at the courts, often a telephone booth, away from prying eyes, Mary strapped it to my wrist, then used a tight wrist guard to both keep it in place and cover it up. I had to disguise that I had strapping on a bad wrist otherwise my opponents, if they knew, would have lobbed me mercilessly. The matchbox and good old Wimbledon adrenalin did their job and by the time I had come through the first two rounds my wrist was feeling fine.

With the help of a course of cortisone injections administered by renowned Los Angeles orthopaedic surgeon and sports medicine specialist Dr Robert Kerlan, I overcame a bout of tennis elbow in time to compete in the inaugural US National Open tournament – boy, a lot of history was made that year. I was eliminated by South Africa's Cliff Drysdale. He beat me 4–6, 6–4, 3–6, 6–1, 6–1. Arthur Ashe and Dutchman Tom Okker struck a blow for the amateurs when they beat all comers to reach the final, with Arthur winning a marathon five-setter. I was bitterly disappointed after my match: not because I lost it, but because I played badly. The '6–1, 6–1' got my goat, indicating I hadn't toughed it out when, usually, I won my five-set matches. My serve had no rhythm and my timing of the ball was out. I didn't dwell, just vowed never to have as lousy a day again.

A series of tournaments in Los Angeles, Texas and Buenos Aires in Argentina occupied the rest of the year. In the final of the hard court Pacific Southwest in LA at the Los Angeles Sports Arena I struck a purple patch of form. It was one of those matches in which everything goes right, and I beat Muscles Rosewall 4–6, 6–0, 6–0. It may just have been the best I ever played – certainly Charlie Pasarell, who is an excellent judge, said, 'I've never seen perfect tennis before, but I did in that match. No errors. Everything in those last two sets was perfect.' My post-match comment to reporters was, 'This is the kind of match you dream about. The kind you play in your sleep.' It was definitely the best match I ever played with a crook elbow!

My tennis elbow was not all that was causing me pain. I was missing Mary badly. I felt awful that we were seeing so little of each other. She was so stoic. Sometimes she could not contain her frustration at being a tennis wife, yet she encouraged me to keep playing, knowing that my time earning money from playing tennis was finite. Meantime, she was handling my finances brilliantly, and with open tennis now in full swing and my having won Wimbledon again, she made another approach to Mark McCormack of the International Management Group to sign me up as a client to win sponsorship deals. Unlike last time, when I was a pro, now Mark could see the upside of taking me into his stable. He sent his executive Jay Lafave to talk to me and he, Mary and I worked out a deal that would see me signed for a number of lucrative endorsements with prestige products.

Less satisfactory from the professionals' standpoint was that in spite of their encouraging words earlier in the year and their decision to follow the other major tournament organisers in making the 1969 Australian championships an open event, Australian amateur tennis officials refused to admit professionals into the 1968 Davis Cup team, unlike the American establishment, which did let their pros in. This unhappy situation lasted until 1973. When Australia took on the United States in the Challenge Round in Adelaide on 26–28 December, our team comprised Bill Bowrey, Ray Ruffels and John Alexander. The Americans won the Cup four matches to one.

The annual Christmas break from tennis couldn't come fast enough. I wanted to be with Mary and her children, and also give my tennis elbow the dedicated treatment it would need if I was to have a clean bill of health for the Australian Open in January. As we wound up our commitments for 1968, the ILTF published its list of rankings, which for the first time meant something because it included all players, amateur and pro. I was ranked No.1, ahead of Arthur Ashe, Ken Rosewall, Tom Okker, Tony Roche, John Newcombe, Clark Graebner, Dennis Ralston, Cliff Drysdale and, at No.10, Pancho Gonzales, which was an incredible feat for a 40-year-old. As far as prize money went, I again topped the list with $70,359.

Chapter 13

Grand Slam II

I COULD HARDLY HAVE PICKED A MORE MOMENTOUS YEAR to try to make sporting history. Neil Armstrong and his Apollo 11 crew landed on the moon, the Vietnam War raged on, the first Boeing 747 took to the skies, Richard Nixon became the 37th president of the United States and Charles de Gaulle stepped down as president of France, The Beatles made their final public appearance and released *Abbey Road*, James Earl Ray and Sirhan Sirhan were brought to justice for assassinating Martin Luther King Jr and Robert Kennedy . . . Quite understandably, with all that was going on, the game of tennis had to battle for headlines, but along the way we managed to make a few.

When Tony Roche and I played the semi final of the Australian Open on 25 January 1969, the first Australian championships of the open era, at Brisbane's Milton courts, we had a point to prove. In the crowd were many local officials who resented the fact that two professionals were fighting it out for a chance to claim the Australian crown in the final of *their* tournament against another pro, Andres Gimeno. We knew that and so, without ever discussing it, we both went onto the court determined to play our best tennis, not just to add the open silverware to our mantelpiece but to hold the flag high for ourselves and our fellow pros.

The old guard of Australian tennis had been dragged screaming and kicking into the open era, and at the Australian Open tournament, their animosity was obvious. The tournament was among the most dispiriting I've ever played in. It was hardly promoted and this was reflected in poor crowds. The facilities for spectators and players were Dark Ages standard and were even worse than some we'd experienced as pros barnstorming through makeshift tin-pot venues in Third World countries. No real effort had been made to get Milton in shape for this major event. The court surfaces were uneven and patchy, and the dressing rooms were just as decrepit as they had been when I was a kid. We professionals were, at best, ignored and, at worst, treated with disdain by some officials. I had the distinct impression that to them we were a necessary evil.

This was my home court, and some of the things that happened at that Australian Open hurt. Former Queensland Lawn Tennis Association president and now LTAA president Big Bill Edwards, under whose auspices the event was held, and some of his cronies even took a day off from the tournament to go to the races. We knew Bill had no time for us as players, or for the concept of open tennis, but by his slack and incompetent staging of the event he insulted us and the tennis community. The player seedings defied belief, with Emmo, Stolle and myself drawn to play each other in the early rounds. There were not enough officials to go around and Bill Bowrey and Ray Ruffels played their quarter final without linesmen. Unbelievable. In the John Newcombe–Tony Roche match, loud music from an official function blasted across the court and Newk and Rochey demanded that the music be turned down because it was destroying their concentration.

The organisers cut off their noses to spite their faces, because instead of reaping a rich financial harvest from this special tournament they barely broke even. Still, we didn't let them, or Milton, get us down and played some really good matches. There was the classic semi final between Rochey and me, and I also had a ripper of a third round match against Roy Emerson. Because of lousy scheduling it was 9pm when Emmo and I went onto the court and after midnight when we finished. I took the first two sets and then, as he always did, Emmo got stuck in and claimed the third. He was serving at 7–6 in the fourth set and seemed likely to win it and take the match to a fifth set that would finish sometime around 2am. That prospect didn't appeal to me, so I dug in too and, to put Roy away, began hitting my returns harder, making them buzz with top spin. Emmo missed some volleys. I broke back and then won three straight games and the match,

6–2, 6–3, 3–6, 9–7. I didn't hang around the court for my customary beer with Roy, because I was scheduled to play Fred Stolle just 10 hours later.

The organisation of the quarter final was, to put it kindly, a fiasco. It was 38 degrees Celsius when Fred and I went onto the court, yet when we checked the drinks that had been supplied for us they were hot because they'd been left out in the sun, and there was no ice available to cool them. Fred and I angrily threatened to walk off the court unless we had cold drinks. I won in three sets after Fred pushed me hard, and the second set stretched to 18–16. That got me a date with Tarcutta boy Tony Roche in the semi final. It says a lot about Australian tennis in that era that the top two players in the world came from tiny bush towns.

Tony was my major rival in 1969 and the man most likely to take my world No.1 ranking. He would beat me in five of the nine matches we played, but unfortunately for him, never in the matches that really mattered. Like me, he was a left-hander and proficient at putting spin on the ball. In that regard he gave me a dose of my own medicine. Tony also had a good swinging serve and a big forehand and while he certainly made mistakes with it, when it was on and carried a lot of top spin he could pull it across in front of you. Tony believed firmly that my time as No.1 was over and that his had arrived. Another reason he always gave me a hard match was that I was unused to facing left-handed spin. On my pro circuit everyone except me, by and large, was right-handed. Facing a left-hander was a novelty for me, whereas Tony, in his amateur years and as a member of the Handsome Eight with left-handers Taylor and Pilic, had faced many.

I don't usually bother reading the newspapers before big matches, and when I learned how *The New York Times* described me in their preview of the final, I knew why. '[Laver is] a mild little man with the look of a drowsy cockatoo off the court, but is a terror on it.' Drowsy cockatoo!

Shortly before we went out onto the court, my brother Trevor called from Gladstone and told me he was just leaving work and was about to drive to Brisbane, and he jokingly asked me to keep the match going till he arrived in a couple of hours' time. Turned out that Trev saw plenty of that semi final.

When we got underway at midday, it was again 38 degrees Celsius with 95 percent humidity. I don't know what temperature it was in the shade, because there *was* no shade. I was glad I'd brought three sun hats. We had towels in an ice box courtside and draped them over our heads every time we changed ends. We took glucose tablets and, before the match, a couple of salt pills to keep dehydration at bay throughout the marathon match, but that relentless blazing sun was always going to take its toll.

Not at all deterred by the small crowd of just 2000 spectators, Rochey and I turned on an intense and at times feisty semi final that many said was worthy of a Wimbledon final, a four and a half hour, 90-game epic that began at high noon and ended as evening shadows fell. We were at each other's throats from the opening serve. In the first set I broke Tony's serve three times, and he decided I wasn't going to get away with that because three times he broke me right back. In the end I took it 7–5. The second set lasted an incredible two hours and five minutes. Again, I had Tony at my mercy, and served for the set at 8–7 and (remember there were no tie breaks then) 19–18 and both times I couldn't go on with the job, dropping my serve and letting him back into the set. I squeaked home 22–20. In the third, he took advantage of some sub-standard serving by me and won 11–9. In our 10-minute break we were mercifully allowed a shower, and as Tony and I stood there in the grubby stall with the tepid water trickling upon our overheated bodies, we both thought how nice it would be if we could just stand there forever. No such luck. All too soon we had to return to the oven. The break favoured Tony more than me. My head was obviously still back under the shower. Before I knew what was happening, he was blitzing me with heavy serves and stiff volleys and he won five games straight and cleaned me up 6–1. When I saw that Tony had the upper hand in that fourth set, I tried to conserve my energy and go for broke in the deciding fifth.

At two sets all, the match was in the balance. My serving was still not what it should have been and Tony, returning beautifully, was breaking me. He was on a roll, yet I was fighting hard. I was doing my best to get my first serves in and race up to the net to put myself in a good position to volley, because Tony was punishing my second serves. I reckoned that because of the intensity of our battle and our physical condition, one break of serve could be decisive and win the match. Tony was seven years younger, and stronger and fitter – at that early stage of the year – than me, but he had never been in a five-set match with me and I couldn't remember, and neither could he, me losing too many of those. (As far as I can recall, I lost only five five-set matches in my career.) And because he was serving second, the pressure was on Rochey. Every time I held serve, the thumbscrews tightened. Suddenly he was no longer blasting me off the court with his serves and his volleys were not quite as hard to handle. His confidence seemed to ebb a little as mine grew. When I served to 4–3, we changed ends and, after a drink, some glucose tablets and a cold towel-down, we returned to the fray.

Tony served, and my attitude was that I would hack and grub my way to return everything he threw at me. As I had learned to do as a pro, I would give away nothing and battle for every single point as if my life depended on it. Forget flamboyant and graceful shots, I was going to get my racquet to the ball no matter what, and scratch and dig and bloop it back over the net at Tony any which way I could. If you can put yourself into that do-or-die zone, it's remarkable how sometimes you can produce a special effort. I was chipping my returns now, squibbing them onto his feet, and they were whizzing all over that sub-standard surface. With me serving at 15–30, I volleyed and he hit a return down my forehand side, and the umpire called it out. I didn't see where the ball had landed, but was happy to take the umpire's word. It was 30-all. Tony, and a number of people in the crowd, were sure the ball was in.

Then Tony was serving at 3–4. If I broke him, I'd be serving for the match at 5–3. It was game on, well and truly. I knew it, he knew it, and everyone who hadn't expired from the heat in the grandstands knew it. Maybe, if he'd been at the match and not at the races, even Big Bill Edwards would have known it. Rochey won the first point, and I won the second, for 15–all. When he missed a volley he was down 15–30. The next point would be crucial. He served beautifully and the ball came down the middle of the court, spinning into my body. I met it with a backhand slice with under spin, and chipped it across the court. Tony chased hard, but relaxed when he was convinced it had gone out. He, and a number of fans with a good view, swore my ball was out by a good 10 centimetres. But there was no call from the linesman. Tony was incredulous. He spun around and glared at the official. The linesman responded by holding his hands parallel to the ground, signifying that my shot was good. The umpire backed up the linesman by announcing, '15–40!' Tony's expression was thunderous. He was very angry, convinced he'd been given a terrible call. I didn't see where the ball landed because of the position I was in when I hit it, but I did have the feeling that I might have put too much on it and it could have gone out. Today, linesmen and umpires have Hawkeye to help them make the close calls; back then such technology did not exist. If the linesman did err, I can feel sorry for Tony, yet that poor linesman had been baking in the sun for more than four hours, doing his best to stay alert, and if he screwed up, I think he could be excused. Certainly in every match, each player gets a share of good and bad calls and usually they even out.

At this point, however, my opponent was in no mood for forgiveness. There was too much at stake. He served hard at me, I returned it, he ran to the net to backhand volley the ball crosscourt to my backhand. Tony, knowing I handled such shots well, moved fast to the left to counter my return. But at this point of the match, with two points to break, I snapped my wrist to load my return with top spin. The ball sang. Even though Rochey had anticipated what I was going to do, there was too much on the ball for his volley, his racquet finding the ball but not controlling it. It clunked into the net. Tony was shattered, by the call that went against him and his inability to return that shot. His game fell apart. I held my serve to win the set, and the match, 7–5, 22–20, 9–11, 1–6, 6–3. When we shook hands at the net, we were each on the point of collapse. We had played 90 games at the highest level. Ours was the eighth longest singles match ever played. At the end we were reeling like drunks from exhaustion and the effects of the intense heat, and when we embraced at the end of the fifth set, I think we were holding each other up as much as offering congratulations. Afterwards, I'm sure, Tony, whose temperament was so good, would have beaten himself up about letting adversity get the better of him. He, as much as any of us, knew that if things don't go your way, that's when you have to knuckle down and play all the harder.

The contentious call was definitely the turning point. Before it was made in my favour the match was in the balance. Afterwards, Tony was still angry at the way he'd lost. It's possible the ball was out, and it's possible it was in. I was in no position to see. If that line call had gone Tony's way, as it so easily could have, 1969 could have panned out rather differently for me than in fact the way it did. My bid to win the four grand slam tournaments could have been derailed right then and there.

In the end, Adrian Quist, along with the crowd, rose above the controversy and was spellbound by the match, writing in his newspaper column that 'there have been many great matches during the last decade but none have surpassed' our semi at that Australian Open. 'It was an epic of courage and physical endurance which see-sawed back and forth until Laver finally scrambled home 6–3 in the fifth set.' Quist wrote of our 'deadly determination' to win; he went on to describe how the marathon second set 'developed into one of the greatest sets played in modern tennis . . . The heat and the slow court took a savage toll of the players' strength, but both Laver and Roche kept attacking on every shot and they were so even that either could have won the set.' Quist expressed his 'great admiration for the courage of Roche. Faced with a deficit of two sets, he never gave up. In fact he lifted his game, serving with even greater speed and hitting passing shots that left Laver standing . . . Laver appeared exhausted but somehow that spirit and courage which comes to every player who has enjoyed success for many years never left him.'

Compared to my semi final against Tony, the final, in which I beat a jaded Andres Gimeno in straight sets – one reporter observed that I played as if I didn't think I could lose while Andres played as if he didn't think he could win – was a disappointing anticlimax. As with other matches in this Australian Open tournament, the crowd for the final was small. A high percentage of those who were in the crowd on final day were members of the Laver clan. As journalist Rod Humphries amusingly observed, 'Almost everywhere you turned at Milton there was the unmistakable freckled face and red hair of a Laver.' As a bonus, Roy Emerson and I downed Rosewall and Stolle to win the doubles final.

One of the best things about playing the Australian Open in Brisbane was that it gave me a chance to spend time with Mum and Dad – not just the usual day or so as we blew in and out of Gladstone and Rockhampton on the pro circuit, but some relaxed quality time at home. As we chatted and recalled old times and all the wonderful things that my ability with a tennis racquet had blessed me with, I realised that my parents were getting on in years. Dad was 70 and in poor health and Mum was only a little younger. While reliving the past was good to do, it occurred to me that our lives were quite separate now – my home was with Mary in America and on the road playing tennis – and planning for the future with my parents no longer had any place in our relationship, and this saddened me. There had been so many lost years. While a number of good young Australian players had succumbed to homesickness and forsook a life on the road for family and career back home, I had chosen to be a tennis gypsy for nearly half my life – travelling the world, making friends, making money – but there was a price to pay. Still, I promised myself that I would try to see more of Mum and Dad in future. That sojourn back in the bosom of my family was a precious time and a good break from the madness and voracious demands of tennis.

And something else hit me like a sledgehammer while I was back home, and the timing of the bombshell was perfect as I immersed myself in my family: Mary called me from California to tell me the wonderful news that she was pregnant. I was going to be a father.

Each year, the winner of the Australian Open singles title wonders if he, or she, can march on to win the French, Wimbledon and United States championships and claim a Grand Slam. In 1969, I certainly did. And if I was able to achieve a second Grand Slam, I would be the only player in history to do so – and even sweeter, for me, was that it would take place in my first full year back after six years in the professional wilderness. I didn't set out on a crusade to achieve Grand Slam No.2, just decided to take each tournament one at a time and see what happened.

Life can be a curate's egg. Good and bad in parts. And one day early in 1969, I experienced both. After a sumptuous roast beef lunch when I was presented with a sparkling trophy for being the American sports writers' selection as the best tennis player of 1968, I faced up to a young Texan named Cliff Richey in the first round of a tournament in New York and came crashing to earth. I had eaten well at lunch, but that had no bearing on the beating Cliff gave me. I won the first set . . . then my game deserted me. I double faulted continually. I wasn't throwing the ball high enough, was rushing my serve. When I did get the ball in, Cliff passed me. He beat me in four sets. This was a reality check for me. I have always believed that hubris comes before a fall and so, yet again, it proved. Rooster one day, feather duster the next. So true.

From time to time my tennis elbow flared, and I resorted to a hydroculator, a canvas elbow pad that retains steam heat after being boiled in a pot of water. I had to wrap my elbow in the scalding contraption for 20 minutes before I played, and then encase my elbow in ice after a match. Because pots were too unwieldy to pack in my suitcase, I bought a new one in every city I played. I became known as the pots and pans man of the tennis circuit.

•

Rex Bellamy, esteemed tennis writer of *The Times* of London, said it eloquently for all of us when he called the French championships the game's finest advertisement. The surface, clay, was gruelling to play on, yet provided the most exacting test of ability and the most satisfying spectacle. He lauded the entry way at Roland Garros as second only to Wimbledon: 'All is grandeur and pathos. The grandeur is public – the protracted, absorbing exercises in tactics, technique and physical and mental stamina. The pathos is private – the drained, exhausted bodies crumpled on the masseur's table or the dressing room benches.' To the eloquent Bellamy the French championships were both great and cruel, the aesthetic potential of tennis being fully explored while the physical cost exacted on the competitors was 'sadly apparent'.

June is French Open month and, in 1969, the first full year of open tennis, Paris was the place to be. Not that anyone needs an excuse to visit that magnificent city. The year before, the inaugural French Open went ahead without many of the top amateurs who, not inclined to go head to head with the despised professionals, opted instead to play a tournament in Germany, leaving Roland Garros Stadium largely to us. This year it was different; open tennis was a fact of life and the money was good, so old preconceptions were discarded and every tennis player who was fit and worth his salt was in the City of Light.

Unlike the previous riot-torn year, in 1969 Paris had reclaimed its serenity and timeless beauty. Whatever political issues that caused the unrest had been resolved to the extent that people could once more walk the streets without running the risk of being beaten with billy-clubs or tear gassed. Sadly, winter weather was hanging on into spring, and it was cold and wet. Going into the tournament, my elbow was bearable thanks to my hydroculator, and I felt strong, fit and focused. Two weeks earlier, I'd beaten Emmo in the $15,000 Madison Square Garden US Pro event, so my form was good.

In my first round match I quickly dispatched Koji Watanabe of Japan, then in the second round I came up against sterner stuff in the 193-centimetre shape of 24-year-old Australian Dick Crealy. Dick was not an especially skilful player but, boy, he hit that ball hard. An upset looked a distinct possibility when he had me down two sets to love. One of my problems was that my top spin, usually very effective on clay, which makes the ball bounce all the higher, saw most opponents playing ground strokes at shoulder level, or head-high. Not the towering Dick. He was taking my top-spin shots just above his waist, which is precisely where he liked them, and smashing them back at me. He was making me run all over the court, and because most of the top dressing had been washed away by the rain or blown asunder by the roaring winds, the surface was dusty and slippery as hell, and I was sliding.

Our match had started very late, extending into the night. Then, around 9pm, rain bucketed down and officials called a halt and announced that play would recommence next morning at 10.30. When we left the court I had pulled back a set from Dick, and it was two sets to one in his favour. I went straight to bed and, as I usually did, slept soundly. I woke at 7 and thought I'd get in some solid practice until match time. Emmo joined me at 9 for a hit on a Roland Garros side court. It was typical of Roy to lend me a hand, even though he was still alive in the tournament. I wanted at least a 45-minute workout to warm me up, banish the cobwebs, and have me ready to rip in when the fourth set got underway. I didn't want to start slowly, because if I had my way there would be two sets played, the fourth and the fifth, and I would win them both. Should Dick win the fourth set, I was history.

When we'd called it quits the night before there'd been a healthy crowd, yet it seemed that 10.30am was just too early for your average Parisian to arrive at the tennis, and when Dick and I played, those concrete grandstands were practically empty, creating a surreal, off-putting atmosphere eerily devoid of the colour and noise that typifies Roland Garros. Dick later told me he was unsettled by playing to nobody, by hitting a great shot and being rewarded with silence. As a pro, I was used to empty arenas. Here he was, a novice on the verge of an upset win against the world's No.1 player, and even if he pulled it off no one would see his triumph. I won the fourth set 6–2 to even the match. I was feeling ready for action and I suspect Dick was still trying to get the sleep out of his eyes. I heard that Dick slept in, and went straight from his bed to the stadium, afraid that if he had a pre-match hit out like I did, he'd leave his good form of the night before on the practice court.

In the fifth and deciding set I raced to a 3–1 lead, only to see him rally when spectators began trickling in and cheering for the underdog. At 4–4 it was his serve, and I knew I had to break him, because I didn't want to be serving a match game at 4–5 in the fierce wind that was now swirling all over the court. He got to 40–30, and his serve was a beauty to my forehand that pulled me out of the court and exposed me for his slam return. I somehow managed to shakily get the ball back to him but, as I feared, there he was, right at the net with all the time in the world to ram home an unplayable winner to go to 5–4. I watched helplessly as Dick wound up to put me away. But, the old story, nerves or a rush of blood or both got the better of him and he hit that ball crosscourt and out of bounds by two feet (610 centimetres). He tried to belt the ball as far away from me as possible and was wide, and there was just no need for that. He fluffed a sitter. It was Les Flanders versus Ashley Cooper revisited. Seeing Dick's shoulders sag, I went on to hit him with every shot in my armoury: I put spin on and made the ball bounce even to *his* shoulders, I used the wind that was at my back to get up to the net fast, knowing it would slow his returns, and as I had done with the giant Sirola all those years ago, I aimed at the tall man's feet. Game to me 6–4, and the match. I bumped into Dick in Brisbane recently and he came up to me and grinned: 'Rocket, remember when I nearly fixed you at the French in '69?' Dick, you nearly did.

After our match Dick went on to have a good career – he reached the 1970 Australian Open final, losing to Arthur Ashe – and played at the major tournaments until he was well into his 30s, after which he became a stalwart of the veterans' circuit. I don't think tennis was ever a life and death affair for him – he played for the love of the game.

Next day I accounted for the promising American Stan Smith in straight sets. He had ousted Arthur Ashe as America's top player for a while, but at that stage Stan's best days, and they were very good days indeed, were in the future.

There was still great rivalry between the amateurs and pros, and this gave the match between Spain's No.1 and No.2 rated players, my pro colleague Andres Gimeno and the amateur Manuel Santana, extra spice. It was their first clash in the open era, so their first meeting since Andres turned pro in 1960. Heating up their rivalry even more were several factors: each was in no doubt that he was the better player; Andres hailed from Barcelona and Manuel from Madrid, two cities always keen to one-up each other; and the two men – in spite of Gimeno being miffed that he was much less well known in Spain than Santana – were friends and one-time Davis Cup teammates. Santana had a brilliant career, leading Spain to Davis Cup victory over the United States in 1965, winning Wimbledon in '66 and the French titles in 1961 and '64, and being awarded his country's highest civilian honour, the Medal of Isabella, presented to him by Generalissimo Franco himself. Not surprisingly, Manuel's nickname was 'Illustrissimo'. So there was much at stake and the match captured the imagination of the public and the players and, the final aside, this clash was the standout match of that 1969 French Open. No surprise that Andres' fellow pros were his biggest cheer squad that day. The much-anticipated match ended in anticlimax when, after Santana dominated the first two sets and Gimeno the third and fourth, Manuel pulled a groin muscle early in the fifth and was unable to continue.

It fell to me to play Andres in the quarter final – where I beat him in four sets, largely due to my sliced backhand, which he had trouble handling – and then, in the semi, Tom Okker, who was almost a Ken Rosewall clone, short, quick, determined, a master of top spin, his big forehand with lots of spin just one of a number of sharply executed strokes. I downed Tom in four. Both Andres and Tom won the first set in their match against me. I was not that concerned. I was too experienced to panic, and simply figured that

I often started slowly, and a tennis match takes a long time to play.

If Tom Okker was a carbon copy of Ken Rosewall, it was my fate to face off against the real McCoy in the final, in a sequel to our French Open final of the year before. Hopefully I could reverse that result. My form was good, and good form is winning form. In the decisive stanzas of my matches with Andres and Tom I had played as well as I was capable of, and in my 6–0 demolition of the excellent Okker in the second set I did everything right. Going into the final, I was confident . . . well, as confident as anyone could ever be when playing Rosewall.

It never fails to give you a jolt when you enter Stade Roland Garros (which, incidentally, was named after a French World War I hero). You walk down a dark tunnel and then, as you enter the stadium, you are blasted by a kaleidoscope of bright colours and the cheers and whistles of 12,000 excited spectators perched in the concrete stands that surround the red clay court. There were no real pre-match pleasantries between Ken and me – perhaps a handshake and a terse 'Good luck.' We were mates for all time, but, as ever when we were on opposite sides of the net, we were deadly enemies. Happily for me, my good form of recent times continued. I took control of the match early and kept it. I had the ball on a string. I was timing and hitting the ball well, hearing that satisfying sound when you're catching the ball in the middle of the racquet. My ground shots were going deep, exactly where I wanted them to go, and Ken was reduced to scrambling and chasing like a man possessed to try to retrieve them. He was pinned to the baseline from where it's a devil of a job to hit approach shots, and I took up residence at the net, easily anticipating his attempts to pass me, and passing him for winners. Some days, for one reason or another, you're on fire, and for me that day, I was ablaze. I won 6–4, 6–3, 6–4 . . . and $7000.

That French Open final may have been my best performance on clay. I served well, not many aces – I always opted for accuracy over speed and, besides, if you gave Kenny speed he'd hit that ball back right down your neck. Perhaps Ken didn't play his best tennis, perhaps I didn't let him. I sustained my form over the three sets and, with Wimbledon just around the corner, I was pleased with that consistency.

Afterwards in the media box I was surrounded by microphones and flashing cameras. I praised Muscles as my toughest-ever opponent, and said that I was in a position to know because I'd played him more than 200 times over the past seven years. Today was my turn to win. 'From the moment we began, I couldn't miss. Usually I was the one on the string as Kenny played me like a yo-yo. Not this time, I had perfect control, and everything I hit was going so deep that Kenny didn't have much chance to do anything but chase and scramble. I could get up to the net all the time, and I was moving quickly either way to cut off his passing shots. I don't know of any match I have ever enjoyed more . . .' And Ken chipped in, 'I missed some easy shots, and Rocket didn't miss any. That was the difference.'

A recurring question reporters asked was whether I thought I could win the Grand Slam this year. 'A Grand Slam is so far away,' I said, 'and there are so many things that could happen – my opponent could be in better form than me, and being fit physically . . . even a heavy cold could be a difficulty.' If someone worked out a way to sustain good form, he'd make a billion dollars.

Form, I found out yet again, with a little help from John Newcombe and Tony Roche, is fleeting. Roy Emerson and I met Newk and Tony in the French Open doubles final, and the world's reigning doubles team towelled us up. As Newk never tires of reminding me to this day, in the fifth set he and Rochey won 13 straight points against us. We'd been getting the upper hand in the set and then everything fell apart. Nothing like losing 13 points on the trot had ever happened to me before and it never did again. When Emmo and I were being presented with our runners-up trophies, I had another of those 'how in hell did that just happen?' moments. I still wonder today. The best I can come up with is that after the singles final and taking the ascendancy in the fifth set of the doubles match, I got casual. Suddenly in that doubles final none of my first serves were going in, this from the bloke whose mantra was to always make sure my first serve was safe, hit at three quarter pace with loads of spin. In that match I tried to be a big hero and blow Newk and Rochey away with booming serves. I began mis-hitting balls that I would normally handle blindfolded. And as my concentration wandered and faltered, John and Tony sensed my mental disarray and went for the jugular.

This was a perfect match not to dwell on, and I never did. It was an aberration.

Before I saddled up for Wimbledon, it was a tonic to go home to California for a bit and be with Mary, who was now six months pregnant. Impending fatherhood – our child was due to arrive on Sunday 7 September, the scheduled date of the US Open final – put tennis in perspective. Feeling that baby kicking in Mary's belly filled me with awe. The prospect of being a father was exciting and terrifying all at once. Mary, of course, already had three children and knew exactly what she was doing preparing for the happy event. I was a novice. I did my best. Becoming a dad preoccupied me day and night, so apart from thinking from time to time that I was on track to achieve a second Grand Slam and how special it would be to be the first player ever to do so, I truly didn't fixate on Wimbledon and the US Open. I would play my best, hope for some lucky breaks, and the cards would fall where they would.

•

During Wimbledon, Mary, by now seven months pregnant, and I rented an apartment in the Dolphin Square complex by the River Thames in London's Pimlico. The place had history. Over the years such luminaries as Princess Anne, Australian actor Peter Finch, former British prime minister Harold Wilson and current Foreign Minister William Hague, not to forget the notorious call-girl Christine Keeler, had called Dolphin Square home. Our flat had a sitting room with a television, a kitchen, bedroom and bathroom with a big bath in which Mary loved to luxuriate when she was feeling uncomfortable. There was a swimming pool in the complex, and our friend the tennis writer Bud Collins was often splashing around in it. Apart from when Mary left a bag of laundry at a local laundromat and neither of us could find the laundromat or my laundry again, Dolphin Square provided exactly the relaxing sojourn I needed, far from the press, and Mary, in her delicate condition, relished the privacy and peace as well. Occasionally we'd stroll with pals to our favourite London restaurant, an Italian eatery called Ponte Vecchio on the Brompton Road. Mostly we'd eat in, a steak, a beer, a glass of wine, watch TV. If I was in luck, there would be a western to take my mind off the next day's match. I never watched the tennis replays.

Hugh McIlvanney, *The Observer* newspaper's renowned sports writer, came to Dolphin Square to interview me during the tournament and reported to his readers on what life was like *chez* Laver:

When Laver returned to his apartment he was carrying newspapers and a bottle of milk. His American wife Mary . . . watching Graham Stilwell's match with Arthur Ashe on colour television. Laver, wearing slacks and a green short-sleeved sports shirt, sat in an armchair and kicked off his shoes, but he took only a casual interest in the compellingly exciting tennis. If he did turn to watch, he seemed to be looking for things that scarcely concerned us. Instead of gasping along with us at a dramatic stroke or a crucial point, he reacted with a warm little smile. He was slightly more distracted when the cameras switched to the Lord's [cricket] Test. 'I don't get obsessed concentrating on Wimbledon. That's destructive. Players can wear themselves out sitting in the stands down there watching the others. You can see by the books and papers scattered around here that life goes on normally. The place to concentrate is on the court. There the rest of the world doesn't exist. All you live for is to get rid of the other fellow. You show respect for him by getting him off as quickly as possible. I don't even do much in the way of exercises away from the court, maybe just a few press-ups and double knee jumps. Your strength should be built up in your formative years from 13 to 18. Afterwards, playing develops the special strengths you need and certainly the amount I play gives you no chance to get flabby.'

It makes me very sad that Mary is not able to write a few paragraphs for this book, telling it how it was in those heady times when she was expecting our first child and I was on track for Grand Slam No.2. A piece she wrote for *The Education of a Tennis Player*, the book I co-authored with Bud Collins back in 1971, will have to suffice:

It was interesting the way Rod and I never talked about the Grand Slam in 1969. We knew he was going for this thing, that he had a goal, and it was good for his game to have a goal. It wasn't superstition . . . we just didn't talk about it. I don't think athletes dwell on something like this. That's the sportswriter's job. Each tournament is an individual matter, that's the way Rod feels. There was no sense lumping them together in his mind. Play them one at a time, to use the cliché. It's always amazed me how loose and easygoing he was, particularly when the pressure built . . .

During a tournament as important as Wimbledon, you might share a bedroom and most of the day with Rod, but he was not really with you. I mean, his mind was somewhere else. He got quiet. He would converse some, but never remember what he'd said. Most people think of him as a quiet person anyway, but this lapse into near-silence was new for me when he took me to tournaments after we were married. Rod and I hit it off right away when we met, and we always had a million things to say to each other. I had to get used to the quietness of tournament time. I don't mean he got moody. Nothing upset him. He's got the happiest attitude I've ever seen, the ideal tempera-ment for what he was doing . . . He never worried about a match or thought much about it until just a few minutes before he went on the court. Then he wanted to be by himself and go over his plans and preparation. Until then, I doubt it even crossed his mind who he was playing. Yet somewhere down there, below his consciousness, something got him revved up and fixed his attention on the job without making

My tennis mates gave Mary and me a fitting arch of honour when we emerged from St Luke's Presbyterian Church in San Rafael, San Francisco, after we were married on 20 June 1966. After being waylaid with Lew Hoad on the way home from a tournament the day before, it was touch and go whether I made it on time.

Mary (with me on our wedding day) was a green-eyed, dark-haired beauty with a love of life's finer things who introduced me to the world beyond tennis.

A welcome breather during my 1969 Australian Open semi final against Tony Roche, a four and a half hour, 90-game epic that was played in blazing Queensland heat. A disputed line call that he believes to this day cost him the match was something else that made Tony's blood boil that day.

In the French Open of 1969 at Roland Garros Stadium in Paris I survived a tough final against the hardest man to play against in world tennis, Ken Rosewall.

Pancho Gonzales: irascible, selfish, temperamental… and a mighty tennis player. Here, at the grand old age of 41, he beats Swede Ove Bengtson in the second round at Wimbledon in 1969.

After falling flat on my face trying to jump the net after a victory in a match early in my career, I tempted fate again when, after I won both the US Open and my second Grand Slam in 1969, exuberance triumphed over good sense.

At that US Open in 1969, I had it all: the title, a Grand Slam, the cheers of the crowd. What I didn't have was a dime to use a payphone to call Mary, heavily pregnant in California, and tell her the good news.

When I brought Mary to Queensland my parents showed her the local sights, and when they visited us and our son Rick in California on their first and only overseas trip, Mary returned the favour.

I won't deny that it was a thrill to meet my celluloid heroes John Wayne and Charlton Heston when Muscles Rosewall and I played in Los Angeles. I was surprised to learn that the stars were as in awe of us as we were of them. I became firm friends with both.

As our tennis careers wound down, Roy Emerson and I opened tennis camps across the United States, teaching beginners and seasoned players training techniques and the finer points of the game. Our venture was profitable, and a whole lot of fun.

184   ROD LAVER

Caricaturists can be so unkind!

John Newcombe (after winning Wimbledon in 1971) carried on the Australian tennis tradition of good sportsmanship and success set by Hoad and Rosewall, Sedgman and Fraser, Emerson and Stolle in the golden age. From 1950 to 1970, Australians won the Wimbledon men's singles 13 times, the Australian championships 18 times, the United States 14 times and the French 10 times. And the Davis Cup 15 times.

BETTMANN/CORBIS

BETTMANN/CORBIS

Victory was never sweeter than when Australia reclaimed the Davis Cup from the United States 5–0 in 1973. Enjoying victory's spoils are (from left) Geoff Masters, John Newcombe, Malcolm Anderson, captain Neale Fraser, me, Ken Rosewall and Colin Dibley.

In the wake of my stroke I had to learn to think, speak, read, eat and walk again and Mary was with me through it all. After I recovered and she fell ill with breast cancer and then neuropathy, the illness that would take her life in 2012, I became her primary carer. Love is a two-way street.

©NEAL PRESTON

MIKE NELSON/AAP/GETTY IMAGES

Being a fighter on the tennis court played a role in helping me battle back from a haemorrhagic stroke that felled me and crippled my brain and the left side of my body in 1998 – that and brilliant doctors and therapists, and the love and care of Mary.

I am humbled when greats of our game such as Pete Sampras and Andre Agassi (at an LA tournament in 2002) say that I inspired their careers.

A sticky situation. They say you've really made it when they put your dial on a postage stamp, and this was the honour afforded Australian women's tennis legend Margaret Court and me in 2003.

In January 2003 I had the opportunity for a leisurely practice match with Peter McNamara at Melbourne Park. Having spent so much time on the road to recovery after my stroke, it was great to be back on the court.

Roger Federer is the greatest player of the modern era, and a true gentleman who treasures the history and traditions of tennis. When I presented him with the winner's trophy at the Australian Open at Rod Laver Arena in Melbourne in 2006, he wept with emotion. Roger, the pleasure was all mine.

On 29 January 2012, to mark the Centenary of the Australian championships, I joined the nine living past Australian men's champions (from left) Frank Sedgman, Merv Rose, Ashley Cooper, Roy Emerson, Ken Rosewall, Bill Bowrey, John Newcombe and Mark Edmondson in parading the Sir Norman Brookes Challenge Cup around the Rod Laver Arena before Rafael Nadal and Novak Djokovic faced off in the final.

In 2012, Roger and I caught up outside the Rod Laver Arena during the Australian Open. With such champions as him, and the likes of Rafael Nadal, Novak Djokovic and Andy Murray, our great game is in the best of hands.

It was one of the greatest honours of my life to be the one chosen to hold the Sir Norman Brookes Challenge Cup high on centre court as the capacity crowd cheered. I like to think they weren't cheering me so much as all of us and the way we played the game.

My heart is in Australia, but for many years, since I married Mary, my home has been in California. Here is Mary and me at our home in Carlsbad in 2011, surrounded and made to feel special by our loving family. Our son Rick stands directly behind me and behind him is my beautiful granddaughter Riley. To Mary's left is Ann Marie, her daughter from her previous marriage. Mary's son Steve stands behind Mary; her eldest, Ron, stands to my right.

My brother Trevor (with me above), sister Lois and me (left, in 2013) are the last survivors of my immediate family. It is always special when we catch up.

Not a day goes by when I don't count my blessings. I've led a fortunate life.

him fluttery. I think that's what was going on when he was so detached: the automatic build-up within.

Keeping busy was his way of consciously avoiding thinking too much about the day's match. He did the shopping, and the laundry and other errands. He had his favorite markets in London, and often at Dolphin Square he would do the cooking. He had to in 1969 because I pulled an abdominal muscle trying to open a stubborn window and was on the casualty list myself for a few days. That doesn't mean he's another Escoffier. He's an Australian – steak and eggs three times a day wouldn't seem odd to him. At least he fixes those well.

Wimbledon in 1969 presented a folksy portrait of the champion that nobody saw but me. The Rocket bustling between his pots and pans, soaking his elbow with the hydroculator one minute and checking on our dinner the next . . . scooping up the soiled tennis clothes for a run to the Laundromat . . . jollying up the pregnant wife and asking if the kid had kicked lately. The hero of centre court was also a domestic dynamo. Sometimes we took the limousine service to Wimbledon . . . More often Rod drove himself. I liked the limousines. Rod drives the way he plays tennis: he keeps things spinning. [Ford always gave me a courtesy car to drive during Wimbledon.] There were hairy rides, but he knows London and he prided himself on taking a different route to the tournament every time we made the 45-minute drive. That was another of his little routines to put his mind on something else.

People used to ask me about his ravished fingernails that he chewed nearly to the elbow. They think he must have been awfully nervous. That was the only outward sign . . . But what he seemed to be worrying about was somebody else. His heaviest chewing was done while he was watching a match. Or television, or a movie. *Butch Cassidy* came close to giving him the look of Venus de Milo. He loves cowboy flicks and must have seen *Butch* 20 times. If he's watching a western on TV I can hear his chomping over the gunfire.

It was a Wimbledon for the ages. With an abundance of tremendous players among the 128 competitors, there were stand-up-and-cheer games from Day 1 on even the outer courts. Daily entry tickets, which cost £2 and 50 pence (yes, you read that correctly!), were almost impossible to come by and hopeful fans slept all night outside the gates to be first in line when the few remaining tickets went on sale. Scalpers cashed in, charging as much as £30 for a centre court ticket. There was one well-known old villain who had been scalping at Wimbledon seemingly since Don Budge was a boy. His office was a shady corner of the parking lot and he was renowned for being able to provide tickets for any match if offered sufficient money. The legend was that he could get you into the royal box, though I suspect that's apocryphal.

There was a marvellous atmosphere in the air as former tennis greats, royals, celebrities, politicians and everyday tennis fans crammed into Wimbledon each day.

We players, too, were buoyed by the intense interest and excitement, and also by the recent formation by more than a hundred players of the International Players Association, whose charter was to enable the players to make their feelings heard to tournament organisers and national associations. In the past the players had no voice, and there was a hope that shoddy events like that year's Australian Open, where the players' rights were not considered, would be a thing of the past. John Newcombe was the inaugural president of the IPA and Arthur Ashe, Niki Pilic and I were on the committee. The year 1969 was an exciting time to be a tennis player.

I mentioned earlier that Stan Smith would do a lot better than he showed against me at the French Open, and I didn't have to wait long to receive a big fright from the 190-centimetre, blond-haired Yank at Wimbledon. Before facing him I was fairly untroubled to overcome Nicola Pietrangeli of Italy and Denmark's Jan Leschly in the first and third rounds respectively, though in the second match, Premjit Lall of India made me work hard when he had me down two sets to love and 3–3 in the third before I recovered to win that set and the last two 6–0, 6–0. Tennis has long been blessed with great writers, and in my era the British had some of the best. *The Times'* Geoffrey Smith was one who combined lyrical and highly original prose with a deep knowledge of the game. In his newspaper the day after the Leschly match, 28 June, he wrote kindly of my performance: '. . . Laver underlined his champion's lineage. [He and Leschly] were men in different leagues. Three services, two of them untouchable aces, and a killing backhand volley down the line . . . a pocketful of volleys and passes. So the whole parade of the Australian's gifts filed past.' Smith wrote that I spread my game before my foe like the irrefutable evidence of a case, 'and the afternoon was lined with silk. Here was the executioner with measuring eye. Top spin passes, backhand and forehand, cross court or down the line, rampant smashes and scything volleys dying to the corners showered on the admiring gallery like the incidentals of delight . . . here was the luxury of creation . . . harnessed genius.' Noting that I was now in the last 16 as I searched for my second Grand Slam, he cautioned that me and my 'hugely developed racquet forearm' must prepare to face the heavy artillery of the big service and power play of 16th seed Stan Smith, 'But unlike Popeye, I doubt if the champion will need spinach to survive.'

Stan's long reach made him hard to pass, he served well and his second serve was as potent as his first. He was always a tough opponent for me, and so it proved at Wimbledon. I started well, and was relatively untroubled in winning the first two sets 6–4, 6–2. Then, the mark of a good player, Stan went on the attack. He started banging my serves right back past me, and his already booming serve became even more powerful. He began to utilise his agility and enormous reach, winning the third set 9–7, and, by out-hitting me, the fourth 6–3. He could smell victory. I was in deep trouble.

In the fifth, Stan had me one game down and was leading 30–0 on my serve when I began my recovery on the back of spinning backhands. I broke him, which made him fight even harder. As a rule, I countered sheer power well, but

Stan was rushing me, and keeping me off-balance. His cocky demeanour and steely expression signalled to me that for him losing was not an option. Seeing such self-belief in the fellow across the net can be daunting. I was serving for the match at 5–3, and still he wouldn't give up and had me reeling at 0–40, giving him three break points. Okay, I told myself, he's stepped it up, now you have to as well. I would get to the net a little quicker, serve a little better, volley a little deeper. Doing all that won me the next five points. When we shook hands after a tremendous match, I knew that Stan, although disappointed by coming up short again this time around, now believed he had it in him to beat me. And in matches to come, he did.

Next on my agenda, in the quarter finals, was Cliff Drysdale, the charming South African who had acquitted himself well against me in the past. He had beaten me decisively in the fourth round of the '68 US Open, including 6–1, 6–1 in the last two sets. He reckoned he won because he had been pinpoint-accurate with his shots, placing them on greener and more slippery patches of grass, while I blamed my defeat on my awful serving that day. Cliff had also beaten me in the West of England Open at Bristol just a fortnight earlier. I confess I was using that tournament purely as a means to reacquaint myself with grass after Paris, but nevertheless his two-handed baseball-swing backhand troubled me. At Wimbledon, Cliff was playing well and already had the prized scalp of Roy Emerson hanging from his belt. Because I believed that only a fool didn't modify his game against a bloke who'd been beating him,

I came up with the tactic of varying my net rushing. In our match, sometimes I'd race up and others I'd stay back. This threw Cliff because he couldn't anticipate what I was going to do and so couldn't plan his shots accordingly. In the US Open, his short angled returns had been landing around my feet and so were difficult for me to volley or half-volley. Now at Wimbledon, by staying back, I was able to move in on them and slam them away. I also attacked his serve, not the strongest part of his game, which had him on the back foot from the outset. He never adjusted to my tactical changes and I won in straight sets.

Arthur Ashe had not had a great 1969. He was going through a lengthy form slump after his triumph at the US Open in '68. Maybe this handsome, tall, articulate athlete, the first American in 13 years to win the US championships and the first black American *ever* to do so, was simply weighed down with too much baggage after that impressive win when, instead of being allowed to concentrate on tennis like other elite players, he became a standard bearer and spokesman for the civil rights movement. Arthur was every-where – at all the tournaments, on the cover of *Life* magazine, a talking head on TV. In those divisive times, he was loved by those who saw him as carrying on a share of the work of the recently assassinated Martin Luther King Jr, but he was also anathema to some in America. Arthur transcended sport. He was a gold standard celebrity. No wonder, in 1969, he seemed to be carrying the world on his shoulders and his tennis results suffered. I have always wondered how good a player he would have been if there had been other black

American tennis stars with whom he could have shared the responsibilities that were imposed on him and, to his credit, that he put his own hand up for. I was critical of Arthur for not allowing himself to realise his potential, but really I had no right to judge.

He qualified to play me in the semi final at Wimbledon despite shaky form. He had only just squeaked home against inferior opposition in his matches so far, but I knew that Arthur was dangerous and he had the firepower on Wimbledon's fast grass to beat me if he was on his game. It was a fact, too, that as the world No.1 at the time I was the bloke everyone wanted to beat and I knew Arthur would rise to the occasion and be a handful. 'Handful', as it turned out, was an understatement. He began that first set at a million miles an hour and I felt like I'd been shredded by a buzz saw. Arthur's return of my serve, whether forehand or backhand, was continually at my feet or past me. He broke my service twice in the first set. Tearing around the court, walloping the ball with immense power, he destroyed me 6–2. He was playing as well as any man can play and although I was playing well, I wasn't in the hunt. Knowing that Arthur's form could ebb and flow in a match, I decided that all I could do was hold on, win a set somehow, and hope that Cyclone Arthur blew himself out over five sets. He's not going to be able to keep this up, I thought. I'd been in this position many times before, when my opponent blasted me off the court, and always my tactic was not to panic, to just hang in there, playing steadily, avoiding mistakes. I would make Arthur work by serving into his body rather than, as he liked it, away from him, and capitalise if he was unable to maintain his form. I was completely confident that I was fit enough to go five sets and I wasn't sure that he was.

In the second set and still hard-pressed to handle his backhand, I hit to his forehand, which was not quite so formidable, and by doing that I began to accumulate some winners. It doesn't look like it when you see photos of the match, but I truly was enjoying this clash, relishing the pressure Arthur applied. The challenge spurred me on, as did the fact that we were battling it out on the grandest stage of tennis, and I began to let loose some bombs of my own. The match has been likened by some commentators to the famous Muhammad Ali and George Foreman Rumble in the Jungle heavyweight championship fight in Kinshasa, Zaire, five years later; George whaled away on Ali over the first six rounds and Ali hung in there, absorbing the merciless punishment, until George got exhausted and dispirited at being unable to put Ali away, and Ali responded by knocking Foreman out.

I then changed tack and began hitting away from Arthur, making him run and scramble to return the ball. His shots began to lose their force. I won the second set by the same margin that Arthur had won the first, 6–2. In the third set, I broke his serve and led 2–0, then, with three fabulous fireball backhands that I had no hope of reaching, he broke back. I began to chip my returns low to make the tall Arthur stretch, and that seemed to throw him because suddenly his volleys started going into the net. I won the third set 9–7.

The tough set seemed to wilt Arthur's spirit. I was now on top. I said after the match that the ball was looking as big as a basketball to me. The decisive moment in the fourth set was when Arthur had me pinned to the baseline and he gently, deftly, tapped a ball just on my side of the net. When it bounced, I was way back. No one at centre court, and certainly not Arthur, believed I could reach it. I ran for that ball as hard as I have ever run and got to it a split second before it bounced a second time, and I flicked it over my flabbergasted opponent's head. He barely reached it and his backhand arced into the net. Arthur wasn't expecting me to pull off that return. Tennis is a psychological game, and this was a blow from which he didn't recover. It was 2–0, and I wanted 3–0, then 4–0 and 5–0 and my killer instinct ensured that I won those games. I took the set 6–0 for a three sets to one victory. I was in my sixth straight Wimbledon final.

Afterwards, Arthur said it was my speed and fitness that beat him in the end. Fred Stolle thought it was something more, something psychological: 'The reason Rocket gets balls like that drop volley is he plays every shot in practice just as hard. It's second nature for him to go after every ball in practice, even the no-chance kind, and not let it bounce more than once. He's made himself want to hit every ball regardless of the circumstances. This attitude transfers to matches. He wasn't that quick as a kid. I think his work on the practice court gave him that extra step.' Fred was on the money, but I have no doubt that my experience as a pro, fighting for every single point because my wage depended on it, and my guile forged on the endless pro circuit, played their part too.

My opponent in the Wimbledon final was my friend and compatriot John Newcombe. Newk was seven years younger than me and he was in form. He had won the Italian and British Hard Court championships that year and just a fortnight earlier he had beaten me in the London Open. He was as confident he could beat me again now as I was that I could overcome him. Going into the match I felt terrific. Without being boastful, I just didn't believe I could be beaten that day, no matter who I was up against.

In the dressing room in the moments before the match, adrenalin coursed through my body, and that was good. As usual, I paced around the locker room and fiddled with my racquet handles. It occurred to me that more people would be watching this match than any other in the history of tennis because it would be screened live on television sets around the world thanks to the communications satellite Telstar. I smiled at Newk, and he at me, and we followed the match referee and locker attendant Bulley, who was carrying our racquets, under the Rudyard Kipling poem on the entrance gate to centre court and onto the scuffed and worn turf punctuated by its gleaming white line markings. Did my legs wobble? Probably, but only a little. I'd say I was more keyed up than shaking in my boots. That was good. I knew that unless I was a tad edgy I didn't play well.

I was a Wimbledon veteran, as was my opponent, and we were lifted and inspired, rather than intimidated, by the experience of playing on centre court. As Newk and

I entered the court, the capacity crowd of 15,000 clapped. We genuflected to the royal box, and I looked up to where I knew Mary was seated in the grandstand, heavily pregnant with our first child, and she was waving at me, looking so beautiful in a bright yellow dress and with a yellow ribbon in her hair. (She hadn't been at centre court for the semi against Arthur Ashe because of her abdominal muscle injury, and had been recuperating in the bath while watching the match on TV.) After a light-hearted warm-up, Newk and I got serious.

I had enormous respect for John as a man and as a player. He was a thinking champion. He always had a plan for winning a match and as his opponent you knew that he'd have thought long and hard about how he could exploit your weaknesses. He controlled play with his accurate and powerful serve and forehand – the writer Bud Collins called it his 'buggy whip forehand' – and had a tremendous volley. He was always putting the most extreme pressure on you to return. He was immensely strong and had a killer smash. While his backhand wasn't quite as effective as his other shots, it was still formidable.

John's strategy became obvious immediately. He would not play his usual fast game, because I handled speed well. Instead, he chipped his returns and lobbed high and deep over my head, defensive lobs to prevent me from finding my rhythm and making me turn round and dash helter-skelter all over the court. My accurate overhead smashes allowed me to win the first set 6–4, although the score did not reflect the intensity of the contest. Newk won the second

7–5 after my smashes, which were winners in the first set, faltered. At a set apiece, the match was anyone's and the crowd was entranced by our deadly cat and mouse game. John broke my serve and went ahead 4–1 in the third set, and his underdog status and wholehearted performance had the crowd on his side. I was undeterred. This was my stage. I had no intention of fluffing my lines. I recovered my serve and my overhead game, and snatched back the momentum. I was punishing Newk's lobs and cracking aces. My serve was humming. I took the next five games in a row and went ahead two sets to one.

Looking back, I can identify the decisive moment that won me that crucial third set and ultimately the match and the Wimbledon trophy. John was ahead four games to two and he was serving. It would have been desperately hard for me to recover from 2–5 down. Newk hit a forehand wide across the court to my right side. I lunged for it and he ran up to the net to cut off any return I might be able to produce. He veered a little to the left, anticipating that if I *did* manage to get to the ball, I would roll a backhand down the line. Thinking fast, I figured that he'd be expecting me to do exactly that, so I did the opposite. I sliced a low under spinning ball crosscourt at an acute angle that surprised and wrong-footed him. It seemed that there was no way it could clear the net and land inside the court, yet it did, wafting gently through the air almost parallel to the net. John thrust out his racquet but it did not connect. The ball landed centimetres within the far sideline. I was stunned. Without actually meaning to, I had pulled off an unbelievable shot.

John was stunned too, and his confidence was dented. Moments later he double faulted. I finished the set, 6–4, with a scything backhand volley.

In the fourth set, my killer instinct came to the fore. I broke John early to go up 2–0. There was a memorable moment when I hit a backhand down the line and John literally threw himself at it, but it passed him. He picked himself up off the turf with an exasperated expression that turned into a huge grin. I think he realised at that moment that today belonged to me. Being the player that he was, John regrouped and fought his way back to deuce. I was angry with myself for not being able to return his serves. Had one of his lobs not gone out by a fraction, he may well have turned the match around, but it was not to be. At my ad in the set, he volleyed to me and faced me squarely at the net, feet planted, ready for wherever my return would travel. I relaxed, focused on the ball, which was once again looking huge and seemingly coming at me in slow motion, and hit my backhand shot down the line for the winner. The final, emphatic, point in the match came when I put away a smash off John's tired lob. I had won 6–4, 5–7, 6–4, 6–4 in two hours and 15 minutes. Of all my four Wimbledon wins, this was the toughest.

John was so gracious in defeat. He later recalled the fourth set incident in his autobiography, *Newk: Life On and Off the Court*:

Rod hit a very good low return off the backhand down the line, and I picked up an excellent volley and hit it sharply across court. I didn't know if he could reach it, but I assumed he would because he was so fast. He did get to the ball, but he was low to the ground and he had very little time to create much. I had 99 percent of the area covered that he could possibly hit to, and I was sure I could cope with anything he did with it. But, of course, Rod found the 1 percent I'd overlooked. He angled his return across court in front of me. I dived to return it but the angle was too acute. The ball took a tiny piece of the line, and that was it.

After the Duke of Kent presented me with the winner's trophy, and I received a cheque for $7200 (what a difference from the rewards of the amateur era!), I savoured some celebratory champagne with George MacCall and John McDonald and their wives at our flat at Dolphin Square – Mary, of course, wasn't drinking alcohol so I was happy to relieve her of her share – before piling into my dinner jacket and then a limo for the Wimbledon Ball. I danced the ceremonial winner's waltz with the women's champion, Englishwoman Ann Haydon-Jones and we foxtrotted to 'Fly Me to the Moon'. All through the waltz I was terrified, because I knew I would have to make a speech, so I thought I would calm my nerves with a little more champagne. Then a little more. The rest of the evening, I'm afraid, is a blur. I'm told I pulled off my speech with barely a stumble. I remotely remember being in a disco called Raffles with Aretha Franklin's 'Respect' pumping out of the speakers, and Mary having a long discussion with Fred Stolle's wife, Pat, about what we were going to call our baby. One of them suggested 'Slammer' and the other 'Forest', because the baby was due to be born on final day at the US Open at Forest Hills. I declared that all names were in contention, except for 'Drop Shot', because we already had a dog by that name.

If I heard anyone saying that, with the Australian Open, the French Open and Wimbledon now in my swag, a win at the US Open in two months would give me my second Grand Slam, forgive me but I sure don't recall it. What I *do* remember is waking up next morning in the bathtub, groggy and dry-mouthed, still wearing my tux, and hearing my staunch protector Mary fending off phone calls from reporters from all over the world, stalling them until I could regather my addled and hungover wits. She'd tell them, 'He's out. Let me see if he's back yet . . . no, he's still out. He'll be back soon.' When she said that I was 'out' she was telling the truth.

One of those reporters, *The Times'* Rex Bellamy, wrote a telling wrap-up of that memorable Wimbledon. Among his observations: 'Wimbledon was dominated by big crowds, record receipts and, in the men's event, the highest overall standard of play the championships have ever known . . .' Bellamy noted that Newk's and my final was the first for five years to go to four sets and said it was the best final to be contested for much longer than that. He called John's challenge a triumph of strategy and tactics. My compatriot, wrote Bellamy, had mixed his game artfully and well, puzzling me with lobs and short angles. Newk had seldom nourished my volley with speed, for which I, he said, had an insatiable appetite. He noted that in this game I was rarely able to hustle Newk as I wanted to, 'but the speed of his reflexes and footwork was breathtaking, and his whiplash of a backhand was always difficult to read.' Most importantly, I had lifted my game in that final to turn adversity into authority. 'Laver played some marvellous shots, among them two memorable forehand passing shots – the first delicately controlled when he had no logical right to be anywhere near the ball, the second a full-blooded drive off an equally full-blooded smash. It may be a long time before we see a champion of his quality again.'

I had hardly had time to give Mary a hello-again hug when our phone began ringing with calls from the International Management Group's CEO and my business agent Mark McCormack and his executives Jay Lafave and Dick Alford, alerting me to offers from companies wanting to pay me to endorse their products. It shows how far tennis had come in just a few years. Back in 1966 when I was a pro, these organisations didn't want to know me. In the United States now, in the open era, tennis was as popular as, and had the credibility of, football and baseball and had consequently become big business. With me on board, IMG also signed up as clients Newk, Margaret Court, Evonne Goolagong and Roger Taylor.

I was glad to have IMG on board. In times past, I had been ripped off by companies whose products I had endorsed and when it came time to pay me for the use of my name, image and time, these shysters did a disappearing act. That was never going to happen with Mark, Jay and Dick at my back. Also, I needed them because I was frankly uncomfortable hawking myself to prospective sponsors. Mary had been a huge help after we were married, keeping track of my endorsement and public appearance work and making sure I was fairly reimbursed. But in that landmark year of 1969, I needed professionals looking after me.

Before I signed on with IMG, my annual non-playing earnings were $25,000. In 1969 they were $50,000. Mark assured me that if I did go on to win the Grand Slam, I would be even more marketable, an attractive proposition to new companies wanting to associate themselves with me, and as such I would be able to ask for and receive bigger fees from my existing sponsors. As usual, IMG was on the money. Here's an example: in 1966 I signed with a small New England footwear manufacturer who made and sold tennis shoes bearing my name. I accepted from them a fee of $1000 plus a 2.5% royalty on the retail price of each pair of shoes sold. Because the manufacturer failed to market the shoes properly, my typical monthly royalty cheque was, say, $7.50. IMG rescued me from that bum deal and placed me with a little company called Adidas.

IMG was also instrumental in organising racquet endorsement deals for me in different parts of the world. In Australia I used and endorsed a Dunlop wooden racquet, and in Europe a Donney wooden racquet. In the United States in years to come I played with a Chemold aluminium racquet. This was when metal racquets were being introduced to tennis after wooden ones had always been the go. Although such players as Clark Graebner, Rosie Casals and

Billie Jean King were proponents of metal and attributed a number of wins to their use, and Pancho Gonzales told me he could hit the ball harder with less effort with his Spalding aluminium racquet, I wasn't a fan. Having achieved so much with wood, why would I change a winning formula? I had, and still have, a soft spot for wooden racquets, and I'm glad I grew up using one because with wood timing is all-important. With a wooden racquet, unless you time your shot perfectly – anticipate what your opponent is going to do so you'll be in position, swing through the ball, make your shoulder turn – it'll have no speed, so I had no option but to work hard on my timing. When it was on-song, I could put maybe 25–30 kilometres per hour extra speed on a ball. Timing was the magic ingredient in my game. I was sceptical when proponents of metal said wooden racquets would be obsolete within a decade. I was wrong. In years to come, after teething problems were solved, I did play with a metal racquet, but in 1969, with the US Open looming and the Grand Slam at stake, I stuck with wood.

I couldn't seem to put a foot wrong in 1969. I had won the three major tournaments to date, and a number of other tournaments besides, although my good form was a double-edged sword because I would have relished an early exit during any of those minor events to snatch a day here and a day there at home with Mary. She needed her husband by her side to lighten the load of her pregnancy. I knew my place was with her, but I was contractually committed to those tournaments and I had to see each one through to the end. Meanwhile, the pundits scratched their heads wondering just what it was about me that saw me win so often that year. *The New York Times Magazine's* Eliot Asinof had a worthy, though, to me, slightly mystifying, stab. *The New York Times Magazine's* Eliot Asinof had a worthy, though, to me at times, slightly mystifying, stab. A winner, wrote Asinof, required a special synthesis of skills and attitude that 'gets at the very guts of a man.' If I had cultivated – and practised – an assortment of excellent and winning shots, so indeed had all the other professionals. On any given day we all possessed the skills necessary to win, although some of us were better at service or an overhead or backhand or volley. The key, mused Asinof, lay with 'the other factor, the hidden factor, the inexplicable and mystical ingredient that solidifies the talent, enabling a man to put it all together, match after match. It is the factor that controls the infinitely delicate reaction of the brain and the related balance of the senses – for this is what sends a shot skidding on the base line and not an inch by it.' Tennis, he pointed out, quite accurately, was a game of inches, and whoever controlled the crucial inch controlled the court.

When I strode onto the court at Forest Hills, New York, in the first round of the US Open in the last week of August, I had won 23 matches in a row, beginning with my first round victory over Nicola Pietrangeli at Wimbledon. The last person to beat me was John Newcombe at Queen's three months earlier. I had been fretting that my winning streak, one that was unprecedented in my career, would come to an end, as purple patches always do, and that when my luck ran out it would be at the US Open at the West Side Tennis Club at Forest Hills. Still, if one has to choose between winning form and poor form, I don't know anyone who'd choose the latter, and if winning form counts for anything, I reassured myself, I had to stand a good chance in the final grand slam tournament of the year.

For all that, my major worry was Mary. I was on the other side of the continent in New York, while my heart was at home with her in California. In retrospect, my concern that Mary's pregnancy continue to go smoothly prevented me from dwelling too much on the US Open and achieving the Grand Slam. We spoke on the phone every day. Helping my focus, too, was my decision not to be so readily available to reporters, who would all be grilling me about the Grand Slam, and to cocoon myself from newspapers whose pundits' pronouncements and pontifications can affect your confidence if you let them. So it was a blessing when Charlton Heston invited me to stay at his luxurious three-floor penthouse apartment in the Tudor City skyscraper complex on Manhattan's east side. He said the apartment by the East River, with views of the United Nations complex, high ceilings, exquisite furniture, art, and a refrigerator stocked with steak, eggs, fresh orange juice and beer, was mine to relax in and use as a Manhattan base for as long as I remained alive in the US Open. I had become friends with Chuck, a tennis buff, in Los Angeles and he was also a good mate of my long-time pal John McDonald, a Kiwi who had played Davis Cup and who would be my minder and helper during the US Open. There was plenty of room for

John at the apartment as well. At night, he and I would have friends over for dinner and drinks, or just hang out watching TV or listening to Aretha Franklin, Dave Brubeck and Jose Feliciano records while I wound and unwound the grips on my racquets, the closest thing I had to a nervous tic. John McDonald is doing it tough nowadays with illness, and I'd like him to know what an important part he played in my US Open campaign. Charlton Heston is no longer with us, but his kindness in allowing me to take refuge in his apartment was a godsend. Chuck was renowned for his heroic roles as Ben Hur, Moses and General Charles Gordon, and his generosity in '69 made him a hero to me.

When I entered the cauldron to play against Mexican Luis Garcia in the first match of the Open, I was at peace with myself. I beat young Garcia, and then the Chileans Jaime Pinto-Bravo and Jaime Fillol without dropping a set. Dennis Ralston, whom I faced in my fourth match, was a different proposition, a living, breathing wake-up call that I was not going to win this tournament without a mighty struggle. Dennis, who had pressed me in the past but was yet to beat me, lost the first set and then, playing the best tennis I had ever seen from him, won the next two. The 10,000-strong crowd at Forest Hills that gloriously sunny afternoon forgave their countryman for some disappointing Davis Cup performances in the past, and cheered him passionately. Their cheers were most ecstatic when he walked to the baseline after we'd had a breather when we changed ends, and when I stepped up there'd be a deafening silence and baleful glares that left me in no doubt that I wore the black hat that day. So to neutralise the crowd's support for Dennis, I fell back on my old Harry Hopman ploy and assumed my position at the baseline at precisely the same time Dennis did. That way I soaked up the cheers that were meant for him, and nobody was going to boo for fear that Ralston would think he was the one copping the Bronx cheers.

I downed Dennis in five sets, 6–4, 4–6, 4–6, 6–2, 6–3. He succumbed to my persistent pressure in the fourth set and his hangdog body language in the fifth told me that his gallant resistance was finished and I overpowered him. We Aussies stuck together and Emmo and Fred Stolle played a part in my win over Dennis when they came to me in the dressing room during the 10-minute break after the third set and told me to toss the ball up a little higher when I served, because many of my serves that day had been finding the net. Their advice paid dividends.

After my match with Dennis, the heavens opened over New York and in 48 hours dumped 16 centimetres of rain. The courts of the West Side Tennis Club became a quagmire. The organisers of this prestige tournament were ill-prepared. The few flimsy tarpaulins they had handy were never going to protect the court surfaces, which, because of the sparse covering of grass over their soil, turned to viscous mud and were not remotely playable. For the next two and a half days, while we waited for the deluge to end, I practised on indoor courts, worked out and had soothing hot Epsom salts baths in the gymnasium of the New York Athletic Club.

We were getting to the pointy end of the tournament, and the quality of my opponents reflected that. In my quarter final against my old mate and nemesis of so many years, Roy Emerson, my rhythm was out of whack and I began sluggishly. Before I knew it, Emmo had won the first set 6–4 on a court that was still waterlogged, which made the balls heavy and sodden. Then Emmo broke my serve early in the second set. I concentrated on settling myself and slowing down, doing the little things right, like keeping my eye on the ball and hitting through it, breathing evenly, getting my serves in by placing them precisely, simply returning back over the net anything he hit at me without necessarily going for winners, punishing his second serve . . . all the tried and tested stuff.

As slippery as that court was, I was moving quickly, faster than Emmo, and battling my way back into the match. I won the second set 8–6, and the third 13–11 on the back of a little good luck. Roy hit a forehand passing shot that he believed was good but which the linesman ruled out. Deuce. I then produced two passing forehands that he was unable to handle to win the set. In my match against Ralston, Denny's shoulders had drooped. There was no way Emmo was ever going to stop fighting, even though he now had to go the distance against a five-set specialist. In the end, it was the court as much as me that ended his US Open. He had a way of dragging his foot when he served and he was chewing up the baseline so much that soon there was no solid section of the court from which to serve. Then he began catching his dragging foot in the sludge.

When it was my turn to serve from the end Roy had ripped up, it was not a problem for me for the simple reason that I did not drag my foot. I was ahead 5–4 in the fourth and serving for the match when I surprised Emmo with my first top-spin lob of our encounter. He was racing in to the net when the ball arced back over his head. The slippery court prevented Roy from stopping and turning to give chase, and he didn't even try – he just kept running to the net, his hand outstretched and grinning that big gold-toothed grin of his.

On his way to our semi final showdown, Arthur Ashe's sledgehammer serve had seen him convincingly beat Manuel Santana and Muscles Rosewall, so he was on a roll. And of course in our match the crowd would be right behind him. With a final depending on the result, I needed no added incentive to beat Arthur, but I had a point to prove against him, because he had been putting it about that it was time for older generation players such as Muscles and me to stand aside for him and his contemporaries Newk, Rochey and Tom Okker. Speaking for myself, I had no intention of vacating the scene for anybody just yet, and I was determined to show Arthur that there was life in this old dog yet. It wasn't an easy assignment.

After I came onto the court at the same time as him to bask in the cheers of his supporters, the Americans who made up the vast majority of the crowd, he went immediately into top gear, much as he had done at Wimbledon. His dynamic serves had me on the defensive and, at 5–4 to him, he served for the first set. Then Arthur's inexperience brought him undone. Instead of coolly and accurately placing a winning serve, he attempted to ace me and the ball sailed out. His softer second serve was easy meat. I did my usual thing of just returning the ball to him firmly but surely, sending back to him everything he hit at me, applying the pressure back on him to hit winners. I was chipping straight down the middle of the court and depriving him of the wide angles he needed to slam winners.

The first set was mine 8–6, and then I won the second decisively, 6–3. In the third, however, Arthur gave a glimpse of the skill and tenacity that were to make him a far better player in years to come than he was in 1969. After he led 3–0, I caught him up and we remained locked together on serve until night fell and play was called off for the day with the score 12–12. We left the court lost in our thoughts. I got the impression from Arthur's worried expression that he would not be sleeping well that night. Arthur knew what he had to do: wrap up the third set the next morning and take the match to five sets. And *I* knew what he had to do, so I planned to blitz him from the outset, win the next two games, the fourth set, and the match.

I won't deny I was nervous, too, and I had no intention of going to bed early, dwelling on what the next day would bring and risking sleeplessness. To help me get my 40 winks, John McDonald and I went out to a bar called the Press Box with a few friends. I had some good food and a couple of beers. When I did put my head on the pillow sometime after 11, I slept like a baby and felt fresh, relaxed and ready for action when Arthur, who looked drawn, and I resumed our match next morning. Also in my favour was that he was serving first. Now, serving after a break or first in a new match is never easy because you've not had time to warm up and get your arm and eye in. This is why I chose to receive when I won the toss in a match – it gave me a good chance of breaking my opponent's serve. Which is what I did, and I held my own serve to wrap up those two games and win the match in straight sets. I was in the final.

That was the good news. The bad was that I'd be playing Tony Roche, who was in tremendous form and dead keen to avenge his loss to me in the Australian Open semi final in January on the back of what he will believe to his dying day was a questionable call. I couldn't help thinking of the parallels between me and Tony, who was, and remains, a good friend: he hailed from a tiny Australian country town like me, and his dad had also been a butcher. I thought again of how Ken Rosewall scuttled his mate and doubles partner Lew Hoad's Grand Slam bid in the US champion-ships in 1956. My fear that my friend Roy Emerson would do the same to me in the final of the 1962 US champi-onships proved groundless, but now I wondered whether it was ordained that this time another mate would end my Grand Slam bid. Then I banished those qualms from my mind. This match would be won by the better player on the day and anything that happened 13 or even seven years ago would have no bearing.

The final was postponed for a day, until Monday 8 Sep-tember, when the rain had eased a little. It now fell steadily instead of teeming. In the countdown, Tony and I sat side by side in the locker room, gear on and ready to play, both on edge, hoping for the sun to pierce the purple clouds above. Out in the grandstands 4000 hardy New Yorkers huddled under umbrellas. I was extra toey because Mary had been due to give birth on the 7th, the previous day, but as yet there was still no sign of our newborn's imminent appearance. Believe me, as time ticked by I gave those leather racquet grips one helluva workout.

As we sat together, two good old mates, surrounded by walls full of framed photos of all the men who had won the men's final at the US championships, including a shot of me circa 1962, we whiled away the time chatting to reporters, who were allowed to join us. I heard Tony tell one:

Rod played me in one of his last amateur matches in 1962 when I was just a kid coming up. I gave him a good go [but] he had other things on his mind. The Davis Cup was coming up and he was turning pro. He was a hero of mine, left-handed like me, you know, and a country boy like me. I had been hoping he'd win the Grand Slam [in '62]. I heard about it on the TV that comes out of Wagga Wagga. Then I read about it a couple of days later. The Sydney papers took a while to get to Tarcutta. It's a bit different between us now. I had one chance to stop him [in the Australian Open in Brisbane earlier in the year], and I might have done it except for a bad call. I'll never forget that one.

Even though he was bone-tired after beating Newk in 169 minutes two days before and I was daisy-fresh in comparison, having taken only a short time to finish off Arthur Ashe, Tony exuded calm confidence and he had every right to do so. That year, he had beaten me five times in our eight meetings.

I used my last bit of change to call Mary on the public phone. She was feeling good but, like me, was wondering what was keeping our baby. 'It'll be just my luck,' she laughed, 'to go into labour when your match is on TV.'

It was mid-afternoon before Rochey and I were able to go onto the court, which was wet, slippery and slow. Since early morning, there had been a helicopter hovering over the court in a bid to dry it off, but all the chopper blades did was suck up more water to the surface and make it even soggier. An important match wouldn't proceed under those conditions today. Yet I was confident that I'd handle the sludgy surface better than Tony because I had played on much worse surfaces time and again as a pro – mud-heaps and waterlogged bullrings where to take a step would be to lift a chunk from the surface – while Rochey was only a recent arrival in the pro ranks and had spent most of his career playing on pristine, perfectly maintained courts. As a precaution, however, before we hit up I fronted match referee Billy Talbert and said, 'If I find myself sliding, can I wear spikes?' He said, 'Be my guest. This is the last match of the tournament so it doesn't matter if you tear up the court.' The spikes were three-eighths of an inch (9.5 millimetres) long but, unlike sharp running shoe spikes, the ends had been cut off and were blunt, so if it became necessary to wear them they would definitely churn up the court. I started the match wearing my normal shoes, thinking I'd wait to see how I went in the mud.

I should have won the first set, but deserved to lose it. And lose it I did. After sliding all over the court, I was serving for the set at 5–3. Tony broke me with a magnificent backhand return, which I couldn't reach on the slippery surface. I asked the referee, 'Can I put on my spikes?' Seeing that the conditions were hampering my game, Talbert gave his approval. Tony chose not to don spikes because he had strained his thigh muscle in the semi final against Newk and worried that he might exacerbate the injury and cramp up with the quick and juddering stops you make when you've got spikes on. Although, because of the spikes, I was moving around the court well, it was so drenched and torn up that my feet were still going in directions I didn't want them to. Rochey won that first set 9–7. I had served five double faults, and I'd not been guilty of serving that badly for a long, long time. At that stage, Tony was looking invincible.

With spikes, I'd learned, you have to lift your feet higher than usual as you move around the court, because if you try to slide to reach a ball they do their job and dig in, which can bring you crashing down. In the end, it wasn't too much of an adjustment to make, and for that, as for so many things, I had Harry Hopman to thank. Back in the early Davis Cup days, he had made us all train in them, lifting our feet high, just in case we ever had to wear them in an important match. I have a distinct memory of a Davis Cup tie at Kooyong in the rain and before it Harry, one of whose many credos was 'be prepared', telling us, 'Get your spikes on, grab your oldest racquet and come with me to the back courts, we're going to get wet.'

Tony began the second set as he'd finished the first. On fire. He held his serve in the first game. Then he led me 30–40 on my serve in the second game and found himself in an excellent position to go on and win the set, which would put him in the box seat for the match. As I readied to serve again, Tony stalled to set himself to return. I settled myself, too. I *had* to hold serve. The entire match, and the Grand Slam, which I confess was now top of my mind, could hinge on it. Usually, as I've explained, I try to serve at medium pace with spin, making sure the ball goes in and putting the onus on my opponent to handle it. This time I did the opposite, the unexpected, and I belted down a boomer, slicing it wide to Tony's forehand. He scarcely got his racquet on it. He had blown his chance to break me. Such chances are rare, and I made sure he didn't get another. The match did turn on that point. I won that game, and as I became more sure of my balance, I began to hit the ball as hard as I have ever hit it. Tony couldn't handle the pressure I was able to exert. I won the second set 6–1.

A half-hour rain delay held up the third set. When play resumed, I won it 6–2. I felt in total control. In the corresponding US final in 1962 against Roy Emerson, I got the flutters for a bit then recovered. It was a mark of how being a pro had toughened me that I never took my foot off Tony's throat in the fourth, and what proved to be the final, set. Hop and Charlie would have approved. My spikes had allowed me to set myself for effective lobs and I lobbed beautifully that day, whereas Tony was hampered by sneakers that offered him little stability on the slippery grass and in the mud and so he struggled to counteract my shots. There was a tiny blip when I was serving for the set and match at 5–2; I made the old mistake of trying to smash away for a winner a sitter of a forehand volley return from Tony when a workmanlike, no-risk response would have done the trick, and I blew it. My second serve was slower and placed perfectly and Rochey's forehand return went long. I had won the US Open final 7–9, 6–1, 6–2, 6–2 in 113 minutes.

I ran to the net to greet Tony as the crowd stood and cheered. Right then is when I broke another of my rules. In my euphoria I forgot my dignity and leapt over the net. Even before my feet hit the ground I felt a fool. I had never been a show-off, a gloater who rubs his disappointed opponent's nose in the mud by celebrating like a lunatic, and this is exactly what I was doing. I remembered how I'd learned my lesson when, as a green and giddy 19-year-old excited by my first victory over a world class player, I hurdled the net when I beat Herbie Flam in Adelaide back in '57 and caught my foot in it and tripped and sprawled ignominiously flat on my mush on the court. Fortunately, this time I cleared the net, but I was ashamed by my showboating and what might have appeared to be a lack of respect for Tony. No, the right thing to do when you win a match, and especially a hard-fought match, is shake your rival's hand and say, 'Tough luck,' or 'It's my shout!'

I had won a second Grand Slam. I was the only player ever to do so. And I had won my Slams seven years apart after being exiled to the wilderness of the professional circuit. At the post-match press conference I announced my decision to put Mary and our new baby (should he or she ever be so kind as to make an appearance!) first from now on and phase myself out of minor tournaments. 'I love tennis – it's my life. But so is my family.' When the reporters put it to me that winning the US Open was a bigger challenge than usual this year because of the Grand Slam pressure, Mary's pregnancy, delays and rain interruptions, soggy courts, the umpire's microphone breaking down – and not forgetting the calibre of my opponents – I conceded they had a point. 'This was probably the toughest competition I've played in.' Which, of course, made victory extra special. Tony Roche, always a good sport, weighed in: 'Rocket managed to get on top, and once Rod gets on top there is not much left you can do. He hit winners left, right and centre. He is playing better than ever. Maybe the $16,000 he won today will slow him down a bit.'

What a journey it had been that year. The wonderful players I had beaten made that 1969 Grand Slam even more special: Rochey and Newk, Muscles Rosewall, Andres Gimeno, Emmo, Arthur Ashe, Fred Stolle, Tom Okker, Cliff Drysdale, Stan Smith, Dennis Ralston . . . champions all. I had won 18 of the 32 singles tournaments I'd entered, notching 106 wins and 14 defeats. As well as the Australian,

French and US Opens and Wimbledon, I won the important South African Open at Ellis Park in Johannesburg, the US Pro Championships in Boston, the US Pro Indoor and the Wembley British Indoor. My Wimbledon win was my fourth straight final win there. I had to get through many, many tough, close matches and somehow, whether by good play or good fortune, I managed to do that. Think about it. If I'd lost *just one match* in all those major tournaments there would have been no Grand Slam. In the four Grand Slam finals, I dropped just two sets. That year, I earned $124,000, becoming the first tennis player to break the $100,000 barrier. Adrian Quist kindly, if a little hyperbolically, hailed my double Grand Slam as 'in my opinion, the greatest sporting achievement by an individual in the history of any game . . . This raises the question whether Laver is the greatest tennis player of all time. It is almost impossible to compare the greats of different eras [but] Laver has tremendous natural skill coupled with the ability to win the really big matches because he does not choke under pressure. All champions possess skill and courage, but occasionally a great champion appears who has the ability to produce his finest tennis when the nervous strain reaches breaking point. Laver is such a player.'

All well and good – as was the trophy and $16,000 prize money and the press conference and the victory party that John McDonald was planning for that evening back at Chuck Heston's penthouse with Dom Pérignon champagne supplied by IMG . . . But surely I knew more than anything else in my life what mattered the most: Was Mary okay? Was I a father yet? I broke free from the throng . . . A phone. I needed a phone. Remember that this was long before mobiles. I found a payphone behind the press stand and scrabbled in my pocket for a dime. It dawned on me that I'd used my last one before the match. I had everything I'd striven for, but all I wanted at that moment was to talk to Mary, who was at our home on the other side of the United States, and to do that I needed a 10 cent piece. I had $16,000 but not a dime. Seeing me panic-stricken, a reporter took pity and loaned me one. 'I'm good for it,' I assured him, brandishing my outsized cheque. I dialled Mary and she told me that there was still no hint of labour pains and she was feeling strong and healthy – and very, very big – and, oh yes, she was so proud of me. I told her I'd be on the first flight out of New York in the morning.

Messages of congratulations flooded in from around the world. Among them was the one from Charlie Hollis that gave me goosebumps, when he said well done, 'now do it again'. That was Charlie. I would have expected no less from my old taskmaster.

Nineteen excruciating days later, days that seemed as long as weeks, our son Rick was born, healthy and happy, at the Hoag Hospital in Newport Beach on 27 September. Some years later, Rick gave me a coffee mug, and on it was inscribed some of the big news events of 1969, such as the moon landing, my Grand Slam and, at the bottom of the list: I WAS BORN. To me, that piece of news should have headed the list. I cherish that mug among my most prized possessions.

On 30 September, the Newport Beach Tennis Club hosted a dinner for me, and there was a good roll-up: Emerson, Rosewall, Gimeno, Roche and Jack Kramer. Each stood and said a few words. Jack made us laugh when he quipped, 'When Rod gets in a jam in a match, he simply lifts his game. He loses occasionally. Unfortunately for many of us here tonight, never at the right time!' I was then presented with a handsome silver trophy. I couldn't help it, my eyes brimmed with tears.

On another level, and being well aware of the fickleness of fame, I was a little bemused by all the attention I received after the Grand Slam. Messages of congratulations flooded in from around the world, and it seemed that whole forests of trees were felled to make the paper on which profiles of me were printed. On 30 November, *The New York Times Magazine* ran a lengthy piece by Eliot Asinof, whose theory was that, with me, first appearances deceived: 'If you had never heard of Rodney George Laver, your first look would confuse you. He walks onto the court with his three racquets tucked under his arm and he seems so slight, so pixie-like, you think he is, perhaps, a misplaced ball-boy with a quick, mincing, pigeon-toed walk. He is lean and light, his shoulders are narrow and sloping. His face is freckled and boyish, and when he turns to profile, you see the sharp, prominent nose that gives it a hawklike quality. If the sun is bright, he wears a broad-brimmed Australian tennis hat, a battered, white floppy thing which he tips jauntily over his eyes like a teenager, or presses firmly over his ears like an old lady on a cold and rainy morning. It is immediately clear he loves that hat . . . Indeed the whole image seems strange.'

Asinof declared that great tennis players were supposed to be big, suave and domineering, like Bill Tilden, Budge or Gonzales, and wondered 'What is this little red-haired lefty tyke doing on the same courts with the best professionals in the world?' But then, he went on, 'he starts to [play] and the image shifts. The slight body suddenly becomes a coiled spring, the legs seem exceptionally sturdy, muscular, quick. Above all, there is that left forearm: huge, over-developed, Popeye-like. You become aware of it as soon as he strikes the ball, the whip-like snap that creates an eerie *thwap*! You cannot help but react, he is so fast, so savage, so explosive; your initial derision turns to exultation as you watch him work.' Asinof praised my concentration and 'ease' (that, I might add, was the end result of relentless practise under great coaches over many years), and he noted that I talked to myself during games. '"Be careful!"' he cries out as he overshoots the sideline or smashes an overhead into the top of the net, "Keep the ball up!" He demands perfection on every shot, until finally he hits his proper groove, whipping shots into all corners of the court with marvelous precision, and he compliments himself on his accuracy, "Ah, yes, that's more like it!"'

In October, influential *World Tennis* magazine ranked me No.1 male singles player in the world, with Rochey and Newk second and third. Ken Rosewall, Fred Stolle and Roy Emerson were also named in the top 10. For Australian tennis, those were glory days indeed. If my head swelled up at all the adulation, my father, typically, reduced it to its regular size. Accepting ABC-TV's annual Australian Sportsman of the Year trophy on my behalf, he told the nation on live TV, 'Rodney was always a good tennis player. We used to play on the court at home, but Rodney was not the best then. His two brothers were better!'

Chapter 14

Back to earth

A LET-DOWN WAS ALWAYS POSSIBLE, PERHAPS INEVITABLE, after that incredible 1969. Physically I felt good – for a fellow feeling his way into his 30s – but I knew that I couldn't expect to be as sharp now as I was in my 20s, and I'd developed a nagging back strain to go with my pesky tennis elbow, another sign of the ageing body rebelling against the pressure I was putting it under. Before and after every match I spent a long time under a hot shower to rev up my circulation. And I'm not sure that my mind was as focused on tennis as it had been before the Grand Slam win, and as it needed to be if I was to continue competing at the top level. What I did know was that my head and my heart were with Mary and our baby boy Rick. I was conflicted. I was the breadwinner in our family, and still enjoying my tennis, yet I resented having to spend time away from them. So I compromised.

I fulfilled my professional obligations, and then some, but tried to be on the road a little less than in previous years by playing fewer of the more minor tournaments.

At the start of the new decade there was a restructuring of the professional organisations. Deciding that there was strength – and more money to be made – in numbers, the two pro groups, George MacCall's NTL, my outfit, and Lamar Hunt's WCT, featuring the Handsome Eight, merged in January 1970 under the WCT banner. Combined, we were powerful enough to stand up to the national organisations and the tournament operators who would not pay us what we believed we were worth. Consequently the WCT boycotted the 1970 Australian Open and the French Open because the prize money was too low to make our participation viable. As much as I love Australia and was looking forward to seeing Mum and Dad and my siblings and mates in Queensland, it was good to be able to remain in the United States in January with Mary and Rick.

The WCT guys competed in a year-long winner-take-all 10-City Classic, which was a round robin of 10 tournaments played in 10 US locations from January to September, in between the grand slam and other tournaments, each one offering the winner $10,000. The first 10-City Classic event was at New York's Madison Square Garden and my opponent was Pancho Gonzales. Incredibly, at age 41, he was still one of the world's best players, as he proved yet again against me. Nearly 15,000 fans packed into the Garden to see us duke it out. When he beat me, the crowd went crazy. Pancho had played to the gallery all match, using their desire to see him win as fuel to drive him on. At one stage he was so pumped up he was bellowing his own name, 'Ricardo!' I was bitterly disappointed to lose, but had nothing but admiration for Pancho, who continued to defy Father Time. As I shook his hand, my Grand Slam seemed a long time ago.

In February we played in an International Tennis Players Association tournament at the Spectrum arena in Philadelphia. Unlike the Australian and French opens, the prize money was healthy, totalling $57,500, with $10,000 for the winner. Some 64 players took part. After the organisers announced that the matches would be played under VASSS rules with its new tie-breaker system, the International Lawn Tennis Federation (ILTF) stepped in and told them they could not play under those rules. We thumbed our noses and went right ahead and used the tie breaker anyway. Unlike some of the competitors, I'd played under the VASSS system before in the pre-open era, and I proceeded to beat Graham Stilwell of Great Britain, Emmo, the curmudgeonly Romanian Ilie Nastase (aka 'Nasty' or 'The Bucharest Buffoon'), Dennis Ralston and Tony Roche to pocket the 10 grand. Between then and Wimbledon, I played in tournaments in Hollywood, Florida, Maryland, Los Angeles, London's Royal Albert Hall and Sydney's White City, where I beat Muscles Rosewall in a tough five sets in the final of the Dunlop Open, as well as Brisbane and Johannesburg. The *Australian* newspaper's veteran sports writer Pat Farrell was in the crowd and liked what he saw. He wrote that in his view, tennis, played the Rosewall–Laver way, was the greatest sports show on the planet. 'Wherever have you seen such shots as Laver played . . . that booming smash in the fourth set, hit when he was actually toppling over backwards, yet untouchable when it flashed past Rosewall? Or that stunning return of a Rosewall volley in the fifth, crawling on his knees and one elbow, yet was able to belt it back for a winner?'

He reckoned that my win was made even more special because I was having an off day, my game 'a tattered, dishevelled mess of errors'. Always a stickler for on-court good behaviour, Farrell praised my calm and observed: 'There is none of the shrieking, jabbering, sweating tennis galoot about Laver. When things aren't going well for him, it seems our wonderful rusty Rocket simply tells himself: "I'm supposed to be a champion. Better knuckle down and prove it."' Well, Pat, that was no more than the Australian way of playing tennis that Harry Hopman and Charlie Hollis had drummed into me and a generation of my peers.

Pat thought that Ken had me beat when I lost the third set, and for the first time since he had been watching me I would end the match on the losing end, but he said that I had dug deeply into the 'bottomless of power' and snatched victory from defeat at the last minute.

Farrell, justifiably, raved about Rosewall and, alluding to how he had prevented his friend and doubles partner Lew Hoad from winning his Grand Slam, called him 'That methodical little thwarter of the great' and noted that he too dug deeply into his reserves of professionalism, skill and courage to try to overcome me. 'He was such an efficient machine that, in the break, he looked insuperable, with his placements, his returns, his unbelievably true handling of the game. He was going to win, as sure as sunrise. And nobody knew it better than Laver. But the first thing Laver did, when they resumed, was the thing that great professionals do when things are at their worst. He refused to go defensive, eschewed safety. He attacked Rosewall as though he was the man whose game was good, who had things going for him, who had not a thought in the world except that this was his championship to win and that he was the only man in the world who could win it.'

Pat ended by saying that he had always thought that nobody having a below-par day could ever beat Ken Rosewall, but he now realised that somebody who refused to countenance defeat always had a chance. '[Laver] stayed there, trying one unbelievable thing after another until [he] overwhelmed Rosewall and left him ragged and as woebegone as Laver should have been himself.'

Another excellent Australian sports writer, Mike Gibson of Sydney's *Daily Telegraph*, wrote that the Dunlop International final harked back to the grand days when John Bromwich and Charlie Hollis' hero 'Gentleman' Jack Crawford were in their prime: 'days when tennis meant guile and rallies and skill. It was a match that showed a lot of us a game we'd almost forgotten. It showed a lot of young people a game they never knew existed. It took us back to the days when baselines grew thin and worn from players running from one side to the other on them instead of just taking off from behind them after their services, like athletes from the blocks. It was a pity there had to be a loser . . .'

The Dunlop Open hosted a 'Rod Laver Day' when fans were admitted free to White City to see me play an exhibition match against Newk, and Pancho played Frank Sedgman in a double bill, and there was a ceremony commemorating my dual Grand Slam. I was interviewed by *The Sydney Morning Herald*'s Alan Clarkson and told him how I had travelled more than 100,000 miles in 1969 playing tennis for 38 weeks of the year, and how I was trying now to wind back that schedule. 'I'm not at home nearly as often as I'd like to be. I have a son, Ricky, five months old now, and it's murder being away so much.' Clarkson provided his readers with the following snapshot of me: 'Laver as a person is relatively unchanged. He's still as Australian as the slouch hat, with not a trace of that easy-to-acquire American accent some of our world-travelling sportsmen seem to adopt.' It was good to read Alan's words, because I was proud to be Australian and tired of forever having to defend myself about living in America. The fact, then as now, is that America is where my family and business interests are.

Mary left Rick with her daughter Ann Marie and her husband Kipp Bennett and joined me in South Africa, and after the event we flew to Australia to see the clan and fish off Heron Island. Then it was back to the US for tournaments in Dallas and Dayton, Ohio, and then Las Vegas in mid-May for the Howard Hughes Pro Invitation Tournament. I was hoping to meet the reclusive billionaire. Unfortunately he didn't emerge from his hideaway on the eighth floor of the Desert

Sands Hotel. I'm certain our paths did not cross . . . unless he showed up in disguise at the tournament that bore his name. Fittingly, the prize money was considerable. In fact, at $17,500 for the winner, at the time it was the richest purse ever offered for a four-day event. I managed to beat the unconventional South African Ray Moore, Fred Stolle and Emmo to book a place in the final against Pancho. He beat me in four sets and consigned me to the runner-up's cheque of $7500. If anything, I thought again, Gonzales was improving with age . . . or could it be that I was not quite as good as I once was? It was reassuring then when, straight after the Howard Hughes, I downed Tony Roche in a 10-City Classic match and banked the $10,000 winner's cheque.

Once all the 10-City Classic matches had been played, the four most successful players faced off in semi finals at Madison Square Garden in June, the two winners to meet in the final in September. I was drawn to play Pancho Gonzales in one semi and Ken Rosewall would oppose Roy Emerson in the other. I avenged my recent defeats at Pancho's hands by beating the charisma machine in three sets, 6–3, 6–3, 6–1. Muscles downed Emmo in five to book a date with me in the final, after Wimbledon and before the US Open.

That 10-City Classic semi wasn't all I won in June 1970. The Queen awarded me the Member of the Order of the British Empire for services to tennis. Gee, I thought, how wonderful to win such an exalted gong simply by playing tennis, doing something I loved, something that was the only thing I *could* do. Other Australians honoured were former test cricket wicketkeeper Bert Oldfield, country singer Slim Dusty, Australian Ballet director Peggy van Praagh and composer Peter Sculthorpe – rather exalted company to hobnob in, if I do say so myself. My tennis commitments prevented me from being in London for the investiture.

While there had been no Australian or French Open for the tennis professionals that year, we all converged on London for strawberries and cream and wonderful Wimbledon in July. I was in good form at the Queen's Club tournament in the lead-up, and beat Newk in the final. Before my first Wimbledon match I told reporter Jim Webster, 'If I lose, I lose, but I'm not going to go down without a damn good swing at it. It's a great tennis tournament and has such great atmosphere. Some players seem to be afraid of the place. They've heard so much about Wimbledon – people saying, "You've got to do well here" – and they get so nervous they can't do well. I like the pressure. I've certainly never felt stronger at any time in my life than I do at this moment.'

I made it through to the fourth round without too many hassles, and that's when I came to a dead halt. Englishman Roger Taylor was a fighter – as Bob Hewitt had discovered to his cost when he came off second best in their locker-room altercation. Thankfully, with me, Roger confined his combativeness to the tennis court, and in our match he won convincingly and KO'd me from the tournament. At match point, I was serving . . . and I clunked those two balls straight into the net. What an underwhelming way to go! This was the earliest I had bowed out of Wimbledon since 1958. In fact, I had made the Wimbledon final six years in a row. Taylor was in turn eliminated by Ken Rosewall in the semi final, and Kenny was himself dispatched in the final by John Newcombe.

Having scaled the Mt Everest of tennis the year before, after Wimbledon I again began to wonder whether I had lost my drive to be the very best. My comparatively lack-lustre results in 1970 were speaking volumes. I'd had some excellent wins that year, and in some of those matches my form was very good, yet I knew that an edge had gone from my game and I was being beaten by fellows I once could have accounted for. After I bowed out at Wimbledon, Mary put my loss in perspective when she told reporters after my earlier than usual elimination, 'Well, at least now we can go out and enjoy ourselves!' And that's exactly what we did.

Consolation for bowing out at Wimbledon came in the final of the 10-City Classic tournament at Madison Square Garden when I played Muscles Rosewall and overpowered him in straight sets to take home the $35,000 prize money. Certainly the 10,000-strong crowd seemed to enjoy the contest if the frequent standing ovations they gave us throughout the match can be taken as an indication.

I saddled up for the US Open after wins in the National Tennis Classic in Louisville, Kentucky (downing Newk in the final), the Rothmans Canadian Open in Toronto (when, in the final, I avenged my Wimbledon loss to Roger Taylor), and the Fort Worth Pros event. Emmo and I had also registered some good performances as a doubles team. All of which augured well for the US Open.

What do they say about best-laid plans? At Forest Hills,

I exited in the fourth round, just as I had at Wimbledon. Talk about a let-down. In 1969 I had won all four major tournaments, in 1970 I won none. The only positive thing I can find to say about that US Open, apart from my solid wins over Australians Allan Stone and Ashley Cooper in the early rounds, was that I was beaten by a bloke in career-best form. Dennis Ralston had always been a top class player, quick, strong and with a fine array of shots. His Achilles heel was that he could lose heart when faced with stiff opposition. In our past matches I knew that sustaining pressure on Denny would lead to victory. Not this time.

I started fast and went to 5–1 in the first set. Normally this is when Denny would have wilted. That day he surged back to 6–6 then won the tie breaker and the first set. His countrymen in the stands whooped with joy. The second set was close as well, and again Dennis was stronger and won it 7–5. I reached for my blowtorch and applied it to Dennis' belly. I kept telling myself that if I could dent his confidence he'd crumble. I won the third and fourth sets to make it two sets all, and had no reason to think I wouldn't win the deciding fifth.

Ralston had other ideas. He went up a gear, and this time it was me who faded. On a break point against Denny in the fifth set, I hit a forehand return, placing it perfectly, right on his toes. Calm as you like, he deftly scooped it up and dealt me a backhand half volley that won him the point. He won the set 7–5, and I was going home. If I hadn't been a victim of it, I would have enjoyed watching this man who had always doubted himself discover self-belief. After the match,

Dennis commented perceptively: 'I don't think losing at Wimbledon and here means the Rocket has slipped . . . but I don't think he or anybody else can dominate the world like he did in 1969. It was improbable that he'd win the Grand Slam again. With everybody playing for money and the number of good players increasing, it's a whole new world.'

Dennis had a good point, as the results in 1970 proved. The top 15 tournaments were won by nine different men. I won the Philadelphia Indoor Open, the Dunlop Open in Sydney, the South African Open, the Pacific Southwest Open and the Embassy Indoor Open in London; Arthur Ashe won the Australian Open and the Paris Indoor Open; the US Indoor Open and the Italian Open were taken out by the wild man Ilie Nastase; Jan Kodes won the French Open; Newk won Wimbledon; Rochey triumphed at the US Pro; the West German Open was won by the consistent Tom Okker; Kenny Rosewall was a popular winner (at age 35) of the US Open; and Stan Smith won the Stockholm Indoor Open. The variety of winners made tennis more exciting. Fans knew that any of us could beat anyone else if the stars aligned correctly. Dennis Ralston might have been right when he said that it was unlikely that anyone would win another Grand Slam. By the same token, people once said man would never walk on the moon or climb Mount Everest. The seemingly impossible has a certain allure.

At Forest Hills in the doubles, Emmo and I won through to the final, only to be ousted by Croatia's Niki Pilic and Pierre Barthes of France. At the presentation ceremony, Charlie Tucker, president of Forest Hills' West Side Tennis

Club, presented Niki and Pierre with a cheque for $1500 and a gold ball trophy, then turned to Emmo and me and gave us a couple of silver balls and the consolation prize of $1000. Perhaps the loss rankled more than I thought, because Emmo saw me looking glum and, beaming one of his huge gold-toothed grins, told me to buck up because, '. . . at least they didn't give us a kick in the arse'. That was true.

For all that 1970 didn't reach the heights of previous years and I slipped to No.4 in the world rankings, behind Newk, Muscles and Rochey, I fared well financially. In winning five of the 15 major pro events, I banked $201,453 prize money, more than anyone else on the circuit, and sponsors seemed unperturbed that I had failed to win a grand slam tournament and continued to pay me to endorse their products. With Mary keeping her eagle eye on the finances, Roy Emerson and I established a series of adult tennis holiday camps in the United States under the Laver–Emerson Tennis (LET) banner. Our first was at the Mount Washington Hotel in Bretton Woods, New Hampshire, a prestigious venue that in 1944 hosted the United Nations Monetary and Financial Conference where delegates from 44 nations established the World Bank and the International Monetary Fund.

My healthy bank balance allowed Mary and me to buy a beachside home in our southern California neighbourhood. After we did, we had serious second thoughts because we began to fear that little Rick would make his way down to the water, so we sold the house and bought another further back from the beach with a safe path to the shore.

With her talent for architecture and decoration, Mary supervised the renovations. Knowing the tragic statistics of youngsters drowning in home swimming pools, Mary and I insisted on draining the water from our backyard pool. For good measure we cracked the bottom of the pool and planted a tree in the fissure. Anyway, who needed a pool when we could walk to the surf? The sight of our 'swimming pool' always made Fred Stolle laugh when he came to visit.

A few years later we bought a home in the neighbouring Newport Beach Back Bay area and had a 14-metre slipway built out into the water at the back to accommodate my 20-foot (6.1-metre) Skipjack fishing boat and, later, a 35-foot (10.5-metre) Egg Harbor fibreglass cruiser I called *Aussie 1*. Mary, Rick, Mary's children and I loved to fish, and sometimes friends joined us to dangle a line over the side. At times it was not hard to pretend that I was back out on the Great Barrier Reef off Heron Island or on the Fitzroy River with my father and brothers in the olden, golden days of the '40s and '50s. Off the coast we caught yellowtail, albacore and dorado, and we enjoyed idyllic weekend picnic excursions out to Catalina Island 35 kilometres off the coast.

We had some of our happiest times then. It was magical watching Rick turn from a baby to a toddler to a strapping boy. I taught him to run and throw and catch and swim, just as my father had taught me. And Mary and I were deeply in love and we cherished every moment we had together. I was still playing tennis all over the world, even if I wasn't absent as much as before, and Mary threw herself into her investing and her art appreciation, and skied on the long powder-snow runs at Aspen and Deer Valley. Life was blissful. After all those years as a tennis gypsy, it was good to have roots, to love and be loved.

Mary was an accomplished hostess and when we were both at home together we had a procession of pals for dinner. Regular guests included Roy and Joy Emerson, and Charlton Heston and his wife Lydia, actor Chad Everett and his wife Shelby, and TV star James Franciscus. Chad and his daughters Shannon and Katherine often played with Rick, and the fun those kids had riding their green machine tricycles is captured in our photo albums. Another friend was the singer and pianist Buddy Greco. We'd played golf together, including in a celebrity event with Sean Connery, South African golf champion Bobby Locke and *Dracula* star Christopher Lee at Royal Troon Golf Club in Scotland, where we got into strife with officialdom for playing outside our allotted time. Buddy liked to say he never played tennis against me. 'I'll play tennis with Rocket when he gets up on stage and plays piano with me.' I told him he'd be waiting a long, long time.

Chuck Heston, Jim Franciscus and Lloyd Bridges were all keen tennis players, and celebrity tennis days in Holly-wood, often for charity, when pro players teamed with a star, were regularly on our calendar. I played with and against the hilarious Bill Cosby, singer Dinah Shore, TV talk-show host Johnny Carson, the singer Ed Ames, and Wayne Rogers from TV's *M*A*S*H*. On the scene were my childhood movie idol, John 'Duke' Wayne, Frank Sinatra's wife Barbara, movie Tarzan Ron Ely, who liked to carry Rick around on his massive shoulders, the singer Steve Lawrence, Gilbert Roland, Efrem Zimbalist Jr and Vice-President Spiro Agnew, whose aim in tennis was every bit as bad as it notoriously was in golf. He once slammed the ball into the back of his own doubles partner, Dinah Shore. Mary played with Spiro a lot and somehow escaped that fate. She and Spiro hit it off well. The Vice-President invited me and Fred and Pat Stolle to visit the White House and we played on the presidential tennis court.

John Wayne lived with his wife Pilar and their kids at Newport Beach. He was more a bridge and gin rummy man than a tennis player. He showed up to the celebrity tennis events and was just one of the gang. John invited Mary and me, and the Rosewalls and Hoads, to his home. As an esteemed member of the Academy of Motion Picture Arts and Sciences, he was sent advance prints of movies before they were released to the public and he hosted movie nights. We saw a lot of westerns and war pictures. I could never bring myself to tell him what a fan of his I had always been and how his cowboy adventures had brought us kids to our feet in that open air cinema in far-off and long-ago Rockhampton. There is a connection between Hollywood and tennis, going way back to when Clark Gable and Bill Tilden were friends. When we were in Los Angeles the stars often invited us to go to MGM or Fox to see a movie being shot.

The celebrity tennis matches raised thousands for charities and there was always a worthy community project to embrace. My friend and best man Kevin Sullivan had ties – purely professional, I hasten to add – with Los Angeles' Chino Prison and Kevin, Mal Anderson and Chuck Heston and I ventured behind bars to play exhibition matches for the inmates. Chuck quipped that he'd never had such a captive audience.

Chapter 15

Money-go-round

MY RUN OF OUTS AT WIMBLEDON CONTINUED IN 1971 WHEN Tom Gorman of the United States, who only the week before had seen me off in a quarter final of the Queen's Club event, vanquished me in straight sets in the Wimbledon quarter finals. Fleet Street was quick off the mark with their obituaries. '[Laver's defeat] resembled a condemned man's walk to the scaffold,' was *The Guardian*'s. 'There was a spell just short of two hours in the Wimbledon championships which marked, I think, the end of a lawn tennis era – Rod Laver conceded his status as the master player of the world,' opined Lance Tingay in the *Telegraph*. To the *Daily Mirror*, my loss seemed to herald the end of the world: 'Everything at Wimbledon paled into insignificance beside the fact that Rod Laver, four times winner of the men's title, was completely, comprehensively, and

crushingly beaten in the quarter finals by Tom Gorman.'
Ouch. As far as I was concerned, the media's reports of my
demise were, as Mark Twain once said, greatly exaggerated.

In July 1971 there was another bust-up between the
International Lawn Tennis Federation and WCT, which
had the 32 top pros on its books. The contretemps was over
our boss Lamar Hunt's insistence that, as well as receiving
prize money, we be paid appearance money for playing at
Federation events, and the ILTF dug in its heels and told
Lamar that in 1972 his players would not be welcome at the
Australian and French opens or at Wimbledon. (The US
Open organisers defied the ILTF ban.) Lamar's response
was, 'Fine. We'll play in our own tournaments.' Some of
us were unhappy at being barred from the grand slam
tournaments, yet we all believed we should stick solid with
our group. So with three of the Big Four tournaments off
limits, I had no choice but to devote my energy to giving a
good account of myself at pro events.

The match I was proudest of in '71 was the final of the
WCT's 20-tournament World Championship of Tennis
event, supposedly to determine the world's best professional player. My opponent was Ken Rosewall and our big
showdown was held at the Dallas Memorial Auditorium
on 27 November. The winner would take home $50,000, a
Triumph Spitfire sports car, a gleaming gold trophy and, to
keep his better half happy, a gold ladies ring and matching
pendant. The loser would pocket $20,000. I'd had the
wood on Muscles in recent times, yet he was never less
than a lethal opponent. We reminisced before the match

on the rocky road we had travelled together as despised pros and then in the open era. We had gone from being kings to outlaws and now here we were, kings once more. We made more memories for our mental scrapbooks in our match.

Mary was there to see the final, having left Rick at our home with a wonderful French governess we'd employed. By now, with colour television replacing the old black and white sets, professional tennis players wore coloured clothing so we could be more easily distinguished by viewers. I usually wore pale blue shorts and a collared polo shirt, but for this match Kenny had bagsed blue and left me having to don yellow. I went onto the court looking, Mary guffawed, like the Yellow Rose of Texas.

The match exploded from the first serve. Ken, playing superbly, better than he had in years, won the first set 6–4. I roared back at him and wiped him off the court in the second set, 6–1. In the third set, Kenny hit a ball that flew off the rim of his racquet and shot like a bullet into his eye, temporarily blinding him. Forgetting the lesson about killer instinct I'd learned so many years earlier when Manuel Santana twisted his ankle and rewarded my sympathy and suggestion that he take his time to recover by doing exactly that and then fighting back to beat me, I rushed over solicitously to comfort my great mate Ken. Of course it was fine to give Ken time to recuperate, I said when the umpire asked if that would be okay. I should have tried to whack Muscles in the other eye! In the seventh game of the third set I found myself in the cushy position of having five break points on Ken's serve, but the wily old fella held his serve, and his nerve, to win 7–6 on a tie breaker. In the next set, the fourth, Kenny broke my serve twice and shot to a 3–0 lead but I found it in me to fight back to take it to 6–6 and yet another tie breaker. I lost that tie breaker 7–4 and the set 7–6. The $50,000, the car, the trophy, the ring, the pendant and the mantle of World Champion were all Ken's, and to make it even more special, the loot was presented to Kenny, celebrating his 20th year as one of the world's finest ever players, by Neil Armstrong, the first man ever to walk on the moon.

Ken was interviewed by *Sports Illustrated* magazine and asked to assess my style. He said this: 'He's exceptional, he's unorthodox and he's someone you couldn't copy. As a champion, his performances and court temperament could be held up as a fine model for younger players. But his playing style certainly couldn't be, because he has shots that few other players can produce. I don't know quite how he does them myself, but it's those wristy strokes of his that win.' Muscles offered that I had so much power in my left forearm that it obviously gave me a feeling of strength and confidence to play those unorthodox shots. Lefties, he went on, were generally expected to have a weakness in their backhands, but that was a weakness I didn't have. 'And the strength of his shots. Very few players on the defensive, or when running to make a recovery shot, can play as power-fully or as quickly as Rod.'

Praise from a master is praise indeed.

I made myself unavailable for the US Open in '71 because, frankly, I was worried about my patchy form of recent months, and thought a little time away from the game would serve me well, let me get my head together, find my rhythm and work on any kinks in my game. My back was playing up too, and I wanted to give it a break. I was also feeling pressure from the media. I suppose my achievements in 1969 had allowed the press to portray me as invincible. I became a bit of a tall poppy and consequently, while other blokes could lose a match and fly under the radar, every time I was beaten, it was big news. Definitely not helping my game, in the United States at least, was having to play with Chemold aluminium racquets. My deal with Chemold, to use their racquets in the US, had just been renegotiated. I kept it very quiet of course, but a couple of times in big matches, I used a Dunlop racquet that I'd disguised as a Chemold.

The catalyst for me withdrawing from the US Open and taking time out from tennis to mend my spirit and a bad back that was seriously hampering me was another loss to Roger Taylor, 7–6, 6–1, during which I, in most uncharacteristic fashion, threw down my racquet and, Pancho-like, smashed two balls high out of the court. Emmo and Newk, always honest and concerned for my welfare, attributed my run of sub-par form to my being tired and lacking confidence, and for so long dealing with the pressure of being No.1. I had a long talk to Emmo, who told me, 'You've got to get out of here, and have a rest from tennis. You'd be stupid to play Forest Hills if you're not mentally prepared. Your game won't be worth a razoo if you continue on now.' According to Newk, 'It's mental. I think Rod's in a transition period when he has to come to grips with reality, as Kenny Rosewall has. He's not over the hill at 33. It's just that he's not going to win every week like he did two years ago. But he still expects to. There are 10 guys in the world, including me, who are much better than we were in 1969, but there's no way Rod can be better.'

I was keeping quiet about my crook back, not wanting to give my opponents ammunition. I was faring badly enough without doing that. Tony Roche, however, knew the score, and told reporters puzzling over my form lapse, 'His back injury is affecting him. He doesn't appear to be walking properly and he needs to warm up for a long time before he can play. That is why he is such a slow starter in his matches and often loses in the early sets – particularly if he hasn't warmed up properly.' Rochey didn't think that Father Time had finally run me down. 'He hasn't been going too well but he hasn't lost anything. If anything, the other players have improved and are now much closer to him. They don't get as over-awed when they play him now. Once upon a time, the players would be psyched out of it before they went on against Rod.'

In January and February 1972, the designated top 12 guys in WCT played each other in what Lamar Hunt called the Tennis Champions Classic, which was an 'around-the-clock' style novelty tournament, organised by Fred Podesta, that offered potentially the richest prize in tennis history. Here's how it worked. Each player was given a number from 1 to 12. Ken Rosewall and I were numbers 1 and 2. We would play each other in the first event, to be held at

Madison Square Garden, and whoever won would receive $10,000, the loser nothing. The winner then moved on to another city to face player number 3, and the victor would take his $10,000 prize money and proceed to the next city to go up against number 4 and so on until all 12 players had competed. The players ranked most highly had the chance to make the most money – $160,000 if either Muscles or I won all 11 matches, plus semi final and final money – than the lower ranked fellows, because we had the opportunity to play more matches, although the losing high ranked players would come away with nothing, of course. So while the Tennis Champions Classic could not compete with the French Open or Wimbledon in prestige and world renown, it sure offered bigger bikkies.

As great a player as Kenny was, he hadn't beaten me in a big event since 1968, so my confidence was high. As it turned out, justifiably so, because in front of a healthy crowd at Madison Square Garden I beat him in three sets. Ten grand down, $100,000 to go. I then downed Newk, who was ranked number 3, in Rochester, New York, then Rochey in Boston, Emmo in Philadelphia, Arthur Ashe at Madison Square Garden to the cheers of 10,000 pro-Ashe New Yorkers, Tom Okker in Detroit, Roger Taylor in Englewood, California . . . I was enjoying this novel concept and kept winning match after match until, at the end of the round robin in February, I had stashed away every available cent of the prize money, $110,000 from 11 matches, while everyone else's coffers were empty. I added $50,000 to that sum when I beat Dennis Ralston in the semi and Tom Okker in the final. My fellow pros would have been well within their rights to mug me. To their credit, they didn't . . . they just made me buy the beers. I could have reminded the guys about all the taxes on earnings I'd saved them from having to pay, but wisely kept my mouth shut.

Although neither of us were spring chickens anymore – in 1972 I would turn 34 and Ken Rosewall 38 – if anything our rivalry intensified. We had another spirited match in the final of the US Pro Indoors at the Spectrum in Philadelphia in February '72. Ken had just arrived back in the US after downing Mal Anderson in straight sets in the final of the Australian Open, giving him his 18th career grand slam title and his fourth Australian singles title. He was, needless to say, in brilliant form, and I was feeling fresh too after my long Christmas break. I had opted to miss the Australian Open so I could be at home with Mary and Rick, and had overcome three fine players in Tony Roche, Bob Lutz of the United States and Tom Okker in the US Pro Indoors lead-up matches. In the final, Ken overwhelmed me early and I regrouped, played percentage tennis to get back into the match, then hit him with everything, including the kitchen sink, to win the encounter 4–6, 6–2, 6–2, 6–2. That year I also managed to vanquish the great Muscles in the final of the Rothmans International in Toronto and the River Oaks tournament in Houston, Texas. I did not fare as well against some of the other champions, and in various other pro tournaments I fell to Marty Riessen and Cliff Richey of the United States, Tony Roche, and the up-and-coming young Australians Ray Ruffels and John Alexander.

I did make it back Down Under in February to take part in the Dunlop Open at White City courts where that little English thorn-in-my-side Mark Cox bundled me out in the third round. Mark had thought so little of his chances against me that he booked himself out of Sydney on a flight leaving next morning, and played the whole match in a long-sleeved sweater because he didn't think he'd be on the court long enough to get warm. He was terrific against me that night, and showed what a gent he was in the post-match interview when he said, 'I was bloody lucky to win. If I was playing at my top and Laver was playing at his, then the result would be about 6–2, 6–1, 6–2.' Mark Cox was a much better player than he gave himself credit for.

There was a lovely sojourn back in the United States in March when Mum and Dad, now both noticeably frailer than when I'd last seen them just a year earlier, came to stay with us for seven weeks, and just as they had shown Mary the delights of tropical north Queensland when she went Down Under, so now Mary was a willing and knowledgeable tour guide for them when they were on her home turf. They had grins a mile wide when they first laid eyes on Rick. This holiday was my parents' only time away from Australia in their entire lives, and their grand tour continued in Italy when I paid their airfare to Rome to watch me play, and win, the Italian Open.

My age-old rivalry with Roy Emerson nearly came to a literally electrifying end while we were teaming in the doubles at the Colonial Pros in Fort Worth, Texas. After washing his shirt and shorts in the bath in his motel room, he touched a metal towel rack that was in contact with live electrical wires. The electric shock Roy received sent him flying back into the bathwater. Thank God the lethal electrified towel rack didn't follow him in.

The most memorable match I played in 1972 was on 15 May against, you guessed it, Ken Rosewall. The WCT season was not contested in a calendar year, and the 1971–72 season wound up in mid-'72 when the eight leading WCT players did battle for $50,000 prize money. Muscles and I won our way to the final at the Moody Coliseum in Dallas, Texas. The place was packed for what was being called 'The Rod and Kenny Show'. The event was staged magnificently with a United States marine hoisting the Australian flag in our honour and a lone trumpeter sounding 'Advance Australia Fair'. To say that Ken and I were emotional is an understatement and we were always going to give that match everything we had. I won the first set, and Ken won the next two (in the second set he demolished me 6–0, and that had *never* happened to me). I levelled matters by taking the fourth set in a tie breaker. The final set was perhaps the hardest fought of all. I had him at my mercy leading 5–4 in the tie breaker, but the little marvel, though dead on his feet, pulled out two magnificent, bordering on supernatural, returns to turn the tables. He won the match 4–6, 6–0, 6–3, 6–7, 7–6, and as we left the court exhausted and shattered, we saluted that extraordinarily generous crowd. It didn't matter that no American contested the final. They had witnessed a classic match, and they knew it.

There had been skill, power, speed, and tactical twists and turns on display. Despite the high stakes and our absolute determination to win, our sportsmanship was impeccable. Kenny, never an emotional guy, wept in the locker room and was so overcome that he left his winner's cheque in the change room. *That* will give you an idea just how moved Kenny was.

Looking back on it, that match had it all: a major title was on the line, we both recovered from seemingly hopeless positions, there was spectacular shot-making, Alfred Hitchcock-like suspense and high tension, big money at stake and a cliffhanger finish. I had to save a match point to put myself in a position to win, and I did that, then Kenny took the match, the 50 grand and all the baubles right out of my hand as brutally as any Central Park mugger. I don't think I've ever been so disappointed after a loss as after that match. I wanted to win very badly.

When I wrote my book *The Education of a Tennis Player*, with Bud Collins, the match was still fresh in my mind. I would like to reprint here what I wrote then – I don't think I can improve upon it, especially as so many years have passed by – to capture the drama of the match and give you a sense of the impact it had on Muscles and me:

All I can say about that incredible final was it took so many twists that I still can't understand how I lost. Two points. I never came so close and lost. But I had my chances and that's all you can ask. I had the serve at 5 points to 4 in the decisive tie-breaker. The odds had switched dramatically to me. I had to win it. I looked at him and he couldn't stand up. Nobody was going to beat me now, after I'd been down 0–3 in the fifth, after I'd saved four break points in the next game to avoid 0–4, and after I'd zinged an ace on match point against me 4–5. I couldn't lose it now. I wouldn't.

And I did. Or, rather, he beat me, that bloody thief, Rosewall.

It had been a shot-making feast throughout, for more than three and a half hours, but after all the sprints and swings and skids I had him. I can tell you the three swings of mine that I regret the most. They came in the tie-breaker with me ahead 3–1. I jerked him out of position and whacked a forehand down the line that nobody could have touched. The tape interfered, and the ball dropped back on my side. Just a fraction higher, and it would have been 4–1. Then I double-faulted. Instead of maybe 5–1, it was 3–3.

Never mind, I told myself, and I got two of the next three to 5–4 with serve. Two points to the championship – and my serve. Great. Concentrate. I was going to go for Ken's backhand corner. Yes, don't tell me – I know all about that backhand. But this time I'd slice it wide and clean him out of the court. He just couldn't move any more to get back in position.

Surprise. He didn't have to move. Terrific serve . . . only the return was even more terrific, a cross-court angle that I'd never seen even from Kenny. I probed to make the half-volley, reached the ball but couldn't control it. Anything over the net would have got me the point with him sagging so badly, but my half-volley went long. It's 5–5.

One more serve and I knew I could outlast him, even if he could carry me to 6–6. He was absolutely dead, and I felt great. Another serve to the backhand corner, and this was Kenny's last stab. Zoom, the ball went down the line and I was passed with plenty to spare. My edge was gone, just like that.

His serve at 6–5, match point. Could he lift the ball to serve it? Didn't much matter. I was glassy over those backhands, and I hardly noticed that he floated a serve over the net. I waved at it with a backhand and tapped it into the net. 'I can't lose,' registered in my mind. 'How . . .'

Kenny was so bushed he didn't make sense in the TV interview . . . They say he was cold and emotion-less, but in the dressing room, he broke down and cried. I wanted to, but I still couldn't believe it.

It's our match forever – his win, but our match – and I feel people will keep talking about it. I won't discourage them.

Tennis pundit Gene Ward, in his column in the New York *Daily News*, praised our three hour and thirty-four minute epic as 'the greatest tennis match ever played'. I was grateful for Gene's words, but I'm sure that Muscles and I, over the course of our long rivalry, played matches that were as good, or very nearly so. We always brought out the best in each other. Next day the television ratings were reported and 21.3 million viewers on 170 NBC network stations had tuned in to the match. There had been high drama when the NBC broadcasters, who just happened to be my friend Bud Collins and Jim Simpson, received an order from NBC-TV headquarters in New York that because it was clear that the Rod and Kenny show would run overtime, coverage of our match would cease at 6pm so the Sunday night news broadcast could go to air at the usual time. Thankfully, as the compelling play unfolded and the NBC hierarchy received feedback that the telecast was rating through the roof and that millions of excited viewers were on the edge of their seats and would be furious if the match was blacked out, they thought again, and the message came through to Bud and Jim: 'Keep going, fellas – we're on to the end!' It was a good decision, for we out-drew the pro basketball and hockey playoffs. Tennis outrating hockey and basketball? That would never have happened just a few years earlier. I'll always believe that if a single match can lay claim to putting tennis on the map in America as an elite spectator sport, that one was it. Tennis could have had no better promotional vehicle. I know the match made me better known than I had ever been. To this day, I still get a little misty-eyed to think I was a part of it, and I'm pretty sure Muscles does too.

The pressure was released in the nicest possible way in July when, in a celebrity match that was part of the

St Louis, Missouri, Holton Classic, the first tournament of the new WCT season in July, I teamed with Charlton Heston to play against Newk and James Franciscus in a doubles match. I think we won. I know we had fun. Jimmy, who played a blind insurance investigator in his television series *Longstreet*, wasn't seeing the ball too well that day, and I'm certain that Chuck, one of whose greatest roles was Moses in *The Ten Commandments*, called on divine intervention to get us home.

Later that month, at the US Pro championships at the Longwood Cricket Club in Boston, I was not seeded in the top 12 players, and this was a first for me. Muscles missed out too. It seemed that we were on the down elevator, while younger men in Newk, Bob Lutz, Cliff Richey, Arthur Ashe (whom I'd beaten 18 times in a row), Marty Riessen, Cliff Drysdale and Tom Okker were now vying for the top tennis spots. Bob Lutz beat me 6–4, 6–4 in the quarter finals. The only good thing about that tournament was it ended just days before the Longwood Cricket Club, which had played such an important role in the rich history of American tennis, was battered by a tornado. Much of the surrounding district was demolished, with houses obliterated and large trees uprooted from the ground. The awesome winds plucked a backyard swimming pool from its foundations and hurled it into the air. It landed six metres away on top of a teenage girl, killing her.

The only grand slam tournament I played in 1972 was the US Open – the ILTF and WCT had buried the

hatchet after Wimbledon, WCT spokesman George Pharr
intoning, 'We have reached agreement for the good of
the game, for the good of the players and for the good of the
public' – and this too, for me at least, proved a tournament
best forgotten. It all began well, when I had easy wins over
lower ranked players John Parish and Butch Seewagen,
then I struggled to eliminate Jaime Fillol, who took me to
five sets. In the fourth round, a round that was becoming
a bit of a hoodoo round for me, I felt a sharp pain in my
back and knew I had exacerbated the injury that had been
dogging me for months. I won the first set against Dennis
Ralston, but with the stabbing pain in my back restricting
me, I lost the next three. I took a month off and underwent
rehab, returned before the injury had healed, and was
thrashed by little-known Ismael El Shafei in the Rothmans
International in Canada in December. I didn't play again
in '72. At year's end, having won five pro tournaments
and $100,200 prize money, I was rated the fourth best
WCT player.

I am nothing if not a realist, and in late 1972 as my losses
racked up against blokes I'd usually beaten in past years,
I realised that at 34 my powers really were on the wane.
Age takes its toll on speed, power and stamina. No doubt
as a result of getting older and the strain I had placed on it
over three decades of tennis, I was still experiencing pain in
my back. I had no intention of retiring, so realised I would
have to use my wiles accumulated over so many years to
compensate for my physical failings.

I was also contending with some welcome distractions. I had immersed myself in family life. Being a husband and father was a deeply rewarding experience. And Emmo's and my tennis camps were going great guns. We had just opened a fine camp at the Mount Washington Hotel in the idyllic alpine village of Bretton Woods in New Hampshire, New England. Mary, Rick and I lived-in at the hotel-resort for the summer. Each week Roy and I put 48 players of all levels through their tennis paces. It was fun, and it was profitable. We staged the Bretton Woods International tournament at the resort, and it was a sign of the times that I couldn't even win my own tournament! I was eliminated in the quarter finals by Cliff Richey.

In 1972 I became the first tennis millionaire when WCT press agent Ron Bookman announced right after I beat Arthur Ashe in a match at Hofheinz Pavilion in Houston, Texas, that I had made $1,006,947 since becoming a pro. Mary, who was there to watch my match, piped up, 'Ron, would you read those figures again? There's a very nice ring to them.' Bookman complied: 'One-oh-oh-six-nine-four-seven.' Those numbers rang like a bell. My winnings – the sum did not include endorsement deals or investments – passed that magic figure in November, three months shy of my 10th anniversary of turning pro at the beginning of 1963. Doesn't sound much when you hear what the best players can make these days, and the Federers, Nadals and Djokovics – and even some much lower ranked players – are multi-millionaires. But in my era, when money was scarce and sponsorship and prize money were worth a tiny fraction of what they are today (Novak Djokovic received $2,551,500 for winning the 2013 Australian Open!), it was a feat. Please don't think my millionaire status had Mary, Rick and me living like royalty. Subtract all those taxes and living expenses over the decade and you'll understand we still had to watch our dollars and dimes. When I was told I had made a million, I realised like never before the great debt I owed to Lew and Muscles who, more than anyone, had encouraged me to take the leap to professionalism even though my presence in the troupe would be a threat to their own earnings.

I returned to tennis in late January 1973 after treating my back to more much-needed R&R. I had no doubt that the marathon 64-player WCT tournaments to be staged through-out the United States and Canada, Germany, Belgium and South Africa from January to May would provide the test it needed. Once more I had given the Australian and French opens a miss to concentrate on doing well in the pro events and resurrecting my ranking. I had my share of wins, and losses too. Still, I made the final eight of the WCT finals that were held at Dallas' Moody Coliseum. I beat Emmo in the quarter final but lost the semi final in four sets to Stan Smith, who went on to down Arthur Ashe in the final.

By now Roy Emerson was my regular doubles partner, and we usually made the final of WCT events. All up, we had won 14 WCT doubles titles since the WCT tour was established in 1971. So we had high hopes when we took on the strong American pair Bob Lutz and Stan Smith in the final of the $80,000 WCT World Doubles Championship in

Montreal in early May. Our hopes were dashed when Bob and Stan beat us in four sets. Emmo was 37, more than a year older than me, and Lutz and Smith were, respectively, nine and seven years younger. Seems every time I played anyone but Emmo and Muscles in those days, there was a major age difference . . . and it was never in my favour!

To escape tennis for a bit I decided to treat myself to a little fun in a 'Superstar Sports Competition' in which prominent sportspeople took each other on in golf, sprinting, swimming and the like. Because we were not permitted to compete in our own particular sport, I wasn't allowed to play in the tennis comp. Nor, we were relieved to learn, would Smokin' Joe Frazier be allowed to box! I did okay, winning the table tennis and placing third in golf, fourth in swimming and third in the 100-yard dash, and coming in third in the overall competition behind the American Olympic gold-medal winning pole vaulter Bob Seagren and the legendary snow-skier Jean Claude Killy. It was a welcome distraction, and I took home $13,100 in prize money.

At the Alan King Tennis Classic at Caesar's Palace in Las Vegas I was knocked out in the first round by my old Australian mate Dick Crealy, who trounced me 6–4, 6–7, 6–0. I've never been one for excuses, and Dick was too strong for me that time, but my ignominious collapse in that final set was due in large part to a painful recurrence of my chronic back problem.

Perhaps, then, I was fortunate when the professionals and the amateur powers-that-be found themselves at each other's throats yet again. The catalyst for the big blow-up of 1973 was when Yugoslavia's Lawn Tennis Association suspended Croatian player Niki Pilic for nine months after he refused to represent his country in the Davis Cup because he preferred to play pro tournaments. The ruling body of amateur tennis, the International Lawn Tennis Federation, upheld the ban but reduced it to a one-month suspension, which included Wimbledon. That wasn't enough to placate the newly formed Association of Tennis Professionals, who believed the LTA and the ILTF were depriving Pilic of his right to earn money from playing tennis, and the ATP held a referendum in which 59 of us, including 1970–71 champion John Newcombe and defending champion Stan Smith, voted to side with Niki and not to compete at Wimbledon. I didn't get to vote because I was in the States with Mary at the time, but I would have voted with the strikers. The press, the public and the All England Lawn Tennis Club wanted to tar and feather us, but we wouldn't budge. Our action was not so much an expression of any affection for the sometimes prickly Pilic as a principled stand by men who believed they had earned the right to control their own destiny. Of the marquee WCT pros, only Roger Taylor and Ilie Nastase played Wimbledon. The final that year was fought out between Czech Jan Kodes and Russian Alex Metreveli, whose national federations forbade them to be members of the ATP or go on strike. While that unremarkable Wimbledon played out, Emmo and I were using our downtime to open another tennis camp, this one at April Sound on the banks of Lake Conroe in Texas.

I made the best of our stand by piling Mary and Rick into an RV and cruising for a month through northern California, stopping each night to camp, ride our pushbikes and fish. It was so good to have a long and uninterrupted stretch of time with Rick. We really made up for all the months I'd spent away playing tennis. Once he had asked Mary where I was and Mary said I was on a plane off to play tennis and he got it into his little head that I actually played matches on board planes. It was nice to put him straight on our family trip.

The WCT lads did front up for the 1973 US Open, and Newk won it. I again fell to youth, when 19-year-old Indian prodigy Vijay Amritraj ejected me from the tournament in the third round. He won in five sets that included a tie breaker, 7–6, 2–6, 6–4, 2–6, 6–4. At least he knew he'd been in a match. (Later I learned that Pancho Gonzales had advised Vijay to hit low to my forehand when I came in to volley, and the ploy worked.) I gave that match everything I had, and kept surviving seemingly hopeless positions, but in the end my serve let me down and Amritraj, a nice kid who became an actor and had roles in the James Bond film *Octopussy* and *Star Trek IV*, punished me for that. Ken Rosewall notched up one for the old guys when he ended Vijay's US Open dream for that year in the quarter finals.

I returned to Australia in early November to play in the Custom Credit Australian Indoors in Sydney. After winning my semi final against Muscles in a match of highs and lows for us both that had some reporters nodding in agreement that, sad to say, at long last we were over the hill, I pulled out all the stops against John Newcombe in the final. Determined to prove that I wasn't washed up just yet, I downed Newk 3–6, 7–5, 6–3, 3–6, 6–4. Then I teamed with the man with the moustache in the doubles final to beat Muscles and Mal Anderson in straight sets. It was nice to be home.

It was even nicer when I was chosen in the Australian Davis Cup team for the first time since 1962.

Chapter 16

For Australia

BEING RECALLED TO THE AUSTRALIAN DAVIS CUP TEAM WAS the last thing I thought would happen in 1973. The powers-that-be were upholding their ban on professionals being selected for the Davis Cup despite the fact that for five years our succession of weak teams had been belted by the United States, whose governing body had no qualms whatsoever about fielding their pros. (When the Yanks lifted the Davis Cup from us in 1968, Harry Hopman, who had captained 16 winning Australian Davis Cup teams, four of them that included me, resigned his post to move to the United States where he coached at Port Washington Tennis Academy at New York's Long Island before opening his own tennis academy in Florida. At Port Washington, he helped promising youngsters John McEnroe and Vitas Gerulaitis reach their potential.) Then, out of the blue, just when the Australian

Davis Cup selectors were looking more intractable than ever about admitting professionals into the team, the decision was taken that all pros were now eligible to represent their country in the Cup.

I put my hand up straight away, as did Newk and Muscles. I had the itch to play for Australia again. Yes, my home was in America, my wife was American and my son was half-American, but I'm an Australian to the core; to this day, after half a century of living in the United States, my passport still has an emu and a kangaroo on its cover and the number plate of my car is AUZZE 1.

I had unfinished Davis Cup business, especially against the United States. Of my four Cup campaigns, three Challenge Cups had been cakewalks. Against the Americans in 1959 it was different. We won, but no thanks to me. I lost both my singles matches to Barry MacKay and Alex Olmedo, and only after Neale Fraser and Emmo righted the ship did we hoist the trophy. I wanted to redeem myself against the US, which, with a strong team that included Tom Gorman, Stan Smith and Erik Van Dillen, seemed certain to defend the coveted trophy.

I knew, being very much in the veteran category, that I would not simply walk into the Australian team. I was ranked No.8 in the world then, and was not playing at my best. So, for the first time in my life, I played the entire Asian circuit as well as matches in Spain and Tehran to try to play myself back into top form. Captain Neale Fraser and I had a straight talk. He asked me how I felt about representing Australia in the Cup. I told him I was keen as mustard to play but concerned that I was no longer up to the intense cut-throat pressure of Davis Cup tennis and I didn't want to let my country down. And what about the blokes who had been carrying the flag for Australia in the Davis Cup preliminary rounds all year and in past years while the pros were outlawed from the team? What about the incumbent players Geoff Masters, Colin Dibley and Ross Case, Bob Giltinan, John Cooper? Would they welcome me, or consider me a blow-in?

Neale told me that if my form justified my selection I'd be welcomed with open arms. The Davis Cup was, after all, about winning for Australia. Yet he admitted that he wasn't totally convinced I should be in the team. He then made it clear that I would need to perform well in the Australian Indoor Championships in Sydney to be considered for the team to play the imminent semi final against Czechoslovakia. I didn't shy from the challenge. I ran long distances, worked out in the gym and made myself fitter than I had been in years, and in the Australian Indoors I beat speedy, sharp-volleying Mexican Raul Ramirez 6–3, 6–4, Muscles in a tight one 6–4, 3–6, 8–6, and, in the final, Newk, after a typically hard struggle, 3–6, 7–5, 6–3, 3–6, 6–4. For that match, I received some timely advice from my boyhood mentor Charlie Hollis, visibly older now but still cutting a debonair figure, who had travelled by train from Rockhampton just to see me play. It was certainly good to have Charlie back in my corner. He had seen that I'd served badly against Muscles and he told me something he had told me back in the old days: 'Leave the big serves to the big guys. Play like a little guy. Play smart.' So against Newk I concentrated on swinging the ball at 75 percent pace, and I served just three double faults. After that match, Neale Fraser came up to me, hand outstretched, and said, 'Rocket, welcome to the team.' The six chosen by Davis Cup selectors Fraser, Esca Stephens and Cliff Sproule were Newk, Muscles, Mal Anderson, Colin Dibley, Geoff Masters and me.

For the rubber against the Czechs that November, my parents came to Kooyong to watch the match. It would prove to be the last time they saw me play, and I hoped I didn't let them down. As I walked onto the court for my opening singles match against Jan Kodes, I saw Mum and Dad, frail now, in the grandstand and for a moment my mind could not help flashing back to Rockhampton and there I was . . . a boy again, playing fiercely against my brothers on our ant-bed court, with my proud parents looking on and calling out advice. Kodes was tough. Of all the Czechs Jan was the best on grass, having won Wimbledon and, just weeks earlier, being only narrowly bested in the US Open final by Newk. I managed to win 6–3, 7–5, 7–5. In the second singles match, Newk was surprisingly beaten by erratic clay court specialist Jiri Hrebec, who chose this occasion to play the match of his life. He was hitting the ball with an almost supernatural power that, frankly, shocked us all.

It was a comfort to have Kenny Rosewall on my side of the net for a change when we played doubles against Kodes and the 192 centimetre 'Ambling Alp' Vladimir Zednik. These Czechs were proving worthy opponents, and Muscles and I escaped by the skin of our teeth, 6–4, 14–12, 7–9,

8–6 to put Australia ahead two matches to one. Coming in against Hrebec in the first of the reverse singles, I was wary, having seen him dismantle Newk. And I was right to be concerned, because he won the first set 7–5. I didn't panic, I worked him out, and took the next two sets from him. Then he battled back to win the fourth. Two sets all. The pressure was enormous. Did Hrebec have it in him to be the giant killer who thwarted our Davis Cup hopes? He didn't but, boy, after I'd won the deciding fifth set 6–4 I knew I'd been taken to the wire. That Davis Cup tie was the highlight of Jiri Hrebec's career. He was scarcely heard of again.

One newspaper reporter summed up my performance in the Davis Cup semi final: 'It is rather ironical that Laver, a latecomer for the Cup team, has been the mainstay of the side after a year of up-and-down performances. He has timed his run perfectly, building up his form through the Asian circuit and the indoor championship in Sydney. He has played a major part in the victory.' That victory won us a date against the United States in Cleveland in the Challenge Round. Bud Collins labelled us 'Captain Fraser's Antique Show', and with good reason: I was 35, Muscles was 39, Mal Anderson was 38 and Newk was the baby of the quartet at 29. To the brash, younger American Cup-holders we probably seemed like easy, and overly seasoned, meat.

Sometimes great things take place in unlikely locations. The Cleveland Public Hall was a cavernous, draughty, badly lit, rundown indoor basketball venue with a carpet court – the first indoor venue ever to host a Davis Cup final.

Wimbledon it wasn't. And, in the depths of December, it was bloody freezing. Making matters worse was that an almost total lack of publicity for the Challenge Round, allied to the crappy facilities, the bad weather and the beloved Cleveland Browns football team playing on TV, meant that only a total of 7000-odd spectators turned up at that inhospitable venue over the course of the tie. That was a shame, because the Cleveland Public Hall, which was justly demolished long ago, was the host of a memorable sporting event when we whitewashed the United States five matches to zip. It didn't matter to us that, thanks to scant crowds and the lack of a public address system, the atmosphere at the matches was deader than Alexander the Great. We created our own vibe. We were determined that when we got on that Qantas flight back to Australia, in our luggage would be the Davis Cup. We were men on a mission, but the Yanks had come to play and had no intention of rolling over for the Australian Dad's Army.

On the opening day, a Friday, Newk turned on a sublime blend of delicate spin and sheer power to beat the always formidable Stan Smith in five sets, 6–1, 3–6, 6–3, 3–6, 6–4. Then came another hard-fought five-setter when I beat my Wimbledon 1971 nemesis Tom Gorman 8–10, 8–6, 6–8, 6–3, 6–1. It was a frantic affair as we tore into each other, charging the net, displaying our array of strokes.

The doubles were on next day. It was a crucial match. If we won it, Australia would have an unassailable 3–0 lead and the Davis Cup was ours. When he was deciding on the makeup of the doubles team, Neale asked Newk and me who we thought would be the best combination. Newk was clearly our best doubles player, and Fraser had to choose between Rosewall and myself to partner him. It was no time for false modesty or worrying about bruising another's feelings. I believed I was best equipped and told Neale so. Both John and I said we thought that while Kenny had a great return and volley, his serve was not as strong as mine. What was vital was that we play our two biggest servers, because Smith and Van Dillen were excellent at bomb returns to break serve and I said I thought these Americans would break Ken's serve. Also, Newk and I separately offered, John was used to playing with a leftie after all those years partnering Tony Roche, and the Yanks might be uncomfortable facing alternate left- and right-hand serves. Neale took our advice on board, then he asked me to play a set against Ken. Muscles was on top early, then I caught him and beat him. Neale announced the doubles team would be Newcombe and Laver. Kenny was bitterly disappointed by the decision, because it had already been decided that Newk and I would be playing the reverse singles, so he wouldn't be playing at all. Kenny is a proud man, and to come all the way to Cleveland as part of the team and then not play hurt him. Newk and I rewarded Fraser's faith in us by thrashing Smith and Van Dillen 6–1, 6–2, 6–4.

The Americans had been taken aback when they heard, an hour before the match, that John and I would be Australia's doubles pair. They were expecting Newk and Muscles or Mal, because they were sure that I would be exhausted after having played a gruelling five-setter the day before.

Perhaps my appearance lulled them into a false sense of security. Stan Smith later commented: 'When I saw Laver out there I thought it might have helped us. I thought he might have been a little bit tired.' As it happened, my fitness regime had me jumping out of my skin.

As we took up our positions, Newk said to me, 'Rocket, when I play against you, I hate it when you move in and really rip your backhand, and much prefer it when you just do your little dinks. Why not rip your backhand today? And it makes me nervous serving to you because your backhand return is so strong. So when the Yanks serve to you today, please step in and hit the shit out of the ball.' As he wrote in his biography, *Newk: On and Off the Court*:

Rod did his best to please me. On the first point of the match, Stan served to me and I returned to win the point 0–15. Just before Rod faced Stan's serve I said to him, '*Now*'s the time. Belt this one back as hard as you can.' Rod, who had the best poker face in tennis, said nothing. Stan served to Rod's backhand, and the instant the ball left his racquet, Rod leaped forward four paces and performed the best backhand return I've ever seen. Suddenly that ball was travelling back at the Americans at warp speed – I couldn't see a ball, just a blur. It was past Erik Van Dillen's nose before he could even move his racquet. The score was 0–30 to us against their serve. Van Dillen's face sank, as if to say, 'I'm way out of my league here.' He was like a boxer who goes out and cops such a belting in the first few rounds of a fight that his one thought is to not get hit again. 'You beauty, Rocket,' I said to Rod. 'They're stuffed.'

Afterwards a distraught Van Dillen mourned, 'If I had had eight arms I wouldn't have won. They put so much pressure on us. It's tough to see your best shots coming back at you even better.'

In the dead rubber reverse singles, Newk accounted for a demoralised Gorman 6–2, 6–1, 6–3, and I finished the job by beating Smith 6–3, 6–4, 3–6, 6–2. That wrapped it up, five matches to zero. It was Australia's 23rd Davis Cup win since the competition was instituted in 1900, and took us to a 15–13 lead over our arch rivals. At the Cup presentation, Dennis Ralston, the United States' non-playing captain, shook hands with his Australian counterpart, Fraser, who was still tightly gripping the good-luck toy koala he had carried throughout the tournament, and said, 'You guys simply played too well for us. You were on every ball. I've never seen Laver and Newcombe play better . . . and I've played them a few times.'

One reporter asked me whether, being married to an American and living in America, I felt a dual loyalty, and I set him straight: 'I am Australian and I play for Australia.'

Next day, we'd be taking the Davis Cup home, but first there was some partying to be done. John Newcombe wrote about our victory party (although it's a wonder to me that he has any recall at all of that particular event!):

Boy, did we party! We had a huge dinner, the beer and wine flowed, and we sang and celebrated all night long. Rod Laver was never a party animal. He is a quiet, undemonstrative man. I have a memory of him that night that I'll cherish till I die. At one point I went to the toilet and there was Rod at the urinal. I went to stand beside him and was about to say something when I saw that he had the biggest, widest grin on that freckled face of his. Rod was just standing there, grinning away. I had no intention of interrupting his reverie so I finished and left him there, smiling beatifically.

That was the last time I played Davis Cup tennis. In 1974, my professional contracts and commitments playing in such events as the professional World Championship, World Teams Tennis in the US, Italy and Spain, and the Alan King–promoted Caesar's Palace tournament in Las Vegas clashed with the Cup schedule so I made myself unavailable. The rest of the time I devoted to family and business. I bowed out at the right time.

Chapter 17

Winding down

Jimmy Connors did not respect his elders. When the hottest, and brashest, young tennis player in the world won the US Open in 1974, he is said to have demanded, 'Get me Laver!' That's what his flamboyant manager Bill Riordan claimed Connors said, anyway, when he was hyping a 1975 showdown between the 22-year-old Connors, with his super self-confidence and pudding-bowl haircut, and me for the so-called World Championship of Tennis. I had nothing to prove against a man 14 years younger than me. I was happy to keep chugging around the pro circuit, not exactly resting on my laurels, but being able to enjoy pressure-free tennis and spending more time at home with Mary and Rick. Still, I'm always up for a challenge, so I said to Bill, 'Tell me more.'

The big match would be played at Caesar's Palace in Las Vegas on 2 February 1975, and broadcast on the CBS television network in the US and on ABC-TV in Australia. Pancho Gonzales was named referee, which enraged Connors because he knew Pancho and I went way back, and in an act of blatant gamesmanship the young lion demanded he be removed. After we sorted that – Pancho remained as ref and was impartial – I told Bill and Jimmy that I was in. Then the spin and hype began. Bill Riordan had been a boxing promoter and he publicised the match as if it was a title fight, a brawl between the champions of two generations, a stoush between youth and experience. I'm sure some of the fans arrived at Caesar's Palace expecting to see us throwing punches at each other. The imagination of the public was captured by the promotional blitz. I was interviewed just before the match and told the assembled reporters, 'I'm doing this because I need a new challenge to get the adrenalin flowing again. When you've done it all and been everywhere it's hard to get up for a regular tournament, even though they're offering big purses. But this is something else, a one-shot deal. I play better when the pressure is on.' Mary told me that since I'd committed to the match with Connors, I was like a kid with a new toy.

Los Angeles reporter Ivor Davis came to visit me at home in the lead-up to the Connors match. It was one of the most wide-reaching interviews I ever gave and was syndicated in newspapers all over the world. It was rare for me to have anyone from the press, except for Bud Collins, in our home. I felt comfortable with Davis and opened up about tennis, business and home life, and took the opportunity to get in a few digs at Connors to build up expectation about our match:

Rod Laver, first tennis millionaire-turned-business-tycoon, wasn't home and wife Mary apologised: 'He'll be back any minute . . . he's doing the kids' car pool today.' It was pleasing to hear that despite his success – and he's had plenty – Rocket Rod is like most of us mere mortals who face daily chores and run routine errands. The winning-est player ever in professional tennis still has to run his son, Ricky, to school. I mean, can you imagine Nelson Rockefeller driving his two offspring to school?

The raw kid from Queensland has built his wrist and forearm magic into a small fortune and although he enjoys the wealth and the fame, the idea of Rod Laver, the business czar, still sits uneasily on him. More and more these days, 36-year-old Rod is directing his energies to boardroom-type activities.

But on February 2 in Nevada's gambling capital of Las Vegas, he's taking the biggest gamble of his life: putting it all on the line against young Jimmy Connors at Caesar's Palace. Connors, 14 years younger at 22, hurled down the gauntlet and Rod, who had been contentedly concentrating on nursing the Laver–Emerson tennis holidays, picked it up. It will be the classic Old Pro versus the Brash Young Upstart – although Rod is not underestimating the brilliant young left-hander who was the biggest money-winner in tennis in 1974 . . .

With son Ricky, aged 5, tucked away in kindergarten, Rod relaxed in the living room of his sprawling, 6-bedroom house overlooking the Pacific Ocean in the beach community of Corona Del Mar about 100 kilometres south of Los Angeles. A winter fog wispily curled in from the ocean as the foghorns blared and Rod, in tailored and flared blue jeans, a blue check shirt and polished boots, talked softly of what tennis has given him, his business ambitions and that crucial Connors game. The Laver–Emerson tennis camps were a smash the first year out. They now have camp sites from North Carolina to California, and at $500 a throw per person (that includes coaching, food and hotel) the money has been pouring in . . .

'I've seen many tennis pros fade into obscurity and near-poverty after their competitive days are over,' explains Rod. 'I've seen a lot of guys plan nothing for their future. Some are not natural coaches or else they don't want to coach so they're equipped to do nothing. And while our tennis days are still very good I'd like to be able to branch off as the competitive days slacken off a bit. So we're building things up now rather than wait till we quit the circuit altogether and then take three to four years to get organised . . . Our playing days are very short, not like a doctor or a lawyer. Realistically, you have to plan for the future . . .'

He shies away at the whole idea of being tennis's first millionaire, explaining: 'I don't think money is what you play tennis for . . . that label is purely the record book talking. I had four great years and the best year anybody's ever had, but it's gonna be topped. These days it doesn't seem hard to find a $100,000 tournament.'

For all his worth, Laver lives modestly but comfortably ('this house is too big'). He drives a chocolate Mercedes 450 SLC and likes to take his American accountant wife Mary with him when he travels. He married her in 1966 ('It's tough to run a romance and play tennis,' he says) and she keeps an eye on his taxes, earnings and business dealings.

The fact that in 1974 he played less top tennis than ever in his career might prove something of a handicap against Connors, admits Rod. 'But by the time of the match I should be in good shape.' Every morning he plays Emerson for about three hours then runs five kilometres on the beach near his home.

The Connors match is crucial for him. 'There's a lot on the line. He's a young kid coming along. I think he's got a lot more to learn. He thinks he's a world beater . . . and he's the first to tell everybody.' Rod is no fan of the flamboyant and abrasive young left-hander . . . 'I think there's a lot more to tennis than a kid playing and talking about it. I let my racquet do the talking. If it's good enough my reputation will stay there. I'm not spouting off saying I can beat the kid. He's darn good. But I think I have a good chance to win. I think I can. Maybe it'll be a good lesson for

him if I beat him. He may become a better player . . .
His repertoire of shots is good but when you look
at his sportsmanship on court that isn't always too
good. He gets carried away with himself and does a
lot of bad-mouthing on court which I don't think is
very nice. I hate to lose. I don't show my emotions.
My style has always been to think out the next point
even if you're playing terribly . . . but keep thinking
ahead. I've played Gonzales and others who are the
masters of the psych. It just gets me mad and I say,
'He'll never beat me!'

I was the outsider and rightly so, but I had no intention of
being road kill for Jimmy Connors, so once more I ran and
trained myself into the best possible shape and brought in
Emmo and Mark Cox, a left-hander like Connors, as my
sparring partners. We worked hard, two hours every afternoon. Mark won two tournaments straight after and put his
good form down to all the training he'd done with us.

The 4000 capacity arena was filled to bursting and there
was plenty of star power. Charlton Heston was there of
course, and Clint Eastwood, Neil Diamond, Rod Steiger,
Dan Rowan and Dick Martin of TV's *Laugh In*, Johnny
Carson and Andy Williams all paid up to $100 for a ticket,
which was big money in those days. I took Jimmy to four
sets, and he won 6–4, 6–2, 3–6, 7–5. Early on, my serving
was awry, which prevented me from storming the net as I'd
planned and putting away volleys. When I did rush the net,
Jimmy passed me with his trademark flat shots. Connors

was well on top at the beginning of the third set and keen to finish the match. I had other ideas. I served three consecutive love games and the crowd was on its feet when I snatched the set. Roy Emerson told me that during that third set, Harry Hopman, who was in the crowd, was in tears as he watched me serving my aces and making passing shots on important points. The crowd, especially in the third set, forgot to be parochial and barracked for the old bloke, and, while Jimmy was generally on his best behaviour, this annoyed him and in his frustration he gave some noisier spectators the middle finger.

The fourth set was a skirmish as we broke each other's serve and there were many deuces. Jimmy outlasted me to win the set and the match. I played as well as I could at that stage of my career, and the match was nothing like the walkover some had predicted. I took pride in being fitter than Jimmy, and he finished the match with painful contractions in his left hand and collapsed with cramps and so, in a way, I had a moral victory. Ironically, the bloke at courtside massaging Connors' legs was Hop.

With the ascension of young turks Connors, John McEnroe and Ilie Nastase to the upper reaches of the rankings, the world of tennis became a less gentlemanly place. They hailed from a new era and, apart from being fine players, they had little in common with the older champions – Pancho being the obvious exception – to whom sportsmanship, grace under pressure and on-court decorum were important. McEnroe, Connors and Nastase wore their emotions on their sleeve. If they were angry or frustrated, everybody knew about it. They were also masters of using whatever tactics were necessary to get under their opponent's skin. This could range from arguments, stalling and insults to physical attacks, such as when Fred Stolle got drilled in the throat by McEnroe. If it meant a win, anything went.

I never had a problem when up against John and Jimmy. Whether they respected what I had achieved or perhaps knew I was never going to be fazed by their antics like some other players, I'm not sure. I can't say the same about Ilie Nastase. Nasty was a talented player who, at the end of his career, would be inducted into the Tennis Hall of Fame, and at that stage he was a better player than me, but some of the . . . well, nastiest matches I ever played were against him. He liked to call me 'Old Man' during matches, and his abuse not only of opponents and officials but also of spectators was outrageous – I told him more than once that the fans deserved better than that. In a pro event in Cincinatti where I was playing doubles with Tom Gullickson against Nastase and the American Peter Fleming, Nasty was on his worst behaviour. He was foot-faulted and screamed at the female umpire. He fired balls off into the stand. When I shaped up to serve to him he'd turn away at the last moment to upset me and throw off my timing. Anyway, he and Fleming beat us, but it was the last in a spate of bitter encounters and I had to make a stand, so after the match I confronted him: 'You're a disgrace! That was the most disgraceful display of tennis I have ever witnessed. You're destroying the image of our game. We all like to win, but not the way you win.

I'll never play against you again, and I don't even want you on our tour.'

I told Jim McManus, who was running the tournament, of my stand and he talked to Nastase, who told him he didn't believe I meant what I said about never playing him again, that I was just upset after the match and I'd relent. When McManus reported this back to me I called Nastase and told him I'd never been more serious about anything in my life. 'If you're playing, I'm not. Simple as that. And I want you to know that a lot of the guys on the circuit feel exactly the same as me.' I was true to my word. I didn't play against Nastase again. Happily, in later years we buried the hatchet and now greet each other civilly when our paths cross.

Even if I didn't always win, I enjoyed the experience of playing against younger men, and really relished taking on the Swedish teenage sensation Björn Borg, who was obviously destined to be an all-time great. Unlike Nastase, he was a pleasure to play against. I played him four times, beat him once, at Houston on clay, and took him to five sets in the WCT quarter finals in Dallas and four in the fourth round of the US Open. By the first time we played each other, Björn had already won the French Open and Wimbledon. I was proud of my victory in the Houston match, and won by doing what I always tried to do, playing from the net. We had a scorcher of a match in May 1975 in the quarter final of the WCT title tournament. *The Sydney Morning Herald* reported that I, 'the sentimental favourite for the WCT title', had been vanquished 6–7, 6–3, 7–5, 6–7, 2–6 in 'a magnificent four hour marathon in Dallas'. Pointing out that at age 36 I was exactly twice Björn Borg's age, the *Herald*'s reporter said we had exchanged 'one stupendous shot after another'. After the match, my fifth WCT failure – making it the only major tournament I'd never won – I told the assembled reporters that this had been my WCT swan song. 'I've had my last shot at it. WCT is a great set-up . . . but I don't think I want to play games as long as that anymore.' WCT chief Lamar Hunt attributed the lengthy matches to the PVC foam-cushioned Supreme Court that tended to keep the ball in play. Lamar said, 'These slower courts mean that the points last longer and satisfy the spectators. But longer points mean a lot more running and when Rod Laver finishes a point, he is in pain. In his case it's not just his age but the jerky style of his game which punishes his body.'

Björn graciously credited me in part with helping him keep his on-court emotions under control after he had been a firebrand as a junior player. He wrote in his 1980 autobiography, *My Life and Game*: 'Rod Laver was my childhood idol but the first time I saw him in person was the 1971 Wimbledon titles when he lost to Tom Gorman. Before that I watched him on TV, but his only influence on me was how he behaved on court, not his strokes. I admired his concentration and straight face. He never got upset.'

●

By this time I was a shadow of the player I had once been, yet, win or lose, I don't think I ever walked off a court not having given my best. It's gratifying that in the years to come people would come up to me and recount their memories of the time I played Connors or Borg in some pro event in the mid-'70s when I was 36 or 38, and how, after seeing me put up a fight, they were inspired to take up the great game even when they were no longer young themselves.

This was the era of exhibition matches, such as when Jimmy Connors went head to head in 'heavyweight championship' events with me and then Newk. And, of course, there was the infamous 'Battle of the Sexes' grudge match on 20 September 1973, between Bobby Riggs, a 55-year-old 1939 Wimbledon champion, and the 29-year-old current Wimbledon women's champ, Billie Jean King. Riggs had enraged women with his male chauvinist remarks about women's inferiority to men and his boast that no woman could beat a man at tennis, even a 55-year-old man. Australian great Margaret Court stood up to him and in May that year they played in what has become known as the 'Mother's Day Massacre', when Riggs took advantage of Margaret's attack of nerves, which saw her serve a succession of double faults, to easily beat her with lobs and drop shots 6–2, 6–1, and got himself on the cover of *Time* and *Sports Illustrated* magazines.

Billie Jean was made of sterner stuff. She told Riggs to put up or shut up, and they faced off at the Houston Astrodome. Some 90 million people watched on TV and a record tennis crowd of 30,472 were on hand to see her destroy

His Piggishness in three embarrassing sets, 6–4, 6–3, 6–3 that had Riggs' supporters averting their eyes. The strutting Riggs, who boasted that he'd eaten so many vitamin pills that he rattled and entered the arena in a rickshaw pulled by scantily dressed models, was reduced to a sorry wreck by the younger, fitter, faster and more skilful King. I was there in that incredible throng at the Astrodome because Houston is not far from April Sound where I was hosting a clinic and, to me, Bobby looked exactly like what he was, a man whose best days were decades earlier. Bobby was a hustler and a self-promoter, trying to eke out a little more fame when he would have been better off out of the game resting on his past achievements. He played badly, hoping his rubbish shots would see him through, and I think he brought Billie Jean down to his level because she was far below her best. Still, she won easily. His ignominy was complete when Billie Jean presented him with a piglet named Larimore Hustle. It all struck me as a bit of a farce. This wasn't tennis as I knew it.

The Alan King tournaments at Caesar's Palace in Las Vegas were highlights of the pro tour. Alan was a comedian and well-known Vegas identity who ran a slick tournament on behalf of the casino. One year I won a Mercedes 450SL and $30,000 and as the photographers clicked away and the high-rollers cheered and laughed at the post-match ceremony, Alan pushed out onto the court a wheelbarrow filled with dollar coins, which I had to pose on top of. A small price to pay for such loot! One of the highlights of playing at Las Vegas was meeting the great boxer Joe Louis, a sweet and charming old gentleman then, who was employed as a greeter at the hotel.

Through all this hullabaloo Mark McCormack and his team were working overtime on my behalf. My name was popping up all over the place on tennis racquets, tennis balls, ball machines, shoes, razor blades, socks, tennis kitbags, watches, sunglasses, suitcases and various items of men's and women's clothing! I checked out all these products before endorsing them. I had no intention of spruiking dodgy paraphernalia. I knew there'd come a time, in the not too distant future, when I would be retired and these offers wouldn't be so plentiful, so I seized the day and squirrelled away the money for my family. I was playing fewer tournaments, and therefore earning less prize money, and my old fear of falling on hard times when my tennis days were over, the fear that had made me turn pro to begin with, continued to haunt me, especially now there was more pressure to be a good provider because Mary and Rick depended on me. The tennis camps with Emmo, property investments and a tennis instruction book I wrote with him, *Tennis for the Bloody Fun of It*, another book, *Rod Laver's Tennis Digest*, and my collaboration with Bud Collins, *The Education of a Tennis Player*, which focused on my second Grand Slam, were my way of keeping things ticking over off the court and into the future.

By the end of 1975, Roy Emerson and I had a number of tennis centres. At various times, as well as at the Pinehurst Hotel and Country Club in North Carolina, Mt Washington Resort at Bretton Woods, New Hampshire, and April Sound on Lake Conroe in Texas, we opened establishments at Murrieta Hot Springs on the highway from LA to San Diego, Palmetto Dunes at Hilton Head Island in South Carolina and one in Boyne Falls, Michigan, near the Great Lakes. There was a hiccup with our camp in Los Angeles near the airport when the court surfaces were destroyed by the plane fuel fumes. We had guest coaches from time to time, and it was a thrill when Lew Hoad dragged himself away from his own tennis ranch in Spain and lent us a hand. The camps thrived, and our feedback from guests was that they departed as better players and had fun into the bargain. As the years went by Emmo and I divested ourselves of some camps and opened new ones, such as at San Vincente, north of San Diego, not far from our home. In early 1977, Roy and I dissolved our partnership while remaining firm friends.

Meanwhile, I was playing in what was known as the Blue Group on the WCT circuit – the others were Rochey, Emmo, Alex Metreveli, Roscoe Tanner, Charlie Pasarell – and we faced each other at events across the United States and in South America and Canada. That year I took an extended break to be with Mary and Rick and tend to business interests.

My Wimbledon swan song was in 1977, when I made a sentimental journey to take part in the Centenary Celebration. I was invited to join other old champions on centre court, where we linked hands and sang 'Auld Lang Syne'. We were united by having done our very best, and succeeded, at the greatest championship on earth. I don't mind telling you I got a little misty-eyed. We had history,

Wimbledon and me. The star of the show was 85-year-old American Elizabeth 'Bunny' Ryan, who'd won 19 doubles and mixed doubles titles between 1914 and 1934. After we all received a commemorative medal, it was time to play. I downed Ireland's Sean Sorenson in straight sets in the first round, but that was as far as I got. American Dick Stockton, 12 years my junior, sent me packing 6–3, 7–9, 6–4, 7–5. In the doubles Newk and I gave Marty Riessen and Roscoe Tanner a good tussle and it took them five sets to dispatch us. No matter about the results, it felt so good to be playing on the green, green grass of Wimbledon again before those polite and knowledgeable spectators and as I trudged off centre court after my loss to Stockton it struck me with some force that this was the last time I would ever do so.

My tennis career was winding down. From 1976 to '78, I played World Team Tennis for the San Diego Friars, who were based nice and close to home. My teammates were a congenial bunch who included Cliff Drysdale, Ross Case, Terry Holladay, and Kerry Reid and her husband Raz, and we played against such outfits as the New York Apples, starring my compatriots Fred Stolle and Ray Ruffels, and the Boston Lobsters, who had Emmo and Martina Navratilova in their ranks. I won some matches, lost some too, but had a wonderful time riding off into the sunset. I was 38 in 1976 when World Team Tennis named me their 'Rookie of the Year'. Who said there's no place for humour in tennis? I would play seniors matches and exhibitions for many years to come, but my last official professional match was on 24 April 1979 when, fittingly, I played John Alexander, who beat me 6–7, 6–3, 6–1 in the first round of the Alan King Classic at Caesar's Palace. If I had to lose, I'm glad it was a fellow Australian who put me to the sword.

For the record, in singles I won Wimbledon in 1961, '62, '68 and '69, the Australian Open (we'll call it the Open even though the Australian championships only became known as such in 1969) in 1960, '62 and '69, the French in '62 and '69, and the US in '62 and '69. I was a member of the winning doubles team at the Australian in 1959, '60, '61 and '69, at the French in 1961 and at Wimbledon in 1971. My partner and I won mixed doubles at the French titles in 1961 and at Wimbledon in 1959 and '60. I claimed the US Pro singles title in 1964, '66 and '67, the Wembley Pro in 1964, '65, '66 and '67, and the French Pro in 1967. I won 52 tournaments in the amateur era from 1957 to '62, 68 in the pro period from 1963 to '67, and 76 in the open era from 1968 until I retired from top-line tennis in 1979. I represented Australia in the Davis Cup from 1959 to '62 and in 1973, and each time we won the Challenge Round.

I never bothered to keep score but Austrian tennis historian Robert Geist did, and according to him I won 75 of the 141 matches I played against Ken Rosewall between 1963, when I turned pro, and when I hung up my racquet. Against Pancho Gonzales, whom I played when he was past his prime but was always a formidable opponent, I won 35–19 or 38–21, depending on which statistician you choose to believe. Roy Emerson and I had a long rivalry as amateurs and then again in open tennis, and at the end of the day I was ahead 49–18. As with Gonzales, I didn't play Lew

Hoad at his best, but in our matches I held a 38–21 lead. I downed John Newcombe 16–5 in the open years. More than these bland numbers, however, what I cherish most is having the privilege of being both fierce rival and good mate of these special men.

Chapter 18

New horizons

AFTER I LEFT THE PRO CIRCUIT, I MADE UP FOR YEARS OF lost time out on the road by becoming something of a homebody. At last I could be a hands-on father and husband, and I immersed myself in the role. After all the sacrifices Mary and Rick had made for me it was the least I could do. I continued to carry out promotional work for my sponsors, which included Adidas and Pro-Kennex, and Mary and I ran our investments. We de-complicated our lives by dismantling a number of our tennis camps while continuing to manage some, and I remained a visiting coach. I played tennis on about 15 weekends a year: exhibition matches and fun events. I also played in and helped organise tennis events for charity.

In late 1979 I took 10-year-old Rick back home to Gladstone to reacquaint him with his grandparents. We found

Dad not at all well, but it was heartening to see him brighten up when we descended on the family home. It was my first visit back to Australia in six years and Rick, my brothers and I enjoyed a fishing trip out on the Great Barrier Reef. That visit was the last time I saw my brother Bob, who passed away suddenly in January 1980, aged just 44, of an aneurism. Then in December of that sad year, my father died. I felt helpless being so far away, back in the United States, when he passed away.

Also in 1980, after we'd had the unpleasant experience of having our Newport home robbed while we were away (the culprit turned out to be a friend of someone we had entrusted to feed our birds), Mary and I went to live on a 50-acre block of land we'd purchased at rural Solvang, near Santa Barbara, up the coast from Los Angeles. It had always been a dream of mine to be a man on the land. Mary, with her brilliant sense of style and decoration, supervised the building of a European-inspired ranch house with pool, spa and tennis court. We grazed a herd of white Charolais cattle. We stayed there till 1984, when, after he'd enjoyed a last taste of freedom on a three-week skiing and cycling adventure in France with friends, Rick became a boarder at the Hunn High School near Princeton University, New Jersey, and Mary and I moved back to Newport Beach.

A few years earlier IMG and I had come up with the idea of establishing a $200,000 Tennis Legends Tour, a series of deadly earnest tournaments in six US cities in which old stagers could relive their glory days while giving fans a glimpse of what we were still capable of on a court.

To qualify as a Legend you had to be aged between 35 and 45 and have won at least one international championship in your career, whether in singles, doubles or mixed competition. We had quite a roster. As well as me, there was Muscles, Newk, Emmo, Fred Stolle, Roger Taylor, Dennis Ralston, Butch Buchholz, Marty Riessen, Charlie Pasarell, Cliff Drysdale and Frew McMillan. The idea caught on, sponsors and TV networks got behind us, and by 1982 the Legends Tour was travelling the world, including Australia, and drawing healthy crowds and positive press coverage. The old buffers, it seemed, were still relevant.

I never tired of tennis, and every time I went onto the court in those seniors matches I was ready to play. Once the match began, pride and my natural competitiveness took over, and I kicked into gear and put myself on the line like in the good old days. Wanting to be close to Mum after Dad's death, I had jumped at the opportunity to play in the Indoor Toyota Open Tournament of Champions at Sydney's Hordern Pavilion in February 1981. It was a Legends event, but there was nothing creaky about the tennis we turned on. Not surprising, really, when you consider that the players on show had collectively won 27 grand slam singles titles and 41 doubles championships. Newk beat me in a tight and typically good-natured match to avenge his loss to me in the Australian Indoors in 1973 when I was on trial for selection in the Davis Cup. Reporter Alan Clarkson was there at the match and our good sportsmanship at a time when the antics of some of tennis' firebrands had brought disrepute to the game had made him nostalgic for less antagonistic days. Delving into his deep experience reporting tennis, Clarkson decided that John's and my shots were as good as we had ever played, while others made us shake our heads in dismay and disbelief. No matter. The crowd had enjoyed our encounter because we players had obviously enjoyed it, and they, like the reporter, were glad that there were no tantrums or monstering of officials. Clarkson wrote that Newk and I were players from the past who were brought up in an era 'when sportsmanship was the essential part of any player's equipment'. He wished only that we were at our prime now.

Writer Skip Myslenski of the *Chicago Tribune* interviewed me and wrote a piece that pretty accurately summed up my state of mind at this stage of my life. Basically, it was about how in my older years I still found pleasure in tennis and in competing on the Legends tour: '[Tennis] is still a joy [for Laver] because he is not haunted by the past, because he is not enchained by that past, because he has slipped grace-fully away from the enchantments of that past and settled comfortably into a life less luminous. He has memories, of course, and there are reveries when his grandest moments replay themselves in his mind; but those instances are brief and not tinged with bitterness, and he is most of all content with a present where his game can still be a joy.'

I assured Myslenski that our seniors matches were quite competitive. None of us liked losing, I said, but it wasn't as if our careers were on the line any more. Consequently there wasn't as much pressure as there used to be, but nor was there as much excitement. I told the reporter that I thrived on the senior circuit and there were times when I felt I could turn back the clock 10, 15 years. 'Some days I feel I could play as well as I ever did, but the margin fluctuates more than it used to.'

I still enjoyed playing tennis, but not all the time. I wanted to be part of the game but nowadays home life was so important to me and, I went on, I was striving for a delicate balance.

So long as I was still playing well, I wanted to compete at a high level, but if I were playing badly, hitting into the stands, doing things that were uncalled for, I wouldn't play. And if injury was hampering me and preventing me from giving my best, I would not expose myself to the public. That, I explained to the journalist, was because I was proud of my reputation and my ability. I had seen others play on after they should have given the game at that level away and it saddened me. 'The public,' I said, 'remembers.'

I told him that when I saw the new generation players such as Björn Borg winning Wimbledon I had no twinges of jealousy that the cheers were no longer for me. 'No. When I see Björn and the others doing so well, it brings back good memories.'

While playing seniors tennis, I signed with Nabisco Brands, which sponsored the Men's Grand Prix pro event that was played all over the world. My work entailed running tennis clinics and giving speeches (I was much more comfortable in front of an audience now than in my old nervy, tongue-tied days). It seemed that people enjoyed hearing about my triumphs and disappointments at the great tournaments of the '50s and '60s and in the white-hot cauldron of Davis Cup. At Nabisco tournaments I shook a million hands, and was honoured to do so.

By the mid-'80s, Australia's world tennis dominance was over. With Pat Cash and John Fitzgerald our only highly ranked players, we had been overtaken by the United States, Sweden, Germany and Czechoslovakia. I was about to return to Australia for a Nabisco Grand Masters tournament in Brisbane in September 1985, and before I flew home I sat down in New York with *The Sydney Morning Herald*'s Alan Trengrove to discuss the state of Australian tennis and the world's best player at the time, the mercurial John McEnroe. To Alan, I expressed my worry that our young players were not putting in sufficient effort. I said that the desire to win every match and a love of tennis for the game itself, were infinitely more important in attaining success than just having a hunger for money, which alone would never be enough to elevate a player into the higher world ranks. Some young Australian players had been tricked by winning big money early in their career to believe that they had no further need to work hard on their game to be the best player they could be. Consequently, they never improved, while dedicated players usurped them and ended up winning more tournaments and therefore more money. Discipline was key, I told Trengrove, and I said that the Australians of my era were *very* disciplined indeed. 'Tennis came first, second, third in their lives. You disciplined yourself to do what was good for your game. Players like Hoad and Rosewall planned their lives so they were ready for every big tournament.'

I conceded that the modern player faced pressures that we never did because of the unceasing struggle to accumulate ranking points via the new computerised system. I offered my belief that while some young players thrived on the demands of the year-long circuit, others found the grind, months on the road living out of a suitcase, too tough to hack and gave tennis away. Also, the need to gather points meant that some players avoided problematical surfaces, such as clay, and so never gave themselves the chance to become proficient on it. Another pressure for up-and-coming players came from the endorsements. They received bonuses if they were in the top 100 players, the top 50 or the top 10. Everything was governed by those points and they too could limit a player's development.

When the subject of John McEnroe was raised I said I was proud when I read that I had been his idol when he was young, and that despite all his antics on the court, I thought Mac was one helluva player. I admired him for his 'competitive and tactical instincts as much as for his stroke-making. He has the ability to win points and change his game'. His racquet work amazed me. And, I continued, 'If Mac is playing a great player, he's pushed a little bit further. You feel that no matter how well someone plays, Mac will find a way to retaliate.' This ability to overcome adversity and always find a way to win, I felt, was lacking in some of the young Australians.

Of course I could never endorse some of the things John said and did on the court. I have always believed that you owe it to yourself, the crowd, the sponsors and the beautiful game of tennis to behave well. I'm often asked to nominate the most abusive thing I ever said to an umpire. It was, 'Are you sure?' Mine was a different era. A world ago.

To inject some interest into that 1985 Nabisco Grand Masters tournament, I joined Muscles, Emmo and Mal Anderson in Brisbane for a meet-and-greet walk through the Queen Street Mall and a thousand fans rolled up to chat and get autographs. I realised then, not for the first time, that in our own small way we tennis players had made a difference to people's lives. I was back in Australia giving talks and pressing the flesh for Nabisco at the Australian Open the following year and in 1987 and both times I caught up with my family.

My great mentor, Charlie Hollis, died in December 1987, aged 77, after a short illness. Charlie was buried in Gosford, north of Sydney, and the obituaries rightly credited his major role in my career, and that of other champions, such as Mal Anderson, Fred Stolle, Roy Emerson, Wally Masur and Mark Edmondson, who benefited from his coaching and work ethic. His obituary in the newspapers was head-lined: 'Charlie Hollis: The Man Who Taught Champions'. No one would disagree with that. Without Charlie I don't know how my career would have turned out. If he hadn't seen me peeping through the chicken wire that night when he was coaching my brothers and told Dad he wanted to give the young bugger a try-out on our home court, my career might not have happened at all.

I was well out of the intense glare of publicity that engulfed the new generation of tennis champions, and

I wasn't minding being a comparatively private person. The fine *Esquire* magazine sports writer Mike Lupica told the story of how, when I was at the US Open in 1988, I passed through the crowd and nobody recognised me. 'The little orange-haired man in a blue golf shirt was asking for directions at the US Tennis Open. He asked a boy at the end of the line: "Do you happen to know where I can find the Past Champions box when I go inside?" "Sorry," the boy said. He asked a woman in white. She didn't know either. The orange-haired man sighed, then smiled, as though it were all some private joke. He finally saw a reporter he recognised and was directed to another entrance. "Who was that, anyway?" the boy asked the reporter. The reporter sighed, "You're kidding." "No, was he somebody I'm supposed to know?" "That was Rocket Rod Laver." "That little guy? No fooling? Laver?" *"No fooling."'*

After school, Rick made his career in computer sciences, based in San Diego. I don't pretend to understand a thing he does! Later, he was posted to Afghanistan to work in satellite communications with the marines and the army. In 1991, Mary and I bought a home right by the ninth fairway of the golf course at the Morningside Country Club at Rancho Mirage, east of San Diego, in the desert near Palm Springs. I had always been a keen golfer and now I had every opportunity to play regularly. Before long my handicap was six and I was playing comp.

Mum's health problems began escalating in 1991, and my trips home to be with her became more frequent. I was a little surprised to see that despite having lived for so long in the United States I was still remembered back home. I was so honoured in 1993 when a bronze bust of me was unveiled by Victorian Premier Jeff Kennett during the Australian Open in Melbourne. I was the first inductee of the new Australian Tennis Hall of Fame, established that year by Tennis Australia. It was gratifying to realise that the golden era of Australian tennis was still honoured by the game's champions. When Pete Sampras, who surely ranks among the best players in history, won the Australian Open in 1994 he was asked to name his inspirations, and he replied, 'Sure, I respected McEnroe's talent and Connors' intensity, but the Aussies, those guys were the great guys.' He said that he had modelled his serve and volley game on mine. 'I feel the Lavers, Rosewalls, Sedgmans were really classy guys and people I've always looked up to. Hopefully I'm getting closer to their level.'

My mother passed away on 12 October 1995, and I felt blessed that I had been able to see more of her in her final years. I was glad, too, that she and Dad had witnessed my career and, I hope, were in no doubt that their sacrifices and loving support and all those endless trips on bumpy outback Queensland roads to far-flung junior tennis tournaments had not been in vain.

Mary and I remained in the desert until 2000, when we returned to the coast, to the town of Carlsbad, about 70 kilometres north of San Diego, and the house that is still my home today. Carlsbad soon became a family affair when Rick and his wife Sue moved there. Life was wonderful for Mary and me. Every chance we got we jumped into our motor home and recreational vehicle and took off, along the entire west coast of California, up to Vancouver, down to the Baja Peninsula, out to Utah. It was good to go to places because we wanted to, not because I had to. I enjoyed the American countryside – the old bush boy in me, I suppose. I still took a keen interest in tennis, and noted how technology and metal racquets were changing the game. I admired current champions Pete Sampras, Andre Agassi and Boris Becker. I played a lot of golf and followed the San Diego Chargers, my local NFL team. I continued to represent my sponsors, working with them on special events, and played seniors and exhibition matches. I was enjoying kicking back.

Inevitably, dashing about on tennis courts for all those years exacted a toll on my body. In 1998, I underwent a hip replacement. I recovered quickly and resumed my life where I had left off. What I didn't know was that another medical problem was lurking, preparing to strike, and it would prove a whole lot harder to recover from than my hip operation.

Chapter 19

Struck down

UNTIL MID-1998, THE 1990S WERE HAPPY AND REWARDING years for me. Years of family enjoyment, relaxation and business opportunities, and, of course, tennis and golf. By then, well into my 50s, I was probably more adept at golf than tennis, it being more sedate, in keeping with my advancing years, and gentler on my battered knees, hips and wrist. I still played against the likes of Ken Rosewall, Fred Stolle, Roy Emerson, Cliff Drysdale, Cliff Richey, Owen Davidson and Colin Dibley in seniors tennis tournaments, sponsored by Carte Blanche credit cards with the individual tennis clubs kicking in a little prize money, and I accepted every possible invitation to make personal appearances and fly my sponsors' flag at tennis events across the United States and occasionally in other countries. I didn't travel overseas all that much because Mary had grown averse to flying. Besides, sticking close to home suited me perfectly. I was enjoying the gentle pleasures that come with getting on a bit after my frenetic striving years as an elite tennis player.

The year 1998 had been typical for me, juggling home and family with tennis and business commitments, and holidaying with Mary in our motor home. In June I did venture overseas, to attend the French Open, and during the tournament I was inducted into the International Tennis Hall of Fame. Then in July, after appearing at some charity events and vacationing on the Baja Peninsula with Mary, I was one of three pros conducting a coaching clinic at the tennis club at Kennebunkport, Maine, on the east coast of the United States. There, I was invited by tennis enthusiast Jerry Weintraub, who produced the *Karate Kid* and the *Ocean's Eleven, Twelve* and *Thirteen* movies, and his wife, the singer Jane Morgan, to play with their neighbour George H.W. Bush on the former US president's hard court at his beautiful estate off the coast of Kennebunkport. As we all went onto the court, Mr Bush said, 'I reckon I should play with Rod,' but Jerry protested, 'You're not getting him. He's *my* partner.' George hit the ball well, which is not surprising as both he and his son George W. Bush, who was destined to become president in 2001, had been coached by John Newcombe at Newk's tennis ranch in New Braunfels, Texas. At all of these events, I felt perfectly fine. There was no hint of the disaster awaiting me.

To mark the Mercedes ATP event being staged at Los Angeles Tennis Center, and the 30th anniversary of

American TV sports network ESPN, I was invited to be interviewed for a program about the foremost sports stars of the 20th century by ESPN presenter and director Alex Gibney at the Westwood Marquis Hotel in downtown Los Angeles. When I sat down in front of the cameras that 27 July, I was just one month shy of my 60th birthday. The first question Alex asked me was where I grew up. 'I'm from Queensland,' I replied. 'Just north of Brisbane is a place called Rockhampton, where it's hot. That's where the crows fly backwards just to keep the dust out of their eyes.' It was all downhill from there.

As the interview proceeded, I was alarmed to realise that my right leg was numb. I pinched it and felt nothing. It was as if it had been anaesthetised. And my right hand and fingers were cold, and my right arm was tingling with pins and needles, as if I'd had an electric shock. I felt dizzy. I had trouble speaking. I halted the interview, stood up, then swayed and collapsed to the floor, vomiting violently. Through all this I was wondering what in God's name was happening to me.

What was happening was that I was having a haemorrhagic stroke, an aneurism. A bulging weak area in the wall of an artery in my brain was leaking blood. Thank goodness for Alex Gibney. He had been present when his father had a stroke and, having heard me using strange words out of context as I was being interviewed by him, then seen me collapse, he knew darn well that I was suffering one too. He phoned immediately for paramedics – fortunately, the University of California Los Angeles (UCLA) Medical Center was just two blocks away and an ambulance was dispatched, siren blaring, to collect me and race me to intensive care in the hospital's neurological department.

Receiving such quick and expert treatment coupled with still being a fit guy saved my life. Much later it dawned on me that had I suffered my stroke far from a hospital – in the Baja Peninsula wilderness where Mary and I had recently been in our motor home, say – I would surely have died. Timing, in life as in tennis, is everything.

Alex Gibney later recalled that when I was wheeled on a stretcher into the emergency ward where a team of neurologists was waiting for me, 'They were checking his mental faculties and [a doctor] apparently asked Rod, "What is your name?" And Rod slurred out, "Rod Laver," and the doctor said, "What is your occupation?" and Rod slurred out, "Tennis player." And then there was a pause and apparently Rod tugged on the physician's jacket, and he said, "I used to be a fairly good tennis player." Indeed he was.'

The ESPN crew tried to find Mary to tell her the news. Trouble was, at the beach house at Carlsbad where Mary was staying to escape the broiling desert heat, we had a silent phone number and I was certainly in no condition to remember it. After some frantic ringing around, someone got hold of Rick's wife, Sue, who called Rick, who phoned Mary. 'Mum, Dad's had a stroke!' he blurted, and Mary, unable to believe that her bulletproof husband could ever be laid low, asked him, 'Whose dad?'

Mary, Rick, Sue and Mary's daughter, Ann Marie, made a hectic journey 80 kilometres up the freeway from Carlsbad to Los Angeles. The traffic was as heavy and erratic as ever, but Rick is a fine driver and he put his emotions and fears on hold and they made it without mishap in less than two hours.

In intensive care, my condition critical, I was given oxygen and 28 CAT scans to keep track of the bleeding in my brain and to gauge whether the leaking from the aneurism was lessening. It seemed it was. If it had continued leaking, I would have had to have brain surgery, which can be dangerous. I was kept under constant surveillance, because further strokes can occur the first few days after a stroke. For a while, things looked grim. My entire right side was paralysed, and my left was only in marginally better shape. I had numerous seizures and my blood pressure was through the roof. My stomach and colon stopped functioning and a tangle of intravenous tubes were inserted in me to compensate. I had a 104 degree (39.5 degrees Celsius) fever that not even lying for hours on a bed of ice could control. My brain was still swollen.

There were times, happily I have no memory of them, when I needed to be restrained because in my delirium I was ripping out my intravenous tubes and the wires attached to my head to monitor my brainwaves. The nurses wanted to fasten me to my bed with straps, but Mary said, 'Don't tie him down. It would kill him.' Amid the chaos, there was one light moment when Mary arrived at the hospital one morning and a nurse said to her, 'Do you want the good news or the bad news first? The bad news is he's pulled his IV out again. The good news is he pulled it out with his *right* hand!' I guess they saw that as some sort of sign that my body was repairing.

I alternated between unconsciousness and delirium, and all the while, Mary, Rick and Ann Marie were at my bedside, holding my hand and willing me to survive. It must have been so hard for them, and terrifying too, to see me so helpless, so close to death. Ann Marie would recall, 'My mum is a very strong person. But when it came to this stroke, that really, really hit her hard. She just kept encouraging Rod, "You're gonna be okay, you know, we're gonna get through this, you're gonna be fine." And then away from Rod she would break down.'

Mary and Ann Marie were so strong for each other. One time, when I wasn't doing too well, they sat together in the garden of the hospital and Mary started to cry. They had no tissues, so Ann Marie said, 'Here, use my coat. We're all in this together. Rod will get through it, and so will we.' They and Rick and Sue stayed each night at the Beverly Hills home of my friend Jerry Weintraub, which happened to be right next to the hospital. Kind and generous Jerry, with whom I'd been playing tennis in Kennebunkport just a week earlier, gave them the run of his beach house.

After two weeks in a critical condition in intensive care, my status was downgraded to merely 'serious' and I was moved to a general ward. It was too much too soon. I had a relapse, with further seizures and brain swelling, and was rushed back to intensive care and reinstated on the critical list.

Word quickly spread that I'd had a stroke. The world's wire services published the following news report:

Rod Laver, perhaps the greatest tennis player of all time, is in a critical condition in a Los Angeles hospital after suffering a stroke while recording a cable TV interview. Laver, 59, collapsed during the taping in a hotel on Monday and was rushed to the nearby UCLA Medical Center. 'His family is with him and he is resting comfortably,' a hospital nursing supervisor was quoted as saying. At the request of the Australian's family, no more information about his condition was released.

Last night, Ken Rosewall, a friend and former rival of Laver, was among well-wishers hoping for a full recovery by the only man to twice claim the coveted Grand Slam. The pair, who shared 15 major titles in the 1960s and '70s, last saw each other seven weeks ago at the French Open, where Laver appeared healthy and in good spirits as he was inducted into the International Tennis Hall of Fame. 'He's the last person you'd expect something like this to happen to,' Rosewall said from his Sydney home. 'But he's a fighter. It's the way he played his tennis. He's a competitor and he'll give it all he's got to get back to being real healthy again.'

Laver, originally from Rockhampton, has been based in southern California for several years. The boyhood idol of current world No.1 Pete Sampras, he swept the four Grand Slam events – the Australian, French and US Opens and Wimbledon – in 1962 and 1969.

Tennis Australia's president, Mr Geoff Pollard, and the Australian Open tournament director, Paul

McNamee, have released a statement expressing their shock and sympathy, while the former Australian Davis Cup great John Alexander described Laver as not only one of the greatest players of all time, but one of the best-liked.

I'm told the hospital's switchboard ran hot with enquiries about my health and there were get-well telegrams, letters and cards from all over the world, including a number from Rockhampton. News crews set up their cameras and microphones in the UCLA Medical Center grounds.

Muscles Rosewall, John Newcombe, Fred Stolle, Ross Case and Pete Sampras all telephoned and left messages saying I was in their hearts and prayers. (In 2003, when Newk had a stroke himself, I sent him a get-well card and he responded, 'Thanks, mate. I knew how much fun you had with your stroke, so I thought I'd better have one too.') Pat Rafter, Sandon Stolle and Bill Norris the masseur kept vigil in the waiting room adjoining my 3rd floor ward, brandishing a 120 by 150 centimetre card signed by more than a hundred players, and every time the doors opened they burst into a noisy and, I'm reliably informed, out-of-tune rendition of 'Waltzing Matilda'. Perhaps it was for the best that I couldn't hear them. Pat recalled his incredulity on hearing the news of my illness: 'Someone said, "Oh, Rocket's just had a stroke." Wow, it sends a real shiver down your spine, just to think about that, it was incredible. He's the last person you'd expect to have a stroke.'

Charlton Heston, wearing a bright red shirt and looking a million dollars, strode into the ward one day to sit by my bedside, which sent the nurses into a tizzy.

My 60th birthday was on 9 August, just 13 days after I'd been felled, and Mary and the family decorated my hospital room with streamers, balloons and hundreds of cards. There was a sad little celebration, even though the guest of honour was away with the pixies. I can think of better ways to spend such a landmark birthday.

I don't remember consciously harking back to my tennis days to summon strength for my recovery. I knew I had been a tennis player, but no details. Everything was so fuzzy. I do remember one of the doctors seeing me trussed up in bed and quipping, 'Well, Rod, I think even I could beat you now.' Dr Martin did tell me that my tennis-playing days were over, which seemed a bit callous. In hindsight, maybe, knowing I was a fighter, he gave me that bleak prognosis to motivate me to prove him wrong by working hard to get back onto a court. As Ann Marie said later, 'The determination that made him the tennis player that he was ensured that he would not let the stroke keep him down. He fought, and he fought with everything he had, like he does with everything in his life.' And Rick added, 'He was the most motivated person the hospital had seen in quite some time. He got better quicker than they thought.'

One day Dr Martin appeared at my bedside with a CAT scan of my brain and declared, 'Rod, there's nothing there!' For one alarming moment I thought he meant I had no brain . . . then he explained: 'No, your brain is blood free. This is very good news.' When the IV tubes were removed, my stomach and colon kicked in and started earning their keep again. I was moved off the serious list and into the therapy unit, although I still couldn't think or speak properly. If I spoke at all, it came out as gibberish, and I spouted words nobody had ever heard before. One doctor reckoned it sounded like Latin and asked Mary if I'd studied Latin at school. She was sure I had not.

I didn't know my name or age. When a nurse pointed to her watch and asked me what it was, I replied, 'Glasses.' For some reason, one of the hardest words for me to say was 'dog'. And when Mary asked me what I wanted for breakfast, instead of bacon and eggs I said, 'Envelopes and eggs.' I had no use of my right arm, hand or leg, and I suffered badly blurred vision in my right eye. There was a clock on my wall but I could not tell the time because I could only see one side of it. Same with my food – I like to joke that I only ever ate half a plate's worth because I could not see the other half. Nor could I feed or shower myself, get dressed or tie my shoelaces. From time to time I'd lie or sit on my right arm, and not know.

After four days there, a nurse wheeled me down to a basketball court on the ground floor and made me stand by my wheelchair while she grasped me by the belt and legs to steady me enough to have a try at holding a tennis racquet in my left hand and hitting tennis balls with it. I had very mixed success at this activity that once I could perform in my sleep. I had to pump a windlass contraption like they have on yachts, and I wound that handle around and around till the sweat poured from me. Soon I was having daily basic therapy. One exercise involved pulling a number of objects out of a little box – a nail, a ball, a pencil – which I then had to put back in the box and tell the therapist which ones I could remember. Early on, I could only manage one or two. He'd say, 'That's good. Now we'll pull them out and put them back again and see how you go.' With practice, I could remember three or four.

I began to improve. Dr Martin told me once I could answer three particular questions correctly, he would let me go home. The questions were: 'Where are you?'; 'How old are you?'; and 'Who is the president?' I had no problems with the first two questions, but with my brain still messed up, I had no idea who the president was. After the doctor had gone, Mary whispered to me that it was President Clinton. 'Remember, Rod, next time the doctor asks you, the president's name starts with a "C".' Sure enough, next day the medico returned and put the question to me once more. I told myself, 'Remember, it starts with a "C",' and then blurted out, 'That's easy . . . it's President Carter.' Back to the drawing board. Mary sighed. She was as keen as me to get out of there.

Then, one happy day, after I'd been able to assure Dr Martin that Bill Clinton was the President of the United States, I was pronounced well enough to continue my treatment at home. When Rick wheeled me out of UCLA Medical Center, the press converged. Mary had tried to get me to our car without them seeing me because she didn't want me to get agitated, but no such luck. The reporters called out, 'How are you doing, Rocket?' and I managed to croak, 'I'm doing okay. I'm getting there.' I was not as confident as I tried to sound.

Once home, I underwent many months of physical, speech and memory therapy. The doctor who had replaced my hip, Adrian Graf Radford, organised a team of excellent therapists to call every day. After each session I'd be exhausted. Because the stroke had destroyed so many of my brain cells, I had to learn again, from scratch, how to think, read, count, speak, comprehend, walk without falling, clean my teeth, dress myself, tie my shoelaces and shower. In time, and not without enormous effort, I progressed from my wheelchair to a walker, and then was able to use a golf club as a cane to steady myself and get around under my own steam. That evening I wrote in my diary: 'I walked today.' It was a red letter moment.

One valuable therapeutic exercise was to take a magazine and rip out the pages with my right hand, crumple them up into a ball and toss them one by one into a wastepaper basket a metre away. In doing that, I was using my right arm, hand, fingers, my brain and my hand–eye coordination. Few things I had ever done were as taxing as this simple exercise.

Learning to speak again came hard too. Eventually I was able to choose the right words and articulate them. To help the process along, my speech therapist fired questions at me: 'Name three golf clubs in the desert.' 'How many southern American states can you name?' 'What street do you live on?' Bit by bit the right answers emerged from my damaged brain.

Now I could use my left hand to gently hit a golf ball with a club and a tennis ball with a racquet. Mary organised for Tommy Tucker, the tennis teaching pro at Mission Hills Country Club near Rancho Mirage, to collect me from our home each morning and hit balls to my good left side on the club's courts. At first I could last only five minutes. Then I worked my way up to half an hour. Tommy helped me to get my feet moving again, and I'd practise the drills in my garage when I returned home. When Tommy wasn't around, Rick hit balls to me, very gently. I performed my occupational therapy exercises daily and worked my way up to laboured 1.6-kilometre walks around my neighbourhood, and folks along the way would call out, 'Go, Rocket, go!'

As I painstakingly battled my way back to health, I summoned reserves of determination, dedication and discipline to work hard that I hadn't called on since my tennis days. Being a natural lefty was a blessing because it was my right side that was affected. First I exercised my left side to fully recover my faculties and then, after three months, I began to concentrate on my still badly afflicted right side. Mary told Bud Collins, 'The therapists were exhausted, too. Rod wore them out, he was so determined to recover. They'd never worked with someone like him. His super determination as a player was showing itself.' A couple of years later I had a funny exchange with Bud. He asked me how I was feeling and I responded that I had a sore right knee. He said, 'That's too bad,' and I said, 'No, it's *good*. This is the first time I've had feeling in it since the stroke.'

Another important element in fighting back was my refusal to succumb to despair. I had been told by my doctors that many stroke sufferers became seriously depressed and that this slowed their recovery. Of course I hated being incapacitated, I resented that the good health and physical abilities I'd always enjoyed had deserted me. But my determination never to be a victim, and to let the love and care of Mary, my family, my friends, the public and the doctors, nurses and therapists do their work, all helped me. My mind paved the way for my body to regroup and repair.

My poor brain. I would get so tired just watching television. I never knew being a lounge lizard was such hard toil. It totally drained me. My therapist told me that my brain had been so damaged that it was overwhelmed by simply absorbing the sights and sounds of a TV program. The antidote was simple: when I felt mentally and physically fatigued, I must go to bed for an hour and lie still, doing absolutely nothing, sleeping if I could. That would rest my brain and give it a chance to recharge. Sure enough, when I rose again I felt better.

Mary made sure I performed all my exercises, and that I went to bed when I needed to, no matter what time of the day it was. Mary was also my gatekeeper when friends dropped by to visit and she shooed them away when she saw I was growing fatigued talking to them. Each night I was in bed and asleep by 8. There were times when therapy seemed all too hard, and my recovery painfully slow. Mary kept me at it.

Gradually, my cognitive abilities returned, and muscle memory, honed over many decades as a tennis player, helped me to get my feet and arms on both sides of my body moving again. I could once more appear at public events – my first was at a children's tennis clinic just nine months after my stroke – potter in the garden, and, in a very limited way, play tennis and golf without someone hanging onto my belt! I could drive my little golf cart. Living on the double fairway at Morningside Country Club golf course, I was able to play the two holes that adjoined our place, No.1 going down and No.9 coming back. I stayed in touch with Mary at all times via walkie-talkie in case I had a mishap. Once, on No.9 hole, I hit my ball into a sand bunker. (The way I was playing I was *lucky* to hit it into the bunker.) I slid down into the sand trap to retrieve the ball and couldn't get out. I could only use one hand to try to drag myself up and out . . . and because the green was so immaculately kept, there was nothing much for me to hold on to. I reached for my walkie-talkie, but stupidly had left it in the golf cart. I was clawing and scrambling up the sandy incline and I could hear Mary's voice squawking over the walkie-talkie, 'Where are you?!' It was quite a while before I managed to extricate myself, and the effort nearly did me in.

My doctors have no idea what caused my stroke. I wasn't an obvious candidate. I didn't smoke and I didn't drink alcohol to anything remotely resembling excess. A couple of beers had always been my limit. I had no stress to speak of in my life. I was fit and strong for my age and was active every day. My cholesterol and blood pressure were at healthy levels. The only black mark was that my brother Bob had died of a brain aneurism in 1980, so there may be something lurking in the Laver DNA that predisposed me to a stroke. Many who knew me remarked that if Rocket could have a stroke, then *anyone* was susceptible. If, as a result of what had happened to me, people started exercising and watching what they ate and drank then that had to be a good thing.

I spoke to groups of stroke victims, told them to be strong and persist, not cut corners, with their therapy. I hoped if they saw how I'd recovered in fairly rapid time, they'd have faith that they could get well soon too. One message I wanted to impart to those recovering from a stroke was that having one does not mean you're an inferior person, which some of them clearly felt. But there is no stigma attached to a stroke. As I learned, a stroke can affect *anyone*, even those who seem to be at low risk.

By June 1999, 10 months after my stroke, I was 90–95 percent recovered. I was able to fly to the French Open where I saw Andre Agassi win the men's singles crown. I was invited to present Andre with his trophy, and when I did, right there in Roland Garros Stadium, he bowed. I was deeply moved by his gracious gesture. By then, I could think, speak and move around. Not quite as well as before, true, but I was more functional, perhaps, than I had a right to be. Sometimes when I was tired, a word refused to come, and my right foot could be unsteady so I needed to be careful, especially when on uneven ground or on stairs. I could play golf, I could hit a tennis ball back across the net – and some-times the ball would even go where I wanted it to.

Many good people did fabulous work helping me to survive my stroke. Without any one of them I could have died. Yet it was Mary, perhaps more than anyone, who pulled me through. Seeing her seemingly indestructible husband rendered helpless must have been a horrifying ordeal for her. Our life, which had been chugging along merrily, changed drastically in an instant. She never complained, just rolled up her sleeves and devoted herself to my recovery. She was gentle or stern, whatever I needed her to be. I will be forever grateful to Mary, and I shudder to think what would have become of me had we not taken the time to stop and chat to each other at Jack Kramer's tennis day in Los Angeles 32 years earlier.

I had no inkling, as my health returned, that just a few years later it would be my turn to repay Mary for the love and care that she had lavished on me.

Chapter 20

The ultimate honour

I FIRST GOT WIND OF THE PLAN TO CALL THE TENNIS STADIUM in Melbourne 'Rod Laver Arena' back in early 1999, when Paul McNamee, the former champion player who was CEO of the Australian Open, sounded me out on behalf of Tennis Australia president Geoff Pollard and Victorian premier Jeff Kennett about getting my approval to name the complex after me. My response was, 'You've got to be joking – what are you talking about? I'm a Queenslander, not a Victorian. And what about Frank Sedgman?' Paul said, 'Rocket, we're serious. We're offering you what we think you and your career deserve.' I thought for a moment and replied, 'Well, you certainly have my approval. But are you sure you're not joking with me?' I was so honoured – in fact, naming the wonderful tennis and entertainment facility after me is the crowning jewel of my career. And I was especially proud because to honour me Tennis Australia and the Victorian Government were turning their backs on big money from companies keen to pay a fortune for naming rights.

I was still not quite up to par after my stroke, so didn't feel able to take the long trip to Melbourne to be there in person for the official opening of Rod Laver Arena in 2000. I made do instead by participating in the inauguration ceremony through the magic of a video link from my home to the arena. Neale Fraser conducted the interview. I was feeling better the following year, and when Rick and I visited Melbourne for the 2001 Australian Open, we stayed at the Grand Hyatt Hotel, which has a panoramic view of Melbourne's CBD, parklands and sports stadia. We arrived late from the airport and went straight to bed in our respective rooms, and when the sun rose next morning Rick drew back the curtains and saw Rod Laver Arena emblazoned in huge letters on one particular imposing and sparkling building. His mouth fell open. 'Rod, I had no idea you were so famous!' Well, he wasn't to know, I don't talk much about my career at home. (For some reason, Rick has always called me Rod instead of Dad. It's just been one of his little idiosyncrasies and it's fine by me . . . I don't care what he calls me, as long as he calls me.) It was such a thrill to go to the arena and walk past the busts of the tennis legends, and I have to say that mine is a pretty accurate likeness. I wished that Mum and Dad had lived to see the stadium. They would have been proud. The facilities are first-rate . . . and, remembering the dodgy conditions we had to play in when I was young, it occurred to me that tennis had come a long way in my lifetime.

As well as hosting the Australian Open each year, the arena is constantly in use by other sports events and rock concerts. I can imagine music fans turning up to see Bruce Springsteen and wondering, 'What band was Rod Laver in?'

Sometimes I have to pinch myself. As well as having the tennis stadium named after me, I've been fortunate enough to receive many other honours. In addition to my career being documented in the record books and the trophies I have won, I was made a Member of the Order of the British Empire, I'm in the Australian and International Tennis Halls of Fame and the Queensland Sports Hall of Fame, I've an Australian Sports Medal, I've been designated a Queensland Great, a Legend in the Sport Australia Hall of Fame, and I'm a so-called Australian National Living Treasure, one of a group of people deemed by the National Trust of Australia to have made an outstanding contribution to Australian society in any field of human endeavour. My face has been on stamps and I've been presented with the keys to Rockhampton. All this, and I'm still alive! I guess I'm truly blessed. I like to think I've received these plaudits not only for playing tennis, but because I've tried to do the decent thing in my career and my life. Whatever I've done and wherever I've done it, I've considered myself to be representing my country, my family and my sport. I would never do anything to drag them through the mud. I played a game I loved, and was able to pit myself against the best in the world. I hope I was a worthy champion.

I have to say that I feel uncomfortable when people call me the best tennis player of all time. That's an honour that's impossible to assign. Fine players trained and played in different eras under different conditions and using different equipment. The changes to racquets, balls, surfaces and clothing, the way the game has evolved over the decades, has been significant and that must be considered when trying to evaluate and compare players. Today's larger-headed, lighter, technically strung, composite metal racquets propel a ball faster and harder than the wooden racquets we used, even though I'm sure with ours we were more accurate. It would be interesting to pile everybody into a time capsule and see some of the past champions at their peak using the modern equipment. After he'd finally retired, Pancho Gonzales said to me that if he'd used a composite metal racquet in his heyday, he'd never have been beaten.

Also, nowadays, there are many more major tournaments played on hard courts, which call for different skills and are certainly tougher on the body than the grass we mostly played on. Serves, too, today are more powerful because players are allowed to jump into the air; our feet had to be planted on the ground. Just the logistics of travelling back in the '50s and '60s would amaze, and exhaust, today's players, who flit first class in enormous jets from Europe to the United States to Australia and back to Europe. When I took off in a four-engine Super Constellation with flames licking terrifyingly out of the exhaust to play in Europe with Harry Hopman and Bob Mark in 1956, it took us three days and two nights to get from Melbourne to Rome after refuelling stops in Darwin, Singapore, Bombay, Karachi and Beirut.

Today's champions seem physically more muscular than we were. A lot of that is down to more advanced training methods. We were told that you would become inflexible and muscle-bound if you lifted heavy weights, so we ran and performed basic push-ups, double knee jumps, agility exercises. Today they do scientifically devised aerobic exercises, stretch, ride the bike a lot, and also lift heavy weights. Today's players' diet is an improvement on ours. Before a match I loaded up on steak and eggs, as I knew no better, while nowadays diets are devised by nutritionists and sports scientists. Oh, and modern players also make so very much more money than we did.

I suppose all any player can ever do is beat the bloke on the other side of the net. All things being equal, who can say whether Donald Budge could have beaten Roger Federer, or how John McEnroe would have fared against Lew Hoad? I certainly can't. What I will not do is put myself on a pedestal because I won two Grand Slams. Just because nobody else has ever done that does not elevate me above other champions. I was simply lucky enough to play my best tennis on a day when it really mattered. A fellow I beat in the Wimbledon final may well have beaten me in a tournament the following week. In my era, any of the top players could defeat anybody else on any given day. The quality of the opposition is often a factor overlooked by people ranking the best players of all time. I was fortunate – or unfortunate – enough to have had rivalries with Muscles, Lew, Gonzales, Tony Roche, Emmo, Fred Stolle and Neale Fraser. No mugs in that bunch. Federer beats and is beaten by Djokovic and Nadal, two mighty players. Sampras was never given a moment's peace when he played Agassi, Rafter, Becker and Lendl. McEnroe, Borg and Connors fought it out at the major tournaments. To be the best you have to beat the best.

All that said, in my opinion two players who stand out from the past and present champions are Lew Hoad and Roger Federer. Although it's possible that age is beginning to catch up with Roger, I believe he is the best player of the modern era, because in his career he has won so many titles, and as I write this he is still playing very, very well at 32 and, on his day, beating the other top players of today, Novak Djokovic, Rafael Nadal and Andy Murray. He's got everything – wonderful strokes (his single-handed backhand is a joy to watch), speed (no one today has his court coverage), precision timing, concentration, amazing anticipation (he always seems to know where the ball will be coming back at him and be there ready), and I can watch his wonderful footwork for hours on end. He is an artist with a tennis racquet. He is mentally strong. On the court, he looks like he is enjoying every moment. He has no ego. To me, he is the complete player and embodies everything that is special about our game. He is another who can always find a way to win. He has his opponent moving constantly. He keeps hitting to the open court, gets him going side to side – out-manoeuvres him.

I enjoy watching Roger play, whereas with a fellow like Jimmy Connors, I admired his talent but I never enjoyed observing him, with his flashy showmanship and bois-terousness. On the court Roger is a true gentleman and what also impresses me is that he reveres the history of our game. It is a tremendous compliment when observers say they can see similarities in the way I played and how Roger Federer goes about his business on the court. It was a pleasure to be at Wimbledon when Roger made tennis history by notching a record 17 grand slam titles, and I'm proud to have taken part in what has gone down as one of the most memorable tennis moments when, after I presented Roger with the Australian Open winner's trophy in 2006 and we embraced on the podium, he was overcome with emotion and the tears coursed freely down his face in front of the world. Later, Roger explained, 'Rod was a big percentage of the reason I got so emotional. To be honest, whether I had won or lost, it would have been emotional because Rod was there.'

It humbles me when I hear Roger and such players as John McEnroe, Novak Djokovic, Rafael Nadal, Andre Agassi and Pete Sampras say that I have inspired them. How could I not be proud when I read Pete's words:

I first met Rod when I was 12 and although I have become acquainted with most of the greats, I know him best of all. We've become real buddies since he had a stroke. We've developed a genuine friendship as a result. We have a lot of respect for each other. My first coach made me model my game on Rod, and I still watch videos of him and the other greats from the past, guys like Ken Rosewall, Roy Emerson, John Newcombe. I looked up to them as a young pro so it feels pretty good to be regarded in the same category as them now. And I think that Rod appreciates that a successful player from the modern era has so much respect and admiration for what he achieved.

I certainly do.

If you've come this far with my story, you could not fail to appreciate how grand a man and player Lew Hoad was. Once you'd been on the receiving end of his power hitting you never forgot it, and his strokes were textbook-perfect. He had a spirit that would never say die. He would have been even better, certainly been at the top of his sport for longer, if not for his chronically bad back.

I also rate Ken Rosewall and the American Jack Kramer very, very highly when I consider players of the past. Kramer is underrated today because, after turning pro relatively early in his career, he didn't play in many grand slam tournaments. And cases can be made for the worth of Newk, Sedgman, Emmo, Roche, Gonzales, Budge, Ellsworth Vines and Fred Perry, and for the players that followed them – McEnroe, Lendl, Agassi, Connors, Borg, Sampras, Becker, Pat Rafter and Stefan Edberg and, in their wake, Murray, Federer, Nadal and Djokovic. I've no doubt that in a few short years we'll be hailing a new crop of champions.

I don't know if Australian tennis will ever again bask in a golden era with six or eight players in the top 10, but I believe we can once more be a power in the game. To achieve that, we must establish world class junior development programs, get more youngsters playing, and then identify and nurture potential champions so they don't fall through the cracks. If only tennis was played Australia-wide, in the cities, suburbs and the bush, as it was when I was coming through. In the 1960s in Sydney alone there were 1500 lit tennis courts in use day and night. Today there is a fraction of that number as high real estate prices and residential and industrial demands have made tennis courts an endangered species. A pipe dream perhaps, but more enlightened planning of new housing developments, based on getting kids back out into the open air, might see a resurgence. I also believe it would inspire the young to pick up a racquet if they had a great Australian champion to emulate. Having coaches of the calibre of Charlie Hollis and Harry Hopman would not go astray either.

Chapter 21

Life's passing parade

MARY'S HEALTH PROBLEMS BEGAN IN 2004, WHEN SHE WAS 76. First came a 99 percent blocked carotid artery that needed to be operated on at UCLA Medical Center, a place I was all too familiar with. She recovered well and our happy life resumed. Then she started having respiratory problems. Then breast cancer. Then she was stricken with neuropathy, a collection of disorders resulting from damage to the nerves of the peripheral nervous system, the part of the nervous system outside the brain and spinal cord. She experienced burning and freezing sensations, pain, numbness and ting-ling in her hands and feet. Neuropathy can harm the heart, blood vessels, intestines and bladder, motor nerves that cause muscle movement and sensory nerves that detect pain and cold. The condition can make legs and arms feel heavy and weak, affect balance, and the sufferer is often overcome with tiredness. It is a dreadful condition, as, over the next years, we were all to learn for ourselves.

As Mary's neuropathy progressed, I became her principle caregiver . . . to the extent that Ann Marie joked that soon the caregiver would be needing a caregiver. Ann Marie and Mary's other children, Ron and Steve, and our own son Rick, and all their families, put their lives on hold to give love and support to Mary. They did whatever was necessary, such as dropping in on us when her spirits needed perking up. I tended to Mary's needs night and day – everything from putting ice packs on her head and soaking her feet in icy or warm water, to administering her medication, dealing with doctors and nurses, and sitting with her, holding her hand – as she had held mine when I had my stroke – while we watched her favourite TV shows, *Animal Planet* and *Mad Men*. It was obvious that her carefree days setting out with me in our RV, playing tennis and skiing were joys of the past. Also off our agenda was globe-trotting. I would have liked to bring Mary to Australia more often than the few times she came, but she was never a fan of planes to begin with and then when she fell ill she needed to be permanently close to treatment and so was simply unable to travel, and I was certainly not about to leave her at home in her deteriorating condition while I flitted around the world.

We took refuge in family life. I had become a grandfather when Rick and Sue had a daughter, Riley, in 2000, and as Riley grew it was plain that she had inherited the sporting gene, for she was a good tennis player and an excellent soccer goalie. I gardened, played golf and tennis, kept abreast of tennis doings, went to the San Diego Chargers games with Rick, kept in touch with close mates and, when Mary's health permitted, I attended tennis tournaments and functions not too far from home. There were a couple of events overseas that I did attend, if only briefly, such as visiting the Australian Open at the Rod Laver Arena and being at Wimbledon in 2012 for the 50th anniversary of my first grand slam, where I was made to feel as special as anyone who ever sat up in the Royal Box. I made sure Mary had the best of care in my absence and I hustled back home as soon as my duty was done.

My wife was a strong and optimistic woman, and despite her awful illness, her love of art and talent for making profitable investments did not flag. Her mind and intellect remained sharp and she was as strong-willed as ever. We still had good times but, boy, it was tough to see the woman I loved, who had sacrificed so much for me, enduring such illness. She had told me how hard it was for her when I was lying at death's door after my stroke, and now I knew exactly how she had felt.

Mary passed away in the early hours of Monday 12 November 2012, at our home in Carlsbad. She was 84. On the day before she died, the family came for a visit. Mary was sitting up in bed with us all gathered around. Riley was curled up beside her. Mary was enjoying her nightly Chunky Monkey ice cream and laughing lots. When the family went home, she was happy and at peace. Sometime around 1am on the 12th, Mary woke up and said a few words to me. Then I laid her down on her pillow, and over the next 10 minutes her breathing grew slower and softer and then she left us.

Mary and I had been together for 46 years. We grew old together but I never stopped seeing her as the beautiful girl with the deep tan, twinkling eyes and dazzling smile. I owe her everything. She gave me love, and widened my horizons far beyond tennis. When we got married some of the players thought she was too old for me. Our age difference didn't matter to us then or ever. With Mary gone, there's a big hole in my world. I know, however, that she would not want me to sit at home and mope. Perhaps now I'll get out and about a bit more. Maybe not be such a stranger to Australia. If someone asks me where I live, I say Carlsbad, California. If they ask me where my heart resides, I tell them Australia.

I still have some commercial arrangements, and when Mary was ailing I routinely turned down invitations to represent these companies in different parts of the world. Now there is no reason for me to say no. After 40 years, Adidas still produces the Rod Laver tennis shoe, nylon mesh with a neoprene sole. Working closely with my manager Stephen Walter, a trusted adviser and good friend, I have some exciting new arrangements in place with several other leading global companies. I'm really proud to have become a Rolex brand ambassador and the ANZ bank's tennis ambassador. Both companies are wonderful supporters of tennis in Australia and internationally. They are of course sponsors of the Australian Open and the (Rolex) Shanghai Masters. Rolex is also the longest corporate supporter of Wimbledon, dating back to 1978.

I was particularly honoured and thrilled when Tennis Australia recently appointed me as 'Ambassador at large' for the Australian Open, for three years from 2014. The other Grand Slam tournaments have been good to me too and I like to reciprocate. For example, I was delighted to play an active role in the United States Tennis Association's program for this year's US Open.

I've also thoroughly enjoyed writing articles for the *Herald Sun* over the past two Australian Opens and this experience was certainly an important prompt for me to have a go at this book.

When I'm out and about, in Australia and overseas, it's always nice, and humbling, to be recognised. Not long ago I walked into Rod Laver Arena, minding my own business on the way to watch a match, and a group of bystanders saw me and burst into applause. The same thing happened at a restaurant in Hervey Bay in Queensland. I was with my sister Lois and her husband Vic and as we entered, a table of 10 started clapping. I was at the market near my home in Carlsbad recently and a fellow in his 50s approached me with the news that when his mother was a young tennis fan she had been in love with me! He said he hoped I didn't mind him coming up to me out of the blue, and I told him that when people stopped remembering, that would be the time for me to worry.

I am always amazed when I look back at my life, and my tennis career, and realise that it all started on Dad's ant-bed court in our yard in Rockhampton nearly 70 years ago. I feel awed when I think of all that has happened in my life, my tennis achievements winning 11 grand slam singles titles and two Grand Slams, taking out a record 17 titles in 1969, representing my country at Davis Cup, and sticking it out through the pro gypsy years – and, even better, being a husband and father, which I rate as my greatest success. I'd forgotten this incident, but when I was profiled on ABC-TV's *Australian Story* in 2012, Rick was interviewed and he told viewers about the time when Riley had to take a family heirloom into class and talk about it. Said Rick, 'She decided that one of Rod's trophies was going to be a good heirloom to bring in. So Sue, my wife, asked Rod, "Hey, can we borrow one of your trophies? Wimbledon, 'cause that's the big one." And then he asked, "Sure, but what year do you want?" Not many people could have [asked] that.' Much of it has been hard work, but what enjoyable hard work. I've grasped my opportunities. Did all of this really happen to me?

As you've no doubt guessed by now, my family is everything to me. Rick is a fine son. He was strong for Mary and me through our illnesses, while establishing his own family life with Sue and Riley. I don't think he ever suffered being Rod Laver's son, as I've heard sometimes happens to kids of prominent people, who often have a tough time of it. Because Mary and I were low-key and level-headed, he took watching me play tennis at big tournaments and meeting celebrities in his stride. It was just no big deal. He and I have always been good mates as well as father and son. Rick was a naturally talented young sportsman and a good, competitive tennis player. Although he's followed my advice in continuing to play because tennis is such a good social activity, something you can do with family, friends and business associates your whole life, he never had the desire to be an elite player. Golf is more his sport and he can hit a ball 300 metres.

Ann Marie is my step-daughter, my friend and my account executive, taking care of my finances and organising payment of my bills. She first took on the responsibility when Mary was too ill to continue in the role and asked her to step in because, as she liked to say, I needed all the help I could get and let's just say that as an accountant I was a good tennis player. Since Ann Marie had a knee replacement, she and I work out together at nearby La Costa Resort and Spa, with its gym, golf course and tennis court. She and her family still live in Carlsbad, as does her brother Steve, and of course my son Rick and his family. Ron, Mary's first child, lives up the coast near Santa Barbara. We're all close and, if anything, Mary's death has drawn us closer. And it's not just Mary's family I embrace. Early in 2013, I made it to my brother Trevor's 80th birthday party in Gladstone. Trevor is dry and taciturn, like Dad, but I'm pretty sure he was glad to see me.

Physically I'm doing okay. I can lose track of my thoughts a little when I get tired, and my right leg is a bit wonky and can go numb at times. Like in 2000 when I was in Paris with Newk, Tony Roche and Fred Stolle, and we were walking down the Champs-Élysées and I suddenly became aware that I was limping. I looked down at my foot and saw why. I had slipped off my shoe under the table back at the restaurant and forgotten to put it back on, and hadn't been able to feel that I was unshod.

My right leg being the way it is, I've learned that discretion is the better part of valour these days, and not to stretch my physical limits. A few months back, Rick and I went fishing off the Carlsbad coast. The tide was out and had exposed some excellent rocks that were ideal for throwing in a line. I started to clamber down the rocks behind Rick, then realised this was not a smart idea. I might never make it out again. 'Rick,' I called, 'go on ahead. I'll watch you from up here.' He said, 'No way, we'll find another spot.'

I've had my right knee replaced – on the inside of the meniscus, bone was gnashing against bone – and now both my hips as well, because of many years of tennis wear and tear. I've recurring wrist and elbow problems, and arthritis in my left wrist and the bones of my left hand, which has now by and large stopped me from playing tennis. I can still play golf when I wrap my hand in an elastic band that keeps all the arthritic bones together. My once muscular left forearm – the one that reminded many of Popeye's or King Kong's – has shrunk to the same size as everyone else's.

Some other players of my era haven't been so fortunate in regard to health, and we've lost some fine blokes over the years. Lew Hoad, my old hero, passed away in 1994 of a heart attack after battling leukaemia. I didn't even know Lew was ill until Paul McNamee called me and told me that Lew had leukaemia and was drifting away. He died on the last day of Wimbledon. A bunch of us – Paul McNamee and his former doubles partner Peter McNamara, Fred Stolle, Butch Buchholz – played some matches at Lew's tennis ranch in Fuengirola, Spain, to honour him and to raise money for his family. Not long after Lew died, the Las Vegas identity tennis promoter Alan King held a dinner and everyone dressed up in costumes. Roy Emerson and I went as swagmen and Mary was Raggedy Anne, with freckles painted on her face. King arrived riding an elephant. It was a fun night, and we all tried to mask our sadness over our fallen mate.

The following year Pancho Gonzales was claimed by oesophageal cancer. After our stormy history, he and I had become friends and I was with him not long before he died. I told him I knew he wasn't doing so well and he replied, 'Don't worry about me. I've had a fabulous life.' Charlie Pasarell, Ray Moore and I were the only tennis players from Pancho's glory days among the mourners at his funeral, which made the sad occasion even more poignant. Gone too are Ken Fletcher, Frank Gorman, Ken McGregor, Chuck McKinley, the towering Italian Orlando Sirola, Barry MacKay, Bob Mark (the young Australian who joined me on my first trip overseas with Harry Hopman), the Grand Slammer Donald Budge at age 84 and, of course, my great mentors Charlie Hollis and Hop himself, who died of a heart attack in 1985. There are others: Chuck Heston, Chad Everett, Lloyd Bridges, Dinah Shore, Duke Wayne, Alan King and James Franciscus have all passed away. The ranks are thinning. John McDonald, my Kiwi friend, who was at my side during the 1969 Grand Slam, is fighting lymphoma. Every one of these people, in their own way and to a greater or lesser degree, had an impact on my career.

It's always special, then, when the old tennis players of my era catch up. I don't see them as often as I'd like, but when we do meet we cherish our time together. It was a very special reunion with old mates in July 2012 when I was invited to Wimbledon to celebrate the 50th anniversary of my first Grand Slam win and a big fuss was made! There were a number of special events, including a function hosted by the Australian High Commissioner at his private residence. At the dinner in my honour we relived great times and outdid each other spinning tall stories.

Perhaps the most special occasion of all occurred on Sunday 29 January 2012, before Novak Djokovic and Rafael Nadal met in the men's singles final of the Australian Open at Rod Laver Arena, when there was a ceremony in which the nine living Australian winners of the title took turns to carry the Sir Norman Brookes Challenge Cup to mark the centenary of the Australian championships. The lights were dimmed and to the strains of stirring orchestral music the grand and gleaming Cup was lowered from the ceiling on a cable. There to grasp it was Frank Sedgman, who held the Cup high and walked a distance around the perimeter of the stadium before handing it to Mervyn Rose. Merv, sporting a bright red cap, completed his own section of the circuit and passed the Cup to Ashley Cooper, beaming and sprightly, who gave it to Bill Bowrey. When it was Newk's turn to parade the trophy he received a hearty cheer.

After Newk, taking the Cup and walking the distance to the next man, Roy Emerson, was Mark Edmondson. Emmo, bow-legged and limping due to the wear and tear on his legs and hips over his magnificent career, handed the Cup to Muscles Rosewall, who lived up to his nickname by lifting it and waving it about as if it was made of balsa. The tournament organisers had decided that I would be the last in line, and so it fell to me to take the Cup from Ken and carry it into the centre of the playing area. The crowd stood as one and clapped and cheered as I lifted it high above my head and brandished it towards the four sides of the court. Not even my qualms about tripping or dropping the Cup could stop me from feeling enormous pride. The nine of us, Australian champions all, combined age 657 years, stood in a line as the National Boys Choir of Australia sang the national anthem.

We old-timers then all shuffled and creaked off up into the grandstand to take our places among the spectators — which, these days, is where we belong – and watched, hearts racing, as Djokovic and Nadal took their positions, and the umpire called, 'Play!'

Index